STRATEGIC
CORPORATE
COMMUNICATION

STRATEGIC CORPORATE COMMUNICATION

Core Concepts for Managing Your Career and Your Clients' Brands

ROSS BRINKERT

Penn State Abington

LISA V. CHEWNING

Penn State Abington

cognella®

SAN DIEGO

Bassim Hamadeh, CEO and Publisher
Todd R. Armstrong, Publisher
Tony Paese, Project Editor
Christian Berk, Production Editor
Jess Estrella, Senior Graphic Designer
Trey Soto, Licensing Coordinator
Natalie Piccotti, Director of Marketing
Kassie Graves, Vice President of Editorial
Jamie Giganti, Director of Academic Publishing

cognella® ACADEMIC PUBLISHING
3970 Sorrento Valley Blvd., Ste. 500, San Diego, CA 92121

BRIEF CONTENTS

TABLE OF CONTENTS

PREFACE

Welcome to *Strategic Corporate Communication*! Whether you are committed to pursuing a career squarely within the field of corporate communication or simply advancing as a professional with strategic communication as an important element of a different career, we hope you find this book and the associated learning experience clear, inspiring, and valuable.

Why We Wrote This Book

As corporate communication professors and practitioners, we are, first and foremost, excited to make accessible some major connections among theory, research, and practice in a still new yet high-impact and fast-moving field. Second, we are proud to offer a core concepts approach that views those chief concerns animating corporate communication professionals' work for clients as the same basic concerns corporate communication professionals need to maneuver to ensure their own career success. We arrived at these core concepts based on our extensive work teaching and mentoring capstone students in corporate communication. Near the end of our book writing process, we were heartened to have our approach somewhat validated when we noticed that the International Association for Business Communicators was using a similar list of items in their delineation of core competencies (https://www.iabc.com/career-center/). We were drawn to a core concepts approach in its facilitation of simplicity and complexity, its allowance for narrow isolation and broad integration, and its capacity for making sense of contemporary situations while still likely holding up in a meaningful way across the coming decades.

We primarily developed this book to support corporate communication majors nearing the end of their studies to unify their learning prior to (in most cases) getting started in corporate communication careers. We also recognize how the book can be of value in courses or majors such as applied communication, business communication, business writing, management, marketing (including integrated marketing and communication), organizational communication, and strategic communication. Further, the book is intended to not only serve students at the upper division undergraduate level but also those studying at the master's level, especially in more applied programs. We see the framework as relevant for all kinds of corporate communication client work and all career stages. We intend for the book to be a reference for readers throughout their careers. Of course, no one book can meet all needs. This book is intended to primarily offer a broad, integrated, and applied view that is substantiated in some landmark theory and research.

A Note About the Use of Title Terms

What to name the book was a tough decision! As will be detailed in Chapter 1: Making Sense of Strategic Communication, the field has many different disciplinary influences and scholars and practitioners largely working with the same core concepts and/or topics; they sometimes use different terms to label themselves and what it is they are working on. While we both happen to be corporate communication professors, we recognize that colleagues sharing our interests sometimes describe their discipline or field as strategic communication, integrated marketing communication, or public relations, the latter even while addressing matters inside and outside of organizations. And these are just some examples of the diversity involved in naming the overall arena! Accordingly, we urge you not to get offended by or dismiss the applicability of this book just because the term corporate communication is not one you identify with or even like. Frankly, the title of the book could very well have left out the term corporate communication and just used strategic communication, as this has better resonance for some in the larger communication field. The downside is that there are many who come from a business background or a European communication background or an area of the U.S. communication field where corporate communication has a strong foothold. Please know that we see the wide range of identifiers at the disciplinary and field levels. We try to be respectful to all established identifiers. Please see our use of the term corporate communication as substitutable in much of the book.

The Design of Individual Chapters

With some minor exceptions in the first and last chapters, each chapter includes the following sections and subsections:

Orienting to the Concept: Offers an initial frame for appreciating the relevance of the core concept

CENTRAL DEFINITIONS: States the main terms needed to grasp the core concept

THEORY AND RESEARCH OVERVIEW: Gives multiple theoretical orientations, along with select research findings for grasping the core concept in reasonable detail

APPLYING THE CONCEPT TO YOUR OWN SITUATION

- Offers general implications as you navigate this concept to advance your own professional standing

- Provides questions to help you reflect on the significance of the core concept for your own career

TOOLS AND PROCESSES FOR SELF-ACTION

- Gives specific avenues for putting the core concept into practice regarding your own career

PROFILE OF INDIVIDUAL EXPERIENCE

- Describes a corporate communication professional and how he or she engaged the core concept for the betterment of his or her own career

- Lists questions to explore the individual case fully and find value for your own situation

APPLYING THE CONCEPT TO YOUR WORK WITH CLIENTS

- Consists of the following subsections applying the concept, especially in terms of highlighted theory and research, to your work for clients

APPLYING THE CONCEPT TO YOUR WORK FOR OTHERS

- Offers general implications as you navigate this concept to advance your clients' standing

- Provides questions to help you reflect on the significance of the core concept for your work for others

TOOLS AND PROCESSES WHEN ACTING FOR OTHERS

- Gives specific avenues for putting the core concept into practice for your clients

PROFILE OF ORGANIZATIONAL EXPERIENCE

- Describes an organization and how they engaged the core concept successfully and/or unsuccessfully

- Lists questions to explore the organizational case fully and find value for your future clients

Chapter Conclusion: Summarizes and offers a final reflection on the course concept

The Ordering of Chapters and How to Use This Book

When working through the complete book for a course, we generally recommend proceeding in the order of the numbered chapters, as references to some reoccurring items across chapters will make the most sense. However, aside from Chapter 1, which introduces the field, the concepts that make up the remainder of the book can be explored in any order because of their highly interconnected nature.

The book is also intended as a general reference and, as such, is designed to be accessed in any manner as needed. Here is a listing of the book chapters (and core concepts beyond Chapter 1):

Chapter 1: Making Sense of Strategic Communication
Chapter 2: Brand: The Positive and Memorable Identity Sought
Chapter 3: Communities: Networks of Support and Impact
Chapter 4: Messaging: Creating Meaning Across Media
Chapter 5: Contexts: The Broad Spaces in Which People and Work Are Situated
Chapter 6: Ethics: The Right and Wrong of Actions Taken (and Not Taken)
Chapter 7: Influence: The Tools for Making a Difference
Chapter 8: Research and Assessment: The Information to Chart and Measure Progress
Chapter 9: Leading and Managing: Taking Charge of the Overall Strategic Communication Enterprise
Chapter 10: Change: Staying on Top of an Important and Fast-Moving Field

An Invitation to Provide Feedback for Future Editions

Whether you are an instructor or a student and whether you like or do not like different aspects of the book, we would welcome your input. Please consider e-mailing us at rsb20@psu.edu (Ross Brinkert) and lvc3@psu.edu (Lisa Volk Chewning) with your thoughts. It will help if you use the following subject line: SCC Book Feedback. Also, please include your full name, your institutional affiliation, your contact details (phone number, mailing address, and an alternate e-mail address). Finally, indicate if you would like to be individually recognized for providing feedback in future editions of the book.

Acknowledgments

The release of this book involved many contributors and supporters to whom we are grateful. At our publishing house, Cognella Academic Publishing, we are most grateful to Publisher Todd Armstrong, who worked with us not just tirelessly but cheerfully from acquisition through all subsequent stages. Todd has a long-standing reputation as a premier book publisher in the academic communication field. All who know him realize he is also a class act as a person. We were very fortunate to work with him. We are also grateful to have worked with many others at Cognella, including Vice President of Editorial Kassie Graves, Project Editor Tony Paese, Copy Editor Melissa Brown-Levine, and Production Editor Christian Berk.

This book received a blind peer review at the proposal stage and at the draft chapter stage. The feedback we received was invaluable in writing and refining the book. We appreciate the reviewers who read our drafts and gave us insightful comments that improved the quality of our work. Among those reviewers are: Angela M. Corbo (Widener University); Matt Crick (William Patterson University); Marya L. Doerfel (Rutgers University); Beth E. Michalec (Penn State Lehigh Valley); Diane M. Monahan (Saint Leo University); Elizabeth A. Williams (Colorado State University).

We thank the following colleagues who generously collaborated with us to create the individual case studies: Angela Balduzzi, Brandi Boatner, John Burk, Sam Gentry, David Goosen, Matthew Johnson, Kwan Morrow, Jennifer O'Neill, Rakia Reynolds, and Nicole Tirado.

We feel fortunate to be faculty at Penn State University and have a special appreciation for various colleagues at Penn State Abington who directly and indirectly supported us in this project. We thank our formal leaders, including Chancellor Damian Fernandez, Associate Dean of Academic Affairs Andrew August, Division Head (former) Roy Robson, and Division Head Friederike Baer. We thank our corporate communication colleagues, including Melvin Gupton, Diane Mitnick, and Surabhi Sahay. We also thank other faculty and staff colleagues, including Karen Carli, Dolores Fidishun, Michelle Haggerty, Eva Klein, Carol Millinghausen, Paula Smith, Tina Vance-Knight, and the entire library faculty and staff.

We thank our many close colleagues in the National Communication Association, particularly those in the Public Relations Division and the Training and Development Division. We extend our appreciation to our close colleagues in the Association for Conflict Resolution, the International Communication Association, the Organization Studies Research Network, and the Philadelphia Public Relations Association.

We thank our former and current students. We are so grateful for the feedback we have received from them over the years on the core concepts approach. We are moved by their hard work and achievements in the corporate communication field and beyond.

Our deepest appreciation goes to our respective families: Colby, Eshen, and Sagan (RB) and Tim, Oliver, Mackensie, and Miles (LVC). Writing a book demands a lot of solitary time. Thanks for your understanding. Thanks for the quiet. And, of course, thanks for being there to joyfully celebrate the completion of the project!

MAKING SENSE OF STRATEGIC COMMUNICATION

Welcome to Strategic Corporate Communication

This book is designed to introduce you to concepts and strategies central to the corporate communication field. What makes this book different than other books is the emphasis on how you can use these principles to plan for, and advance in, your own career, as well as when working with your clients.

To that end, each chapter follows a similar format that is designed to help you delve into the field from both a personal and professional perspective. Chapters open with a focus on important definitions and a review of theory relevant to the chapter topic.

- We then move on to a focus on how you can use this information in your own career planning. Not only do we take a deeper dive into some of the information covered at the beginning of the chapter, but we also give you practical ideas for how you can start to apply this information to your life now.

- Following, we tie the content and skills covered in the chapter to the work environment and provide insight and ideas for how you can use it when working with clients in the future.

- To help you picture what it all looks like, we also include one personal profile and one organizational profile in each chapter.

- Finally, chapters conclude with a series of questions and activities designed to help you put what you are learning into action. Many of the activities in this text can be used to help you assess where you currently stand in terms of your own reputation and career readiness, such as performing a social media audit, setting up an informational interview, and finding a mentor.

It is our hope that this text will increase your self-awareness relative to where you are now and where you want to be in five years while providing you with a tool kit to get there.

This chapter explores what it means to be strategic, traces the development of the field of corporate communication, distinguishes between strategy-related goals and objectives, and positions strategy as the unifying theme of the overall book. You will begin developing your own professional strategies, as well as analyze and make proposals for the communication strategies of organizations.

Theory and research in this chapter will focus on creating a foundational understanding of the concept of strategy and the overall corporate communication field. While the chapter will not delve deeply into theory, it will cover a history of the field, as well as establish baseline knowledge of strategic communication skills and tactics, such as goals, plans, partnerships, and assessments. While each of these topics is revisited throughout the text, they will be introduced in this chapter as part of a process-oriented view of strategic communication.

Communication is at the heart of who we are, and what we do, as humans. It is how we assign meaning, create identity, and share values. If you really think about it, *you can't not communicate* (Grossman, 2012). Everything you say is verbal communication. Your gestures, facial expressions, tone of voice, and appearance constitute nonverbal communication. Even silence is a form of communication—for example, when you are giving someone the "silent treatment."

And it's not just humans who communicate. We have entire fields of practice built around the idea that *organizations* can communicate. Corporate communication, marketing, public relations (PR), and integrated marketing communication are all professional fields built on the idea of communicating organizational goals with groups of people called stakeholders. Stakeholders are any group of people who can impact, or are impacted by, the organization (e.g., customers, donors, employees).

Arguably, anytime we communicate with goals and purpose, it is strategic. But what does that mean in terms of your personal and professional life? And how can you use strategic communication to build your career and help your clients be successful? This chapter will cover the basics of strategic communication and what that means when you work in a communication-based field, such as corporate communication. By the end of this chapter, you should understand how strategic communication fits into your life, how it can enhance your professional opportunities, and what it means to be part of the corporate communication field.

Orienting to the Concept: What It Means to Be Strategic

To be strategic means being goal oriented and having both long- and short-term plans aimed at reaching positive outcomes related to your goals. Being strategic can help us both personally and professionally. For example, strategically planning your career can help you to ensure that you set measurable goals, consider all of the important variables, and make informed decisions along the way to getting a job. This could include identifying what industry you want to work in, what salary you want, and then taking the classes, making the contacts, and acquiring the skills that you need to get there. Compare that to someone who doesn't really think about his or her career during college, chooses a major "just because," and then scrambles to find something a month before graduation. While both students may end up with a job, it is very likely that the strategic planner will find a job that is more suited to what they want to do and pays better than will the student who waits until graduation. Strategy can be employed on behalf of organizations as well.

On a large scale, it involves planning and executing the goals of the organization and then sharing those goals with others.

This section of the chapter defines strategic communication related to both personal and professional settings, corporate communication as a field that employs strategic communication, and what it means to be part of, and work for, an organization.

CENTRAL DEFINITIONS

STRATEGIC COMMUNICATION

As we discussed previously, strategic communication can take place on both the individual and organizational levels. We are going to focus on both levels throughout the text. On the individual level, strategic communication is planned, and targeted communication is aimed at achieving positive outcomes for specific goals.

While strategic communication on the organizational level can be defined in the same way (i.e., planned, targeted, goal-oriented communication), the term strategic communication can also be used to distinguish a work function in organizations. For example, it has been defined as "the practice of deliberate and purposive communication that a communication agent enacts in the public sphere on behalf of a communicative entity to reach set goals" (Holtzhausen & Zerfass, 2013, pp. 72–84). The act of strategic communication is generally rooted in the organization's strategic plan and focuses on enabling the goals and objectives of the organization (Holtzhausen & Zerfass, 2015, p. 4).

CORPORATE COMMUNICATION

Corporate communication is a field that employs strategic communication to coordinate internal and external communication processes with the goal of creating positive stakeholder relationships and furthering organizational goals (Elving, 2012).

ORGANIZATION

If we are going to talk about strategic communication on behalf of organizations, it is helpful to define exactly what an *organization* is. At its simplest, an organization is a form of social organization (i.e., a collection of people in a set relationship with each other) within set parameters aimed at a specific mission. Typically, when we talk about organizations, it is a social unit related to business, government, or social advancement. The most common types of organizations that we encounter in corporate communication are corporations, nonincorporated businesses, government institutions, nongovernmental organizations (NGOs), not-for-profit organizations, educational institutions, religious institutions, health-based organizations, institutes, and more.

Reputation is the "aggregate evaluation constituents make about how well an organization is meeting constituent expectations based on its past behaviors" (Coombs & Holladay, 2010, pp. 168–169).

THEORY AND RESEARCH OVERVIEW

Corporate Communication as a Field

While the word "corporate" can be interpreted by some to mean a for-profit company, especially a large for-profit company, we interpret the root "corp" to be related to "corpus," Latin for "body" and, therefore, referring to the whole of an organization regardless of its size and for-profit or not-for-profit status (Elving, 2012). Therefore, we focus on the integrative aspect of corporate communication rather than on communication solely related to the single organizational type known as a corporation.

In this section, we will focus on the origins and evolution of corporate communication, as well as the most common functions of contemporary corporate communication.

ORIGINS AND EVOLUTION

Corporate communication is a broadly based field that has roots in management communication, organizational communication, and PR/marketing. Management and organizational communication typically focus on leader/employee or employee/employee communication, whereas PR and marketing typically focus on communication with external stakeholders (Bronn, 2008; Van Riel & Fombrum, 1997). Traditionally, each of these functions existed separately in organizations, creating an artificial divide between the internal and external operations of the organization. Corporate communication recognizes that the internal/external are not only interrelated but also overlap as information and communication technology (ICT), and the ways that stakeholders use media have led to convergence that has blurred many previously existing boundaries. Corporate communication integrates these communication functions to focus on a holistic approach to communication with internal and external stakeholders, adopting a more long-term perspective not focused solely on sales or the bottom line (Bronn, 2008) but rather focusing on the overarching areas of corporate identity and corporate reputation, as well as the orchestration of internal and external communication (Van Riel, 1997). In practice, this involves breaking down silos between different functional areas of the organization, such as marketing, management, media relations, and human relations, and focusing on strategies to translate organizational goals into internal and external processes to accomplish those goals, including communication focused on creating shared meaning between the organization and stakeholders.

By this definition, corporate communication *is* strategic and *employs strategic communication* with a variety of stakeholders to accomplish goals and create and communicate organizational identity and vision. Contemporary corporate communication draws on a variety of communicative fields and benefits from the interplay and overlap of traditional disciplines. The reason behind this shift can, in part, be explained by the changing nature of organizations over the last 100 to 150 years. The modern organization came into being during the Industrial Revolution and emphasized hierarchy, segmentation, and replicable methods. Employee input outside of the managerial level was not prioritized, and communication was primarily top-down. Media during this time was limited to mass media, and organizations were able to operate without a lot of external interference or accountability. As the 20th century progressed, organizations took on more matrix (even communication across levels and departments) and horizontal (flatter, less hierarchical with lateral communication) structures, which allowed for multiple flows of communication in the organization, including upward (employee to supervisor) and horizontal (group work, task forces, and interdepartmental without the intercession of supervisors). In some horizontal models of communication, the customer or client is included in the production process. Changes in media, most notably the growth of the Internet and social media sites (SMS)—both internal and external—brought more transparency and accountability to the organization. It also gave internal and external stakeholders a public voice related to the organization. Accordingly, the strict divide between *internal* and *external* has become increasingly fluid, creating the need for a more integrated approach to organizational messaging and stakeholder relations.

TYPICAL FUNCTIONS OF CORPORATE COMMUNICATION

The field of corporate communication continues to evolve as our business and social environments change. Just as the advent of corporate communication as an integrated function came about as the structure and role of organizations changed, the functions associated with corporate communication are affected by the sociotechnical landscape in which the organization operates. Table 1.1 includes the predominant corporate communication functions at this time.

Strategic Communication in Action: An Overview

A useful way to understand the full scope of strategic communication is to break down the term to the root of its two words. *Strategic* has an array of meanings and associations, including planned, goal driven, deliberate, power based, influence, decision making, and critical thinking, and, in terms of organizations, it is associated with organizational survival and the study of the organizational environment (Hallahan, Holtzhausen, van Ruler, Vercic, & Sriramesh, 2007). While these terms associate strategic with the idea of rationality, Hallahan et al. (2007) argue that it is also tied to change, organizational learning, and inclusion. Because humans do not create strategy in a vacuum but rather are informed by their lived experiences,

TABLE 1.1 Typical Functions of Corporate Communication

Public Affairs (PA)	Liaising with the government to affect policy creation and change.
Investor Relations	"A strategic management responsibility that integrates finance, communication, marketing and securities law compliance to enable the most effective two-way communication between a company, the financial community, and other constituencies" (National Investor Relations Institute, 2003).
Branding	Creating and communicating the organization's story in a way that reflects the organization's identity and reflects shared cultural values with stakeholders.
Community Relations/ Corporate Social Responsibility (CSR)	Liaising with members of the community in which the organization operates to create and maintain positive relationships. This can be extended to CSR, which involves enacting prosocial dialogues or initiatives that extend beyond the organizations bottom line.
Media Relations	Liaising with mass media representatives (i.e., journalists) to secure and influence the presentation of the organization in publication. Can be proactive and reactive.
Digital/Online Communication	Stakeholder communication enacted via web-based applications, such as SMS, organizational websites, and enterprise management systems. Includes content curation, stakeholder communication, and social listening by and for digital outlets.
Employee Communication	Communication that specifically engages employees, including management communication, human resources, and mediated communication systems, such as intranets, digital broadcasting systems, and enterprise management systems.
Marketing	Focuses on the movement of goods/services from the organization to the end user. Can include a focus on customer behaviors, promotion, packaging and design, market analysis, and more.
Public Relations	Uses strategic communication to build and maintain positive stakeholder relationships across a variety of mediated and interpersonal contexts. Creates the public persona for the organization.
Event Planning	Planning and executing interpersonal events for internal and external stakeholders. Can support other functions, such as investor relations (e.g., annual shareholder meetings) and community relations (e.g., community events such as races or fundraisers).
Issues Management/Crisis Communication	Separate but related functions that deal with the analysis and definition of issues that could affect the organization and communication are centered on organizational learning and restoration when issues are triggered into a full-blown crisis

strategy can be influenced by gender, race, culture, and previous experience (Halla-han et al., 2007). *Communication* is the conveyance of information and co-creation of shared meaning. Thus strategic communication is a way to affect change toward goals by deliberately creating shared meaning with stakeholders. Because neither the strategic communicator nor the stakeholder comes from exactly the same place, this will likely be a process of negotiation over meaning that involves both planning and adapting, which underscores the importance of feedback, listening, and empathy in the strategic communication process.

In corporate communication, strategic communication is often employed to build stakeholder relationships and maintain a positive reputation. Reputation is built around the components of organizational identity, or how the organization views itself, and how well the organization is meeting stakeholder expectations based on both direct and indirect interaction with the organization (Coombs & Holladay, 2010). When there is alignment between organizational identity and stakeholder expectations and values, organizations generally enjoy a positive reputation. When there is misalignment, organizational reputation suffers. This misalignment can occur when an organization acts in a way that violates stakeholder expectations or when an organization doesn't properly communicate that it *is* acting in accordance with stakeholder expectations. We will talk more about reputation in Chapter 2 and focus on how to fix this alignment in the following section on strategic planning.

STRATEGIC PLANNING

As we established earlier, to be strategic is to be deliberate, purposive, and goal driven. Strategic communication begins with an organization's strategic plan, or blueprint for action. Strategic planning involves creating a medium- to long-term plan for the organization based on an analysis of the internal and external environment. Strategic plans often span 3–5 years or longer but can be broken down into smaller segments and (re)evaluated periodically. While there are many models for strategic planning, they all focus on the following elements:

- Situational analysis

- Goal setting

- Planning

- Execution

- Evaluation

Strategy can be both deliberate and emergent, and organizational planning often involves both (Hallahan, 2015). That is, the organization can begin with a clearly specified plan, but personal agendas and perspectives of organizational members, along with a changing internal and external environment, can shift priorities at any point in the strategic planning process. Thus strategic planning involves long-term thinking but also the flexibility to adapt as necessary.

Communication professionals also strategically plan communication campaigns related to organizational goals. While strategic plans as described previously are long-term plans for the organization, campaigns are shorter term communication endeavors that communicate different elements of the strategic plan and other related organizational actions to various stakeholder groups. Campaigns are *strategically planned* and follow the same process described earlier, but they are not the strategic plan.

A PROCESS-BASED ORIENTATION

Based on the preceding definition of strategic planning, it is clear that planning is not a one-time act but rather a *process*. Processes are a multistep series of actions linked together by a common end goal that takes place over a set amount of time. Processes are often replicable and, therefore, can be repeated with similar results time after time, unless one or more of the steps are changed.

The strategic communication process has been characterized as a RACE: research, action, communication, evaluation (Cutlip & Center, 1952; Marston, 1963). The process begins through research. As we will discuss in Chapter 8, research involves gathering facts that help the communicator understand the environment in which his or her organization is operating. This can involve a routine process of scanning the environment or regularly checking sources, such as newspapers, blogs, and social media, for mentions of the organization or issue around which communication is needed. Alternately, research can involve conducting in-person interviews, surveys, a communication audit, or other methods. In the action step, you use the data to identify a problem or issue, set your goals, and create a course of action. For example, if your client is running a new and innovative CSR program but scanning the environment shows that nobody relevant to the industry is talking about it, you have identified your problem. Based on that, you would create a goal to increase awareness and discussion of the CSR program with specific publics in specific outlets within a specific time frame. Following, you would create objectives, strategies, and tactics to reach your goal. You would then communicate what you are doing using multiple specific media targeted at chosen stakeholder groups. Finally, you would evaluate your efforts by again conducting research and comparing your pre-action findings to your post-action findings relative to your goal. If executed well, you should find that your intervention created increased awareness and discussion of the CSR initiative among targeted groups. We will discuss research and evaluation in much more detail in Chapter 8. Goal setting should be SMART: specific, measurable, attainable, relevant, and timely. Notably, if you can't measure your objectives, you will never really know if you've achieved your goal. See Table 1.2 for a breakdown of goals, objectives, strategies, and tactics.

TABLE 1.2 **Goals, Objectives, Strategies, and Tactics**

Goal	Long-term, overarching purpose. What you want to achieve.
Objective	Measurable, finite purposes that move toward the completion of goals.
Strategy	The plan for how you will reach your objective.
Tactic	The tasks related to implementing the strategy.

It is important to note that although a process is generally linear, or step-by-step in a specific sequence, you can also go back and revisit steps throughout the process. For example, you may get halfway through the action stage and realize that you need more research. So, rather than pushing ahead, the smart thing to do is go back and conduct a little more research. This could help you refine your question or problem statement or reassess your goals. Likewise, you can conduct minieval-uations throughout the process to gather feedback, as well as a larger evaluation at the end to measure overall goal achievement. And, because communication always changes the environment, the strategic process is cyclical; once you have finished your communication intervention, you have altered the environment and, therefore, must start the process all over again.

APPLYING THE CONCEPT TO YOUR OWN SITUATION

Why It Is Important to Be a Strategic Communicator

Strategic communication is the purposeful use of communication to fulfill a mission (Hallahan et al., 2007, p. 3). Thus being a strategic communicator means that you are consciously orchestrating your intrapersonal (internal thought), interpersonal (communication with others), and mass (one to many, such as on social media) communication to achieve your goals. Being a strategic communicator requires you to think long term and, therefore, see the bigger picture. Rather than thinking one step ahead, you think one, three, or five steps ahead by creating a goal and then working backward to figure out how to achieve it. By starting with your goal and then creating objectives, strategies, and tactics to achieve your goal, you are less likely to get lost on your chosen path.

Being a strategic communicator enables you to identify and procure what you will need to achieve your goal(s) at various points in the process. Through strategic communication, you can achieve the following:

▪ Know and understand who you are and what you offer to the world (Chapter 2)

▪ Identify and engage with people who can help you reach your goals, such as mentors and organizational contacts (Chapter 3)

- Create messages that effectively tell others who you are, what you stand for, and why you are an asset (Chapter 4)

- Understand your *context* or how you are situated relative to your environment (Chapter 5)

- Impact those around you positively and ethically (Chapter 6)

- Be influential within your chosen sphere (Chapter 7)

- Procure and use various sources of information to help you set your goal and create your long-term path, as well as analyze your choices and progress so that you can course correct when necessary (Chapter 8)

- Gain self-awareness so that you can lead yourself and others (Chapter 9)

- Successfully adapt to a changing environment (Chapter 10)

As you work on developing your skills in strategic communication, it could be very helpful to explore other communication courses at your campus, even if they don't *seem* to relate to strategic communication. The better you understand communication as a holistic concept, the better your communication skills become.

Exploring Professional Roles in Corporate Communication

Professional roles related to strategic communication relate to the functions outlined earlier in Table 1.1. Ideally, corporate communication enjoys a seat at the management table, as corporate communication is as much about creating an organizational vision as it is about executing it. Thus within the field of corporate communication, individuals can occupy roles ranging from tactician to director. Some of the top career choices in corporate communication include social media director/strategist, communications director, content marketing manager, digital communication editor, PA director, human resources specialist, and much more. Many roles exist within an organization whose mission is not corporate communication (known as "in-house"); however, you can also work for a communication firm that takes on corporate communication-related tasks for clients.

Corporate communicators are verbal, analytical, and creative. They often enjoy working with words, the nuance in meaning, solving a puzzle, and working with others. Many times, corporate communicators are *"people* people" (i.e., people who love being around others), but there are many roles behind the scenes as well.

To get an idea of the breadth of the field, or to see where you might fit within it, visit a job search website, such as Monster, and type in the phrase "corporate communication." Click on some of the job descriptions and see what tasks are associated with the job and what skills are required. Think about your current goals. What jobs are a match for you? What skills do you have left to acquire?

QUESTIONS:

- What type of communicator am I?

- How have I already demonstrated strategic competencies when representing myself?

- What strategic competencies do I most need or want to develop given my professional direction?

- Who do I most admire for their strategic abilities, and how might I best learn from their example?

Tools and Processes for Self-Action

COMMUNICATION SELF-ASSESSMENT

Communication is a multifaceted process that involves creating shared meaning with others. While originally operationalized as a simple process of sender, message, and receiver (Shannon & Weaver, 1949), contemporary communication scholars recognize communication as a much more complex process in which participants cocreate meaning through every turn, with other factors, such as noise (any type of distraction) and mediation (technology such as phones or social media), as part of the process. Thus knowing how to communicate competently is rooted in many different factors and is a skill that everyone should purposefully build. Communication competence is "the ability and willingness of an individual to participate responsibly in a transaction in such a way as to maximize an outcome of shared meanings" (Littlejohn & Jabusch, 1982, p. 29).

There are many publicly available communication assessments online, and it is likely that your career and professional development center also has communication assessments available for you to take. Try finding one and taking it, or perform an informal self-assessment in the following areas:

- **Verbal communication.** Verbal communication is any communication rooted in message and word, and it can include spoken, written, and signed language. It encompasses a wide variety of communication skills, including creation, delivery, and adaptation of messages. Littlejohn & Jabusch (1982) refer more broadly to "communication skills" that fall under verbal communication, including graphics, public speaking, and design and implementation of information and media systems.

- **Nonverbal communication.** Nonverbal communication includes pitch, tone, eye contact, dress, gestures, and facial expressions. Our nonverbal communication can reinforce or contradict our verbal message; for example, think about the difference in saying "I'm fine" with a smile versus a frown. Nonverbal communication has also been characterized as a "relational message" in that it represents an intersection between our emotions and the ability to portray those emotions in a culturally appropriate way (Chesebro, 2014).

■ **Emotional intelligence.** Emotional intelligence is "the ability to monitor one's own and others' emotions, to discriminate among them, and to use the information to guide one's thinking and actions" (Salovey & Mayer, 1990, p. 189). It relates to the appraisal, regulation, and utilization of one's own and others' emotions and can encompass verbal and nonverbal communication, empathy, flexible planning, creative thinking, redirected attention, and motivation (Salovey & Mayer, 1990). Someone who is high in emotional intelligence is able to identify and assess how they are feeling regarding a situation or communication partner and adjust actions accordingly. In addition, a person high in emotional intelligence will take into account what other communication partners are feeling as well.

■ **Listening.** Listening is "the process of receiving, constructing meaning from and responding to spoken and/or nonverbal messages" (International Listening Association, 1996, as cited in Vickery, 2018). If we think of communication as something that is constitutive or reconstituted in every communicative act, then listening is just as important as speaking in terms of contribution toward creating shared understanding.

SETTING STRATEGIC PERSONAL GOALS

Earlier we talked about the importance of goals. Now it is time to set some of your own. Think big and work backward.

1. Where do you see yourself 5 years from graduation? Ideally, 5 years post-graduation, you will have entered your chosen profession and moved up the ranks at least once. Take some time to brainstorm what that profession is and what kind of responsibilities and title you want within that profession. *Be as specific as possible.* You may have to do some online research or even interview people in the communication field to hone in on possibilities. Try job search websites, your college career development center, and your professors. Once you are done brainstorming, choose your most desired possibility, and write it down at the top of a piece of paper in all caps or bolded with a marker. This is now your *5-year goal.*

2. Now brainstorm the smaller steps you will need to get done to achieve your 5-year goal. Again, this will take some outside research. And again, be as specific as possible. Based on the steps you come up with, create a *short-term goal* (what you want to achieve in the next year) and a *midrange goal* (where you want to be in 3 years). Write each of these farther down on your paper, leaving about one third of the space of the paper between each goal.

3. Now, fill in the *strategies* you need to enact to achieve each goal.

4. Finally, what are the *tactics* you will use to enact each strategy?

PLANNING FOR THE FUTURE IN TERMS OF EXECUTING MY GOALS

Throughout this book, we will discuss different ways that you can work toward your professional goals. The communication audit in the previous section will help you outline what your goals are and the steps you can take to achieve them. While these goals and steps will be specific to you, there are some broad categories that you should consider as you set out to create the strategies and tactics to achieve your goals.

- **Know yourself.** Who are you? How do you want to meld your personal identity with your professional identity? Why have you identified corporate communication as your chosen field, and what exactly do you want to do within the field? These are all questions that will both inform your goals and help you execute them. One of the key things that you can do is to do a "self-assessment" of who you are on a periodic basis. Keep the assessment in a journal or somewhere else where you can easily access it. Try taking the assessment every 2 to 3 months. Notice how it changes. As your assessment becomes more consistent, you will be able to work toward creating a personal brand or identity that you want to project in your professional career. We will discuss this more in Chapter 2, but before you can create your brand, you have to know who you are.

- **Resources.** The word "resource" is loosely defined as "means," "recourse," and "ability." In practical terms, resources are the tangible and intangible assets that you need to accomplish your goals. The most common resources are information, money, relationship, and access. You need to identify *what* resources you need to be successful and *how* to get them. This will involve firsthand research, such as talking to instructors, career counselors, alumni, and professionals in your chosen field. It will also involve secondary research, such as checking job websites and the websites of organizations you would like to work for someday, as well as reading about your chosen industry.

- **Connections.** Once you know what resources you need, then you should connect to them. If you need information, who can you go to in order to get that information? If you need money, how can you get it, and who can help you get there? This will involve assessing and strategically forming your networks, which we will discuss in detail in Chapter 3.

PROFILE OF INDIVIDUAL EXPERIENCE:

Sam Gentry

Sam Gentry, global social media governance and activation lead at General Motors, understands the importance of strategic communication for both personal and organizational purposes. Having been in the communication field since 2017, he still vividly remembers the role that strategic communication played in his transition from college to early career. Planning and setting goals were critical steps in his path from student to professional. He says: "When I was a college freshman I sat down in my counselor's office and said I wanted to work for General Motors when I graduated. While I didn't follow the path that I anticipated would be a logical one for the job I have now, I think that it's extremely important to set goals and share them with those close to you who can help enable you and hold you accountable."

Mr. Gentry works for General Motors's Social Media Center of Expertise, a central team responsible for social media strategy and governance for all of GM's brands. He works with stakeholders across the enterprise to ensure that GM effectively leverages social media to its

FIGURE 1.1 **Sam Gentry.**

full extent, from conducting marketing and managing PR to gaining customer insight and providing customer service. Strategic communication plays a role in everything he does. Says Mr. Gentry: "Strategic communication is important in my day to day work life because our team is responsible for interfacing with many parts of the organization that don't have a direct reporting relationship to our team. Therefore, I need to consistently be aware of how I tie our team's initiatives back to the business objectives that our stakeholders are held responsible for by their own leadership and craft communications that make those connections clear."

Mr. Gentry draws upon experiences from college in order to effectively enact strategic communication across a variety of settings and situations. For example, working on a state-level legislative campaign provided "direct" experience, such as creating advertisements and doing debate prep, but also offered valuable indirect experience learned by going door-to-door in support of his candidate. Says Mr. Gentry: "Knocking on a complete stranger's door to ask for their vote is something that gives you great experience in self-confidence, recovery, the ability to read a situation, and practice sticking to key messages that is a great intro for a communication-based job." Additionally, his experience studying abroad while in college gave him a great appreciation for working with people of diverse backgrounds, which has proven helpful in his role as liaison to GM global markets. He says: "My experience getting immersed in cultures different from my own taught me valuable lessons around being aware of certain sensitivities and expectations in the workplace. Additionally, my exposure to other languages helped me be stronger when understanding those who use English as a second language and also increased my own awareness of the way I speak back to them."

In terms of advice for current students looking to make the transition into the communication field after graduation, Mr. Gentry suggests employing strategic communication to make and leverage connections. Just as strategic communication rests on content, or what you say, it also involves who you communicate with and how you do it. "Networking, from my experience, is really about being able to effectively leverage the connections that you have, while building new relationships along the way. On the first day of a Communications class when I was in school, my professor mentioned that she had completed a fellowship with GM in the past. After class, I asked her if she had any connections at GM that I could reach out to, and years later I'm still here at GM. There are a lot of people who love to play 'connector,' so I would definitely advise that you leverage them as well as be a connector for others when possible."

Questions:

1. How can you apply the principles of Mr. Gentry's setting of personal and professional goals to your own experience?

2. Based on what you read in this profile, what elements of strategic planning have played the biggest role in Mr. Gentry's success. How can you apply that to your own situation?

3. Often in Corporate Communication we think of the importance of mass media over interpersonal communication. How did interpersonal communication play a role in Mr. Gentry's journey? How can you apply these principles to your own journey?

APPLYING THE CONCEPT TO YOUR WORK WITH CLIENTS

What Does It Mean to Communicate on Behalf of Someone Else?

Whether you are working in-house or for an external client, you will not produce content in your own voice. Rather, you have to adopt the voice of the organization (e.g., in social media posts, employee news blasts, the annual report) of specific members of the organization (e.g., when you are writing a speech for a chief executive officer (CEO), or chief financial officer, or representing an organizational officer in the media). This means that you have to understand not only the goals of the specific situation about which you are communicating but also the larger level vision and identity of the organization and, when applicable, the personality and voice of the person you are writing for.

How you do this comes down to research. Research can and should include a combination of first-person research, such as interviews, and secondary research, such as previous organizational speeches, campaigns, and marketing materials. The following information should be gathered when writing a speech for someone else:

1. Information about the person's background and experiences with the organization and the topic of the speech

2. The person's goals for the speech

3. Anything specific that the speaker wants to be included in the speech

4. Anything specific that the speaker wants to leave out

5. The kind of emotion the person wants to evoke

6. Determine if the speaker has any personal speaking quirks or catchphrases

As you talk with the person you will be writing for, it is useful to pay attention to the way he or she structures his or her sentences, the cadence with which the person talks, and anything else that is unique to the person's speaking pattern. This will help you as you compose sentences that will sound as if the speech giver wrote them him or herself.

Related, if you are writing for internal or external media, you may want to add a quote from a high-ranking member of the organization who is relevant to the topic you are writing about. For example, if you are writing a story for the organization's newsletter about an upcoming community event sponsored by your organization, you may want to make the story more interesting by quoting the PA director. However, the responsibility of creating the quote is often not given to the PA director but rather the person writing the article. In this case, rather than interviewing the PA director, you could create a relevant quote that is fairly neutral and then submit it to him or her for approval.

Developing a voice for the organization is a much more detailed process. As we proceed through the book, we will cover different elements of how to write effectively for the organization. However, some of the basics include the following:

- **Continuity.** It is important to create continuity in how the organization "speaks." Therefore, you should research previous materials, such as CEO speeches, campaign materials, social media posts, slogans, internal and external reports, and more.

- **Goals.** Consider what you want to accomplish with the specific materials that you are creating. While an organization should have an overall voice, it is natural that how that voice is enacted will change based on the goals and type of communication (e.g., print, social, audio).

▪ **Purpose.** Related to goals is the purpose of the material. Purpose is what you want to evoke in the listener or reader, such as to engage, educate, or inspire (Schwab, 2011).

▪ **Character/persona.** How would you describe your organization? Playful? Authoritative? Down-to-earth? What would the organization sound like if it were a person? What is the internal culture of the organization? Create a persona for your organization and then create materials based on that persona (Schwab, 2011; Solis, 2010).

▪ **Tone and language.** Separate but related, tone and language are the way that the brand "speaks" (Schwab, 2011). Is it personal or clinical? Complex or simple? Tone and language will be informed by, and a direct expression of goals, purpose, and character.

QUESTIONS:

▪ Which organizations do I want to support with my strategic communication talents and efforts?

▪ How are these organizations performing from a strategic communication standpoint?

▪ What are the best opportunities for helping these organizations achieve new strategic communication successes?

Tools and Processes When Acting for Others

COMMUNICATION AUDIT

A communication audit is a process by which organizations evaluate their current communication efforts with internal and external audiences. It is a comprehensive analysis of what an organization is doing well and where it can improve. There are four broad steps to conducting a communication audit: establishing the scope and framework, the discovery process, the distillation process, and interpretation (Cornell, 2015).

Establishing the scope and framework of the audit is the first step because it directs the rest of the process. In some ways, it is analogous to setting your goals for the audit: what is it, specifically, that you want to find out, and how widely do you want to search? At this time, you should also determine which stakeholder groups you want to include in the research. While communication audits aim to capture internal and external audiences, you should decide if you want to include all employees, management only, nonmanagement only, or other groups. Similarly, for external stakeholders, are you concerned with customers, shareholders, media, or other groups? Finally, establish what methodologies you will use (Cornell, 2015). You can choose quantitative methodologies, such as scale-based surveys; qualitative methodologies, such as focus groups; or both. We will discuss more about different types of research methods in Chapter 8.

The discovery process is the active research phase and includes a combination of primary research, or research collected by you, and secondary research, which relies on third-party sources, such as the media or institutional documents (Cornell, 2015).

The distillation process is the analysis stage, where you comb through the data and look for patterns or categories and make comparisons. Since communication audits consider both internal and external audiences, comparing data between the two groups can yield insight into the alignment between organizational identity and public perception, as described previously.

Finally, during the interpretation process, you draw conclusions about what the data means and what action steps the organization should take. Findings are generally compiled into a formal report to be shared with organizational decision makers.

PROPOSALS TO CLIENTS AND PROSPECTIVE CLIENTS

Client proposals are written plans that are submitted to a client (if you work for a communication firm) or to the appropriate department/decision maker (if you work in-house) to propose a communication action plan to address a problem or opportunity. Within the client proposal, you are communicating (a) that you have identified a problem (e.g., declining sales, losing market share) or opportunity (e.g., new program or product), (b) what you propose should be done, and (c) why you are the right firm/team to do it. Most plans follow a problem/solution or opportunity/benefit format. Sometimes you will be recruited to write the proposal, and other times you will enter the proposal as part of a bidding process. If you are working in-house, you may create the proposal unprompted based on a problem or opportunity that you see within the organization or at the request of a department or manager.

There are several layouts that you can use, but the basics cover the following:

- Executive summary

- Information about the background and qualifications of your firm/team. If you are in-house, this may detail which organizational members or departments you are pulling into the project and could also be positioned later in the proposal since your audience is already familiar with you and your qualifications

- Overview of the opportunity or problem. You can add facts/statistics found in your research to support your assessment

- Steps to address the situation or problem, including

  - Goals/objectives

  - Strategies/tactics

  - Key messages

  - Time line

- Evaluation

▪ Budget

▪ Conclusion

You might have noticed that this looks a lot like the RACE process. Although research isn't articulated here, research is the step that enabled you to identify the problem or opportunity, possibly through a communication audit as described previously.

To get an idea of what is involved in generating a proposal, think back to your goals. What kind of organization do you want to work on behalf of? Is there a particular area (social media, media relations, internal communication) you are most interested in? Do some research on that organization and identify a problem or opportunity for them. See if you can create a proposal based on the problem or opportunity.

PROFILE OF ORGANIZATIONAL EXPERIENCE

Walmart

What do you think of when you hear the word "Walmart?" The name conjures the idea of savings and value for some, and wage issues and bad shopping experiences for others. Walmart started as a family store in Rogers, Arkansas, in 1962. The company's founder, Sam Walton, believed in the model of discounting, which involves acquiring large quantities of inventory at a discount and then selling at a reduced rate (Gilbert, 2012). This model proved successful, and Walmart grew rapidly, going public in 1970. In 1983, the company expanded to include Sam's Club, a membership-based warehouse store. Walmart, now Walmart Inc., has evolved into a sprawling multinational corporation with more than 5,000 stores in the United States and 11,700 retail units worldwide (https://corporate.walmart.com/our-story/our-locations), making it roughly the size of the state of Maine (Neff, 2011). Walmart sells goods ranging from groceries and personal items to clothing, toys, and electronics, making it a one-stop shop for approximately 100,000,000 customers per week. As you will read in this case study, Walmart is a great example of the importance of internal and external alignment, and how (mis)communication can directly impact reputation.

Despite its financial success, Walmart has faced a number of challenges over the years, both internal and as a result of the changing external environment. While Walmart's slogans have focused on employees ("Our people make the difference") and saving consumers money ("We save people money so they can live better"), these two areas have been a place of misalignment between organizational identity and public expectations and values, leading to reputational damage. Indeed, Walmart CEO Doug McMillan is quoted as saying, "At some point, Walmart became big, and societal expectations changed. And we missed the memo" (Green, 2018). Issues associated with Walmart included poor employee treatment and pay, poor customer service, dirty stores, accusations of sweatshop labor, and being known as a behemoth that destroys communities by putting smaller "mom and pop" shops out of business without giving anything in return (Gilbert, 2012; Irwin, 2016).

To address these threats, Walmart made several changes in its company policies and communication, including the following:

- **Going digital and telling its story.** The company culture, set by founder Sam Walton, originally focused on serving customers by saving them money but not engaging with stakeholders outside of the shopping experience (Pollitt, 2014). In recent years, the company has made a shift from focusing only on discount prices to telling the Walmart story to both internal and external stakeholders through sites such as www.walmartfacts.com, eight Twitter handles ranging from @walmartveterans to @walmartgreen to @walmarthealthy, paid advertising, and internal platforms, such as Workplace by Facebook and other internal communication tools (Goldman, 2017; Pollitt, 2014). In addition, Walmart has shifted its advertising strategy to a narrative-based approach, telling the stories of employees who have graduated from one of the company's internal training programs, Walmart Academy, and launching a campaign based around the tagline "Wal-Mart saves the average family $2,500 per year. What will you do with your savings?"

- **Improving employee relations.** In addition to improving employee communication through internal newsletters and intranet platforms, Walmart invested upwards of $2.7 billion in higher wages, scheduling improvements, and employee training, including internal programs, such as Walmart Academy and Pathways (Corkery, 2017; Taylor, 2017). The average pay has increased approximately 16% for nonmanagerial full-time employees, and employees are provided more predictable scheduling (Peterson, 2016). There is also a clearer path for advancement within the company (Peterson, 2016).

- **Improving the in-store experience.** In addition to improvements in employee wages and training, Walmart has invested money in store renovation and addressing common complaints, such as empty shelves and dirty stores (Peterson, 2016). As a result, Walmart's customer service scores have improved, and they are seeing increases in sales and store traffic (Peterson, 2016).

- **Focusing on community and sustainability.** In 1972, the company established the Walmart Foundation, which by 2005 had grown to be the largest corporate foundation in the United States in terms of giving cash (Soderquist, 2005). The foundation provides grants, scholarships, and volunteering under the pillars of opportunity, sustainability, and community

(Walmart Foundation, n.d.). Each store, club, or distribution center is given discretion over how to spend its giving budget, which enables them to give directly to local community projects (Soderquist, 2005). Walmart has also addressed sustainability through the building of green stores, reducing packaging, and working with the sustainability fund to reduce greenhouse gas emissions and create a sustainability index for the products that they sell (Atamian, 2017). The same size and scale that has been considered a downside in the past, in terms of damaging community infrastructures, is a benefit because it allows Walmart to negotiate meaningful deals in terms of renewable energy and its supply chain (Atamian, 2017). These changes are having a positive impact. According to a HuffPost article, "Walmart is known for low prices. Now, the company is being recognized as a leader on the fight against climate change" (Atamian, 2015).

▪ **E-commerce.** A more recent challenge to Walmart has been the external threat from Amazon. Amazon's main areas of growth between 2016 and 2017 included pantry (up 38%) and grocery items (up 33%), and its top sales were in home electronics (Thomas, 2018), three of Walmart's primary sales areas. To combat this threat, Walmart upgraded its online shopping experience in three ways (Green, 2017). First, they started offering free two-day shipping on offers over $35, which matches Amazon's non-Prime shipping policy. Walmart has also started free grocery pickup for online orders. Finally, they offer pickup discounts for some items that shoppers buy online but pick up in the store. They also acquired Jet.com, an online retail company that offers discounted prices and uses smart-cart technology to provide discounts when shoppers bundle certain items. Walmart is set to implement similar technology on Walmart.com in the near future (Green, 2017). Walmart's e-commerce sales have risen by 50%, indicating that stakeholders are both aware of, and taking advantage of, these features.

Although Walmart still faces reputational challenges and external threats, strategically shifting its internal and external communication to tell its story through a variety of media, including via its employees, has reconciled at least some of the misalignment between its identity and the way the public perceives the company, allowing it to create the beginnings of a new narrative for the future.

Questions:

1. Compare a commercial from 2008 (https://www.youtube.com/watch?v=-FODPzxzdaEs) to more recent commercials: (https://www.youtube.com/watch?v=JJivCX2sUmc&feature=youtu.be). Which strategy do you think is

more effective? Why do you think storytelling can be such an effective part of strategic communication?

2. What elements of the strategic communication process can you identify in Walmart's communication strategy?

3. It took a combination of internal and external changes to improve Walmart's reputation. In what ways does this case study highlight the importance of a holistic communication approach that focuses equally on internal and external stakeholders?

Chapter Conclusion

In this chapter, we set the stage for a better understanding of what strategic communication is, why it is important, and how it fits into corporate communication. Hopefully, you've started to think about how you can communicate more strategically and how you might fit into the corporate communication field. If you still have questions, don't worry. As we move through the book, we're going to unpack much of what we talked about in this chapter in more detail, giving you guidance about how you can develop these skills for yourself and put them to use for clients. We begin in Chapter 2 with a focus on one of the most important outward-facing concepts in corporate communication: brand. As brands are closely linked to identity, we will show the importance of working with clients to build and maintain a positive and memorable brand, as well as creating a professional brand for yourself as you start your career.

Key Terms

Communication audit

Communication campaign

Communication self-assessment

Corporate communication

Goal

Objective

Organizational identity

Reputation

Strategic

Strategic communication

Strategy

Tactic

Chapter Discussion Questions

1. What is the link between internal and external communication? How do they both contribute to brand reputation?

2. What does it mean to be a strategic communicator on a personal level versus an organizational level? What areas of overlap can you identify? What are the differences?

3. How would you prepare to create a document in the voice of an organizational executive? What are the most important factors to consider?

4. Who are your stakeholders? How does what you learned about strategic communication in this chapter affect your view of communication with these groups of people?

Chapter Activities

1. Create 3-, 5-, and 10-year goals for yourself. Fill in your objectives and strategies.

2. Visit a job search site, such as Monster, and search for jobs using the keywords "corporate communication." What types of jobs interest you? What skills do you need to develop to get those jobs? Create a strategic plan for developing the necessary skills to apply for those jobs.

3. Conduct an external communication audit for the organization of your choosing. Find its mission statement on its corporate website and compare the organization's stated mission to its external communication. Is its communication in alignment with its mission? What recommendations would you have for this organization?

Recommended Readings and Resources

This humorous video demonstrates the importance of effective strategic communication:

https://www.youtube.com/watch?v=JwjAAgGi-90&feature=related

A listing of the major professional communication associations. Browse the sites for each association for information about academic and career paths related to strategic communication:

https://www.professionaldevelopmentpath.com/professional-communications-associations/

PR Daily is a source of news about strategic communication trends, topics, and happenings:

https://www.prdaily.com/Main/Home.aspx

CLIENT PROPOSAL

   I. Title Page
- a. Includes company name, contact information, and logo
- b. Client name and contact information
- c. Title for proposal
- d. Date

  II. Cover Letter
- a. Company introduction
- b. Overview of special characteristics
- c. Closing

 III. Table of Contents

 IV. Executive Summary
- a. Why you are sending the proposal
- b. What you can offer

  V. Proposal
- a. Problem or opportunity you are addressing
- b. Anticipated outcomes
- c. Time frame

 VI. Action Steps
- a. What you will do
- b. How you will do it
- c. Estimated time line and benchmarks

 VII. Pricing

VIII. Detail Outline
- a. Specifics of time line and payment in concise outline form

 IX. Legal Information/Agreement and Signature Page

https://blog.pandadoc.com/how-to-write-a-proposal/

BRAND
The Positive and Memorable Identity Sought

This chapter addresses the concept of brand, including its evolution in meaning to represent the overall identity of an individual or an organization, and its relationship to allied, sometimes nearly synonymous concepts. Attention will be given to the birth of brands and the management of brands in good and bad times. Consideration will be given to the basics of personal branding as well as what it means to manage major organization brands.

Theory and research in this chapter will draw from a range of sources, including interpersonal communication in sociology, narrative communication in business, and crisis communication in corporate communication. Despite the roots and original scope of each of these approaches, all will be shown to be relevant to brand communication management for individuals and organizations. Case studies will show the interface of individual and organizational brands regardless of whether the focus is on positioning an individual or an organization.

Orienting to the Concept:
Personal and Professional Brands

"Brand" may be a term more commonly associated with the field of marketing, but we feel it is the most useful identity-related term for this book and the interdisciplinary field of corporate communication. This is because brand conjures the most vivid aspect of identification for a given entity (i.e., individual or organization) and is generally understood as getting positioned by both the entity itself and the various stakeholders it engages.

Brand and closely allied concepts, such as identity, image, and reputation, matter because, first and foremost, the individual professional and the individual organization must be recognized as existing before they can be clearly understood as capable of acting and being acted upon. Brand is, therefore, foundational. And even though it can come into being without strategic awareness, a lack of strategic thinking and acting around brand is rarely, if ever, the case for entities that are continually successful in a competitive environment.

When studying to be corporate communication practitioners, we tend to take it for granted that brand development, protection, and enhancement for organizations is at the heart of what we do. Yet our own personal brands, however modest, give us the credibility to take on this work for others, and this aspect can sometimes be overlooked. It makes sense to carefully consider how we see ourselves as professionals, how we want others to see us, and how they actually see us. This can be a daunting process, especially when we feel like we are just getting started in our careers or we are contemplating a major repositioning of our careers. You may ask yourself, "How do employers even know I exist, let alone know that I have valuable talents to offer?"

Even if our own personal brands are in order, what is it exactly that we are trying to do for clients? We might be adept at spotting an organization in crisis or see an opportunity for an organization to more effectively use a media platform to reach stakeholders, but are we so sure of ourselves in knowing what it is we are protecting or extending? Sometimes it is easy to overlook the obvious. To sharpen our own thinking and more clearly articulate ourselves to clients, it is extremely helpful to clarify brand-related terms and theories, as well as get some experience in applying those terms and theories.

CENTRAL DEFINITIONS

IDENTITY

"Identity" is an entity's self-concept (Argenti, 2016; Goffman, 1959), whether that entity is an individual or an organization. "Identity" is how we want to be seen, particularly by those we judge to be important to us, such as key stakeholders. Identity can change across time, but, even when this is the situation, it is likely to have at least some enduring aspects.

IMAGE

"Image" is how an entity is perceived from an external perspective, especially by important stakeholders, at a certain point in time (Argenti, 2016; Benoit, 2015b).

REPUTATION

"Reputation" is generally understood as how stakeholders view an entity, and while this definition of the term is virtually synonymous with image, it has long been seen as a more respectable term than image (Coombs & Holladay, 2010). A more precise definition of reputation is that it is an evaluation of an entity's performance of meeting stakeholders' expectations (Coombs & Holladay, 2010). "Reputation" has also been defined as an assessment made across time (Cornelissen, 2014).

BRAND

"Brand" is what an overall entity is essentially known as. A key finding from the study of reputation is that an entity's distinctiveness is highly important (Fombrun & Van Riel, 2004), and, accordingly, cultivating a brand for the overall entity can be a valuable undertaking. The terms "identity," "image," and "reputation" may be more central to corporate communication as a scholarly pursuit, but there are several reasons why we concentrate on "brand" in this book. "Brand" has deep emotional connotations. A "brand" may not only be engaged but also co-created (France, Merrilees & Miller, 2015). "Brand" can be argued to subsume the concepts of identity, image, and reputation. In this sense, it can be viewed as the most important aspect of identification. Elevating the concept of "brand" in this book is also justified since employees use terms such as identity, image, and brand interchangeably (Harvey, Morris & Santos, 2017) and, therefore, use of these terms is quite malleable. The term "branding" is also relevant to this book because it has been applied to individual professionals (e.g., Kissel & Buttgen, 2015).

THEORY AND RESEARCH OVERVIEW

Brand Work as Performance—Goffman's Identity Theory: Dramaturgy and Impression Management

Erving Goffman was a qualitative sociologist who closely studied human interaction. He used dramaturgy or an overall theatrical metaphor to explain how we think about ourselves and relate to others. His close observations and compelling descriptions of interactively managing one's personal identity continue to affect theory, research, and practice in various fields, including communication. Goffman authored several acclaimed and influential books (with some addressing topics beyond self-identity). His most important book on self-identity and, therefore, the most valuable for our purposes is *The Presentation of Self in Everyday Life* (Goffman, 1959).

One of Goffman's main distinctions in *The Presentation of Self in Everyday Life* was between front stage and backstage. In an actual theater, the "front stage" consists of the areas in which actors are visible to the audience. "Backstage" consists of the areas only accessible to the actors and those others involved in staging a performance because these areas are out of view of the audience. Actors often go to considerable effort to perform their roles in ways that meet audience expectations. And the audience itself plays a certain role in terms of exhibiting expected behavioral norms. A performance goes well when there is agreement among all characters—the actors and audience alike—that everyone is behaving as they should and remaining in character while interacting on (the front) stage. When backstage or in a back space, actors may step out of expected roles, but when on the front stage or in a front space, behavioral expectations are high.

When applying Goffman's dramaturgical approach to everyday life, it is important to emphasize that we are all actors, and the processes of identity and meaning management are interactive and ongoing. Even at the time that Goffman wrote, he acknowledged that things are complicated by the fact that any given actor plays different roles and is often strategic in making behavioral choices most likely to lead to a successful performance with a particular audience.

In the more than half-century since he wrote his landmark book, the application of Goffman's dramaturgical approach has been further complicated by a considerable collapse of front and back spaces with the rise of electronic communication

(Meyrowitz, 1985). Public figures, such as business leaders, politicians, and celebrities, are safest when assuming they are always at least potentially on the record because the physical contexts used to define front and back spaces are destroyed with audio and video recording equipment, the rise of social media, and a sense that others' actions in private settings can be shared, and individual behavior should hold up to overall norms regardless of the context in which it first took place or was intended to take place. Think unexpected leaks and the crises they trigger for individuals and organizations. Goffman would point out how they are often instances of back-space interactions unexpectedly leaked into front spaces.

In the context of corporate communication, front space can be generally understood as all that is accessible about a brand to one or more external audiences, and back space is the internal communication operation that is unavailable to external audiences. Again, this is a tenuous distinction at a time when insider and outsider divides are weak.

Goffman's concept of "impression management" is worthwhile to point out because it highlights the strategic nature of establishing, maintaining, and rehabilitating identity. As Goffman described it, an actor effectively communicates with an audience by using verbal and nonverbal means to present a socially ideal version of the role he or she is adopting. The actor is carefully controlling his or her behavioral performance and the meaning of that performance in a front space. For Goffman, it was clear that actors could not sustain such control of performances and the overall impression management process without the ability to retreat to back spaces. From a contemporary standpoint, it is remarkable that actors not only have less control of the front-space and back-space divide with a given audience but also have less control over which audiences are able to access a given performance.

FIGURE 2.1

An actor unable to meet societal expectations in terms of a front-space role performance can either attempt to hide this failure or potential stigma or retreat into or proudly embrace a stigmatized position. Much of Goffman's later work explored the nature of deviance and stigma.

While Goffman's work primarily addressed the interpersonal level of communication, his theoretical contributions can arguably still be very applicable to larger levels of social interaction, including the organizational level.

Brand Work as Storytelling

Much has been written on work identity as a narrative process. A leader in this area is Herminia Ibarra, a professor of leadership and learning at INSEAD, one of the world's top business schools. As Ibarra and Barbulescu (2010) have summarized, an effective story creates meaning (Gergen, 1994; McAdams, 1996, 1999) and makes it more likely that identity claims will be accepted (e.g., Ashforth, 2001; Van Maanen, 1998). Representing ourselves through stories is important throughout our careers, but it can be especially vital and challenging during times of transition (Ibarra & Lineback, 2005). It can be helpful to remember to focus on the coherence of your overall story at these times yet not overlook transformation as an explanation for discontinuity (Ibarra & Lineback, 2005).

Ibarra and Barbulescu (2010) have articulated a detailed model of narrative identity during career transitions, such as entering and leaving an organization or changing occupational roles. These authors view us as having narrative repertoires. When going through a transition, we go through a process of telling, adding, reshaping, and dropping stories from our repertoire. Stories are more likely to be maintained in the repertoire if they are coherent, have cultural legitimacy, and are participatory for those hearing them. A varied yet coherent repertoire with effective identity work performance carried out over time is indicative of a successful transition.

Brand Across Time—Punctuated Equilibrium Theory

The authors Abratt and Mingione (2017) point out that clarifying corporate identity is vital to and precedes the determination of strategy and strategic marketing. For them, corporate identity involves all the following elements: who we are, what we are, our expression of choices, our mission, and our values and beliefs. Ideally, identity for an organization appears to stakeholders as singular. However, an effective identity is differentiated from other entities' identities in seven respects: (1) ownership, (2) vision and mission, (3) values and beliefs, (4) business, (5) personality attributes, (6) external image, and (7) strategic performance (He, 2012 in Abratt and Mingione, 2017).

Again, as Abratt and Mingione (2017) have concluded, while organization identities can sometimes seem stable, they are best understood as possibly including relatively enduring labels, but these labels inevitably undergo changes in meaning (Goia, Schultz, & Coorley, 2000; Balmer, 2015). In reviewing the literature, Abratt and Mingione (2017) have determined that there are two main reasons organizations need to change identities: environmental and internal misalignment among identities. Environmental change can involve any or all the following elements: social, economic, technological, political/legal, sustainability, and ethics.

Given the nature of organizational identity, Abratt and Mingione (2017) advocate for the punctuated equilibrium theory (PET). This is a theory developed over time by several contributors, including Tushman and Romanelli (1985) and Gersick (1991). PET regards organization identity as shifting between periods of slower, incremental change and faster, disruptive change. The slower, incremental times can be characterized as evolutionary periods when equilibrium and alignment are emphasized. The faster, disruptive times can be explained as revolutionary periods when more massive changes are in order.

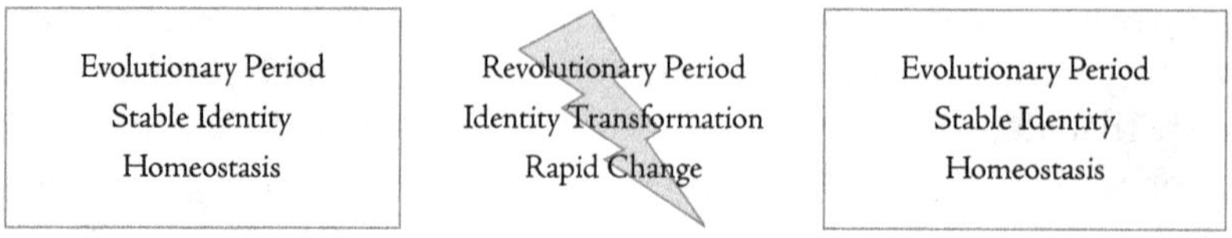

Evolutionary Period	Revolutionary Period	Evolutionary Period
Stable Identity	Identity Transformation	Stable Identity
Homeostasis	Rapid Change	Homeostasis

FIGURE 2.2 **Punctuated Equilibrium in Organizational Identity**

Image Repair as One Strategy When Confronting a Brand Crisis

Coombs (2012, p. 2) has defined a crisis as "the perception of an unpredictable event that threatens important expectancies of stakeholders and can seriously impact an organization's performance and generate negative outcomes." A crisis' most serious potential outcome is the threat to the organization's brand and, thereby, a threat to the organization's very existence. What can befall organizational brands in crises can also befall personal brands in crises. Crisis communication is closely related to risk management and reputation management, with risk management concerned with the minimizing of vulnerabilities and reputation management attempting to influence perceptions of crisis responsibility (Coombs & Holladay, 2015). Crisis communication, as a major area of study and application, covers crises from preventative efforts through post-learning and tends to emphasize the role of strategy and meaning-making (Coombs & Holladay, 2015).

Image repair is a strategy for a brand in crisis. Image repair in these situations matters because credibility is almost certainly on the line. Benoit (2015) has made the case that image is about perceptions and image repair theory is a messaging strategy for dealing with matters that involve responsibility and offensiveness. Benoit (2015) has provided a detailed typology of messages, and the selection and construction of a given message should take into account the following criteria: What needs the most attention? What will the most important stakeholder group accept as true? What evidence and resources does the entity have at its disposal, and what is the optimal medium for communication with priority stakeholders (Benoit, 2015b)?

APPLYING THE CONCEPT TO YOUR OWN SITUATION

THE IMPORTANCE OF A PERSONAL BRAND

1. **Existence.** Your very own professional brand matters for several reasons. First and foremost, basically, identity markers are necessary to have any level of visibility in the professional world, to simply exist on the professional landscape. The presentation of your name, the arrival of your resume, the fact that you are ready to participate in an interview demonstrate that you are a person claiming professional status. And, of course, even these fundamental communications will begin

to trigger qualitative impressions in those you meet. In this way, having a brand is unavoidable if you are seeking work. And, by implication, if you are bound to at least have a default brand, why not try and exert control and influence over how others see you by aiming to deliberately craft your brand?

2. **Basic credibility.** A second primary identity function of a personal brand is to successfully establish foundational credibility in your field. Do you have the required accomplishments to at least be an entry-level professional if seeking a salaried position? Do you communicate in ways that are understood to fit within the range of what is acceptable for the category of professional you are seeking to be? Are you someone to be taken seriously for the position you are targeting?

3. **Positive distinction.** A third function of a personal brand is to claim positive distinction to not only be one among many qualified people but also to outshine others, at least in a localized setting. If you are a distinctive candidate, you bring unique value that makes you more than credible in a generic sense. Here you are not just wanted because you can get the job done. You are wanted because you are you; you are different than others in your category.

4. **Potential for exceptional audience visibility.** A fourth function of personal brand is the potential for exceptional reach with one or more relevant target audiences. Highly effective personal branding means you are likely very recognizable in a net positive sense beyond the narrow circumstances of winning or succeeding in a certain position. You stand out in the eyes of a wide array of people who matter to you professionally, people who directly engage or could directly engage your brand.

5. **Potential for offering and being rewarded for high value.** A fifth and final function of personal brand explored here is the potential for your carefully crafted professional brand to be one that brings very high value, perhaps even the highest value, in your professional category. You provide outstanding service or produce results, and you can be compensated accordingly for your talents.

YOU ARE A PERFORMER

Personal brand comes alive in its embodied performance and closely related communications. It is not uncommon for corporate communication students and professionals to have been artistic performers of one type or another in their pasts. Even if you have not performed in or fulfilled a production role in a play or a recital or a YouTube video or done something similar at some point in your past, you are probably quite comfortable with the idea that corporate communication work often involves performance. Accordingly, representing yourself, representing your own professional brand, is not just like a performance; it is a performance, or a whole series of performances.

An effective performer convincingly portrays a certain character. The character has a coherence about all his or her behaviors and other communicative manifestations. To be a highly regarded professional is to be known for your character and to be consistent in not only your obvious actions but also in other aspects, such as your dress, demeanor, business card, and online presence.

While this is clear when an actor moves between front and backstage, it can be less clear when a professional is in a front space versus a back space. Professionals need back spaces to compose themselves, to polish their talents, and to prepare their work. Back spaces are valuable for working through conflicts and for doing the deep preparations required for outstanding front-space performances. Professionals sometimes work in traditional shared offices, sometimes work from home, sometimes work on the road. All of these can function as back spaces. Yet all of these can be front spaces too. How is potentially dangerous back-to-front space leakage avoided? What are the front spaces that truly matter to a given professional? How can performances in these front spaces be brought to the highest level possible?

For a professional, the very idea of a valuable front space and a commanding performance in that space are closely tied to being in front of the right audience. Some corporate communication professionals find it helpful to distinguish between primary target audiences and secondary target audiences. In this framework, primary target audiences are those that can potentially hire the professional to perform work, and secondary target audiences are those with whom the work is carried out. Make no mistake, the interaction between the corporate communication professional and a primary target audience is often one of significance and may be considered a high-stakes performance, even if it is a performance for just one or two people.

SHAPING YOUR STORY IS VITAL

Stories help us create meaning and offer the potential to make our professional identities credible—for both ourselves and the audiences that matter to us. A professional exists as one or more stories come into being. In the case of corporate communication professionals, stories can be derived by others, or each of us can at least attempt to shape our own story. Why not seize the opportunity? It is not about starting from scratch. Story strands or fully formed stories litter our personal biographies. Each of us needs to draw from these to create one or more signature stories to convey our professional identity. When developing a signature story, it can be helpful to remember to account for all five story elements: character, setting, plot, conflict, and resolution. Of course, it is only a great story if it connects you to your audience in its details and performance. And expect to rework your story throughout the course of your career, if not the course of a week.

BASIC MANIFESTATIONS OF A PERSONAL BRAND

Manifestations of a personal brand include your resume, your nonverbal personal presentation, your oral statement of professional introduction, and your portfolio of work samples.

Some see a resume as a straightforward and objective statement of a person's professional accomplishments. From a corporate communication point of view, it is important to see it differently. Yes, a resume must be factual in terms of accurately stating dates and any listed affiliations to organizations. These might be termed "hard constructions" that have been widely shared across our society over a considerable amount of time. However, there is often plenty of room for legitimately steering a resume for one or more audiences. In condensing a lifetime of professional relevance into one or two pages, there is much craft in deciding what cannot or should not be included in the document. And for that which merits mention, the shaping and positioning of language is potentially powerful in its possibility.

Nonverbal personal presentation can be a challenging topic to address in part because of the prejudice that many have experienced in this area, in part because the United States and many other Western countries put an emphasis on an individual's right of self-expression and in part because of the continued trend toward more casual dress, including street style, in many professional environments. Even with populist revolts against so-called political correctness in many countries, it remains entirely unacceptable to judge someone on his or her race, ethnicity, gender identity, sexual orientation, economic background, religious or non-religious identity, and disabilities.

There are some relatively stable aspects to how we self-represent. There are also less enduring choices we make about how we self-represent considering what we each interpret as meaningful given our overall identity. Sometimes, we regard these less enduring choices as still non-negotiable. Other times, we look at these choices as very negotiable and even strategic in terms of not necessarily reflecting our deep identities as much as potentially influencing those around us. Groom, dress, and accessorize as you must to be true to yourself. And consider how room for choice making in these areas can possibly be advantageous in terms of advancing your positive and memorable professional brand and the other brands you are seeking to advance.

Your oral statement of professional introduction is a 30-second to 2-minute monologue that states who you are professionally, what you have accomplished professionally, and the value you seek to provide a paying or otherwise sponsoring client. When combined with a request or proposal, it can be thought of as a personal pitch. While the oral statement without a request or proposal is largely informative, the personal pitch (i.e., oral statement with a request or proposal) is clearly an attempt at persuasion.

Your portfolio of work samples can consist of one or more of a wide variety of projects you completed in traditional courses, internships, or paid positions. These projects can be in hard copy or electronic format and can highlight any one or a combination of your competencies. In determining whether to use a hard copy or electronic format, consider what will be easiest for you to present and most impactful for your portfolio audience. Remember that electronic items can be rendered in hard copy form (e.g., a screen capture printout of a social media posting) and vice versa (e.g., a scan of a hard-copy letter). It is generally a good idea to showcase a range of talents in a range of media. For instance, no matter your academic and professional emphasis, strongly consider giving some evidence for your writing and visual design talents. While the fullness of your portfolio can impress, it is probably most important that you communicate the overall high quality of your work. Even if you are seeking an entry-level position, try to include work that reflects your ability to analyze complex situations and make strategic recommendations, as well as your ability to execute much more basic tasks. Before including work from internship sites and job sites, be sure to get proper permission to take creations outside of the regular work environment and share them with others.

PREPARE FOR PROFESSIONAL STABILITY AND CHANGE

You have probably already begun to anticipate how your professional story will change as you continue to develop your educational credentials and workplace victories. However, do not expect even, linear growth in your career trajectory, related main story, and overall brand. One or more of your educational accomplishments or client projects may bring transformative growth. There may be times when you voluntarily pull back in your career. There may be disappointments and setbacks in work and life. And the context of our field or our overall culture may shift so profoundly that your brand needs to be reformulated and repositioned. It is also very likely that new possibilities that are invisible to you right now or do not yet exist for anyone in our world at this time now will become available.

READY YOURSELF FOR CONFLICTS AND CRISES

Since our field is one that others rely on in times of serious brand-related conflicts and full-blown crises, it seems reasonable that each of us should take steps to prepare for such conflicts and crises in our own careers. There are brand-related conflicts and crises that can affect pretty much any professional. These include an individual's brand that is threatened by close association with an organization with a tarnished brand. You may also be affected by a layoff, regardless of the reason, from a salaried or contracted position. Also, there are almost certainly potential conflicts and crises more likely for your type of professional brand. For instance, if you are a social media professional and you get caught posting something inappropriate, what will you do?

QUESTIONS:

- What do I most value about myself as a professional?

- What is my desired personal brand?

- How do I already exemplify my desired personal brand to my stakeholders?

- What is my personal brand story, and how might I enhance it?

- What personal brand work is most important for me to undertake in the near future?

Tools and Processes for Self-Action

BASIC BRAND SELF-ASSESSMENT AND EXECUTION

Which of the following boxes are you able to check as far as your audience's general sense of your own brand? (a) You exist (basic professional visibility); (b) you are credible (basic professional value to offer); (c) you are distinct (recognized as having some degree of unique value to offer); (d) you are exceptionally visible; (e) you are especially valuable. No matter your positioning, take stock of the following: (a) your personal and professional history, (b) your personal qualities and values, (c) your passions and talents, (d) your personal and professional goals, and (e) some stories that best reflect who you are. Use these explorations to create or refresh the following manifestations of your personal brand: (a) your resume, (b) your non-verbal personal presentation, (c) your oral statement of professional introduction, and (d) your portfolio of work samples.

USING REFLECTION AND REFLECTIVE LISTENING TO DEVELOP YOUR BRAND

Because a career involves hard work ideally grounded in self-motivation and innate or at least long-established talents, it is worth taking time to ponder the essentials of what defines you professionally. In terms of your own passions and competencies, reflection can occur on your own or in conversation with those who know you well and whom you deeply trust. Because careers also involve serving others, it can also be very helpful to develop your brand by listening closely to the goals and unmet needs of those to whom you want to provide value. This can mean setting up a kind of informational interview or just talking more casually. In any case, prepare to listen carefully and have some of your existing assumptions challenged by what you hear. Sometimes it is helpful to meet one-on-one with individuals who have known you for a long time to get insights into what may make you uniquely powerful as a developing professional. Sometimes it is helpful to meet one-on-one with established industry professionals who can help point the way given their insider knowledge and your ability to articulate your core characteristics, talents, and interests for their consideration.

PERSONAL BRAND BENCHMARKING

While it is never okay to steal someone's intellectual property nor, arguably, is it ethical to broadly adopt someone else's brand as your own, even while staying in the bounds of the law, it is not unreasonable to study the strategies of top leaders in your sector or even successful professionals just a few years ahead of you and learn from them. For instance, how do the most highly regarded individuals in your field anchor their brand stories, and what media platforms do they use? Benchmarking of any kind may work best (and best keep you out of trouble) when you focus on patterns across a collection of brand leaders rather than seek to imitate anyone. In this respect, benchmarking can turn into the identification and application of best practices to your branding situation. Recognize that benchmarking can be used for any brand situation, such as initial development and launch, steady growth, and transformations and crises.

PROFILE OF INDIVIDUAL EXPERIENCE:

Rakia Reynolds

Rakia Reynolds is founder and CEO of Skai Blue Media, a full-service PA agency whose clients include Comcast NBC Universal, Dell, and Serena Williams. Ms. Reynolds is an exemplar of personal branding since she has been wildly successful at developing her personal brand, as well as her organization's brand. Rakia Reynolds—the individual—has been recognized as a top leader by *Elle* magazine, PBS, and other media outlets. She has also been featured in a Dell advertising campaign (Dell, 2017).

FIGURE 2.3 Rakia Reynolds

It may be tempting to look at Rakia Reynolds now and assume she has followed a straight line to the pinnacle of personal branding, but that is not the case. After completing her undergraduate degree in international business and marketing, she moved on to graduate work in consumer behavior but also branched out into counseling psychology courses. This led her to work in higher education for 5 years before reorienting toward the concept of brand in all she did professionally. She made what felt like a huge leap of faith and became a TV producer for MTV Networks. Ms. Reynolds summed up this early part of her career and three notable roles that followed: "I went from educator to producer to ideator to mother to entrepreneur."

Currently, Rakia Reynolds most likes to describe herself as "trailblazing entrepreneur," an African American businesswoman forced to find her own way. "There weren't any other women of color who I knew starting businesses as creative influencers that I could look up to when I began my journey." Ms. Reynolds seized the opportunity to be distinctive about her personal presentation, including how she dressed and accessorized, to advance her brand. She explained, "For a number of years, I wore a different hat almost every day. That was my way of telling people I was a woman with many different talents." Four years later, she made a style shift that she maintains to this day. Ms. Reynolds talked about gaining insight into an important overall brand principle that triggered a new clothing commitment: "I realized I am an authentic leader, which means being transparent to my clients and my team about the good, the bad, and the fugly—fucking ugly. So, I decided to consistently wear our brand color, which is blue. Blue is the color of trust, honesty, and sincerity."

Simultaneously building a personal brand and a closely related organization brand can be tricky. It helped that, from the outset, Ms. Reynolds had a plan for separating and relating the two. "I made a very concerted effort to create two distinct brands. There was Rakia Reynolds and there was Skai Blue Media. The story was always Rakia Reynolds as the hands behind the brand. I didn't want Skai Blue Media to be Rakia Reynolds. I wanted it to be Rakia Reynolds who built this awesome company called Skai Blue Media."

Given that Rakia Reynolds is a name brand representing name brands, you might think that her professional life is highly stressful, but no. Ms. Reynolds's efforts to develop her authentic self have made her work easier and truly joyful. "The most rewarding part is that I get to be me! It's the difference between being a freestyle lyricist and a rapper who must endlessly practice their stage routine because someone else wrote the lyrics. The most challenging part is seeing people who are inauthentic and have to work really hard before delivering their brand to the masses."

While Rakia Reynolds is proud of her achievements, she is also very aware of how she needs to keep progressing: "As the technology landscape continues to rapidly change, I will need to track how media content and consumption evolve and adjust my brand communication to maintain visible and consistent messaging regarding my honesty, transparency, and authenticity."

Questions:

1. How does Ms. Reynolds exemplify Goffman's concept of identity work as performance, and to what degree is she performing effectively? Please provide two examples.

2. Select any two role shifts in Ms. Reynolds's career and, for each, suggest how she might have had to creatively extract one or two stories from an old role to establish initial credibility in her new role. For example, how might experiences as a university educator prepare her for becoming a TV producer and how might experiences as a TV producer prepare her for becoming an entrepreneur?

3. Referring to PET, how can you make a case for the number of times Ms. Reynolds made revolutionary personal brand shifts versus evolutionary personal brand shifts?

4. How do you think being a trailblazer has made Ms. Reynolds's professional journey easier and/or more difficult for her?

APPLYING THE CONCEPT
TO YOUR WORK WITH CLIENTS

GETTING OTHERS TO SEE BRAND AND BRAND
MANAGEMENT OPPORTUNITIES EVERYWHERE

An organizational brand is certainly communicated in the name of the entity as well as in its visual depiction, including the name of the entity combined with a logo and catchphrase. Other ubiquitous forms of brand communication include design of physical locations, websites, social media, advertising across platforms, and visibility of senior leadership and/or other notable brand ambassadors. This is an extremely abbreviated listing. Brand is at least indirectly communicated in everything organizational members do. Recognizing the branding opportunity is the first step to seizing the opportunity. It may be evident to you, but it will likely not be evident to most of those with whom you work.

GETTING CLIENTS TO OWN THEIR BRAND STORIES

Brand story ownership for your clients means making sure they understand their brand stories and are motivated to share them whenever possible. Sometimes you will have the chance to facilitate a process in which clients shape their brand stories. This can easily lead to a strong feeling of brand ownership for those who take part. But this kind of process is not always possible. Very often a brand basically exists already, and clients need to be introduced or reminded of its appeal. Here it can be helpful to highlight instances of the brand story at its best and reaching across time and space, possibly by emphasizing the purity of its origins or its deeply positive present-day impact on external stakeholders. Clients or other key members inside the organization can, subsequently, feel a strong connection and feel like they want to bring the brand forward in their own activities for the organization. It is a good thing when clients have a brand story and love it, but it is not enough. It is also important that they bring that story forward in all their work. Here the concept of performance can be crucial.

GETTING CLIENTS TO GRASP BRAND
COMMUNICATION AS PERFORMANCE

Corporate communication students and professionals tend to understand the value of the metaphor of performance for making sense of their work, even if they do not see their work as actual performance. However, some clients can find this point of view difficult to see. They may think they are being asked to be insincere or, worse, plainly unethical. Or they may think they are being asked to do something that is socially acceptable but difficult for them because they are not actors in the traditional sense. It can sometimes be helpful to explain brand communication performance as an organization or a representative of the organization putting their best foot forward. Expectations for what that looks like depend on the identity of the organization, the audience, and the situation itself. To have good brand communication is to have a strong commitment to doing things in a way that best reflects the organization to which you belong. It is a carefully considered and deeply sincere way of being. It may take effort to determine what it means to behave in this way and then learn to behave in this way, but it can be personally, as well as organizationally, rewarding. Of course, it does not only happen in person; it happens with brand manifestations. It can still be helpful to see these other communications from a performance mind-set, for example, as carefully created props.

GETTING CLIENTS TO APPRECIATE AND RESPOND TO THE NEED FOR BRAND TRANSFORMATION

There can be a crazy irony in helping clients fall in love with their brands and then later challenging them to move on from them. In most cases, a client's or a client organization's brand will be managed effectively with an incremental approach, especially if you have a long-standing relationship with them, and they are not in a particularly volatile sector. Yet the need for disruptive change to a brand will come eventually and likely sooner than anyone on the inside of the brand wants to anticipate. The arrival of this kind of need is often nothing less intimidating than an invitation to have a chance at surviving by committing to painful and resource-intensive change, all without a guarantee. Corporate communication professionals can help by normalizing brand transformation during the "good times"—times of near stability. Corporate communication professionals can also be helpful in doing as much as possible to design brand evolution strategies for clients that essentially amount to smart incrementalism that makes hard brand shifts less necessary or less severe or less risky. Corporate communication professionals can also be a support by making the brand transformation process as clear an opportunity and as managed a risk as possible.

GETTING CLIENTS TO MEET BRAND CRISES HEAD ON

A crisis is a moment of reputational damage or at least a serious threat of reputational damage. Here brand protection is not just a nice thing or even a matter of potential concern. The concern is now. A crisis successfully navigated does not necessarily result in brand transformation. It may simply be a case of disciplined execution with the result that the existing brand stays intact. There are many instances, though, of crises spurring brand transformation. Whether a transformation is thrust upon a client, likely imminent, or worth contemplating given a crisis situation, the corporate communication professional often finds it is his or her job to make sure that the client is acknowledging the crisis reality and is engaged to assess the situation and likely take some related course of action.

QUESTIONS:

- How does your client organization describe its brand story, and what other brand manifestations mean the most to them?

- How is the brand seen by its stakeholders, especially its most valued stakeholders?

- How can your client's brand story be improved or transformed?

- How can your client's stakeholders be more effectively connected to the brand?

Tools and Processes When Acting for Others

STRATEGIC PLANNING FOR BRAND EVOLUTION

Although you may play a role in helping create and launch new brands, it is probably more likely you will support existing brands. Further, you will likely be focused on narrow initiatives to involve one or more internal or external stakeholder groups rather than looking after the overall brand. Nonetheless, your work will remain important because brand opportunities and challenges are present in every situation involving stakeholders.

When in a brand caretaker role, it can be helpful to begin by clarifying the overall brand and its likely direction in the near to midterm future, as this will point to the general direction for more localized efforts. Addressing brand in more focused areas is often done best when time is taken to gather information and consult with all likely affected parties, including peripheral stakeholders, prior to taking disruptive action.

CREATING BRAND NARRATIVE

A major goal of many corporate communication professionals is to engage stakeholders to generate positive brand-related stories and, by doing so, extend the brand. This process involves clarifying the basic brand, developing opportunities for brand extension that have parameters but are not too tightly controlled (so as to empower and motivate), engaging one or more stakeholder groups in the effort, managing the process, making the most of outcomes, and learning from the overall effort.

ORGANIZATIONAL BRAND BENCHMARKING

There is much to be learned by scanning the organizational brand landscape and identifying brand leaders and branding trends. While it is valuable to consider the brands of allied organizations and competitors within the same sector as your client organization, a very broad consideration can also be enlightening. By looking beyond your organization's sector, you may find fresh benchmarks.

Crisis management is not only about what actions are taken after a crisis emerges. It also involves scanning the entity's crisis landscape, decreasing the likelihood that certain crises will happen, and even recognizing that some crises are a near certainty and planning accordingly. Brand crises can develop internally or externally. Taking time to prepare in advance can pay dividends even when the nature of eventual crises is not forecast with precision. Preparation invariably leads to the development of systems that can be adapted. Proactive brand crisis efforts can also pay dividends if you champion them and are seen as doing a good job.

PROFILE OF ORGANIZATIONAL EXPERIENCE:

Nike

Nike is one of the world's most recognizable, desirable, and profitable brands. Known for a name borrowed from the Greek goddess of victory, with its distinctive Swoosh™ logo and many powerful slogans, including "Just Do It," its identity can seem clear, dominant, and unified. Yet the company's brand was not clear at the outset, and it continues to navigate branding turbulence, including some that it intentionally initiates.

In his memoir *Shoe Dog*, Nike creator and founding CEO Phil Knight (2016) recounted how his shoe business existed long before Nike was born. And it was longer still, sometimes years, before other key elements of the brand emerged. Nike started out as Blue Ribbon in the mid-1960s and was simply a distributor of Japanese athletic shoes in the United States for 7 years. As Mr. Knight and others involved in the start-up began talking up their Tiger shoe in the late 1960s, they began referring to the shoe's innovative fabric as "swooshfiber" (p. 138). It was also around this time that Mr. Knight bumped into Carolyn Davidson, a struggling graphic designer from Portland State University, who offered to do some design work. Mr. Knight got her name and number on a piece of paper but forgot about it.

As Mr. Knight (2016) noted, it was not until 1971 that Nike truly was born. Knight's relationship with his manufacturers soured, and he and his team decided to make their own shoes. Because the company was under pressure to generate a supply of shoes and keep its income flowing, it needed to quickly figure out what logo to put on its first original shoes and what to name them. Knight reached out to Ms. Davidson, a now occasional designer of ad copy at Nike, to come up with designs that involved motion. After receiving input on some rejected offerings, she presented something that looked like "a wing" or "a whoosh of air" (p. 181). The now classic Swoosh™ had been developed. And Ms. Davidson was presented with a check for $35.00 (and, many years later, paid much more generously for this extraordinary work). Various animal names and the name Dimension Six were cast aside when Bob Woodell, a member of Knight's inner circle, literally had the name Nike appear to him in a dream, and it stood out, just barely, for Knight when he was on the phone with the factory making his first original shoe order.

In the decades that followed, Nike's core brand remained largely unchanged and spread across the U.S. and around the world. New brand elements were added, including the "Just Do It" slogan in the late 1980s. And there have been controversies that threatened the brand to which Nike was forced to respond. These included serious allegations of labor abuse in the manufacturing of Nike products in Asia and a culture of sexism in the leadership ranks in the United States.

In 1992, an exposé in *Harper's Magazine* documented how Nike was paying some of its workers as little as 14 cents per hour (Ballinger, 1992). This was the start of years of protests and bad press for Nike, not only because of the core issue of working conditions at some of its factories but also because of its embrace of a stonewalling strategy. Notably, Nike eventually turned things around and, at least on this issue, has become a leading example for other companies. By the mid-2000s, Nike was publishing a groundbreaking yearly corporate responsibility report that detailed labor conditions at all of its production facilities (Ritson, 2005). Nike went through a protracted PR crisis on this issue of labor standards and only emerged as it embraced full disclosure (DeTienne & Lewis, 2005).

A more recent challenge facing Nike concerned the treatment of women in its leadership ranks. This came after years of Nike touting its support of women. In 2018, the *New York Times* published an investigative article on wide-spread discrimination against women in the organization (Cresswell, Draper, & Abrams, April 29, 2018). This included women being blocked from leadership positions in top company divisions, such as basketball, blatantly sexist language used in internal communications, and the human resource department failing to effectively respond to serious accusations. Nike's CEO subsequently committed to taking the issue seriously and instituting changes beyond some already made (Draper & Cresswell, 2018). Within a matter of days and after the results of an investigation, the departure of an additional five senior managers was announced (Cresswell & Draper, May 8, 2018). Remarkably, Nike's "Teflon brand" allowed it to weather this storm with women's impressions of the brand even less affected than men's impressions (Segran, 2018).

Notably, Nike has not only responded to tensions regarding its general brand identity; it has introduced tensions by promoting diverse brands within its overall brand. As customer connections to brands have become more mobile, Nike has honed its SNKRS app and sales of specially branded limited edition shoes (Ringen, 2018). The "sneakerheads" who are attracted to these shoes are a small percentage of all buyers, but they have an outsized effect on the overall sneaker market (Ringen, 2018).

Questions:

1. Nike, Inc. is named after the Greek Goddess of victory. What are two branding insights that Nike, Inc. could gain by considering itself the metaphorical embodiment of Nike the goddess within the framework of Goffman's dramaturgical approach and our present day context?

2. Referring to PET and the Nike labor and sexism-in-leadership crises, make an argument for whether these events should be described by Nike as causing incremental or revolutionary changes to the brand story. And should attempts at these classifications by Nike be similar or different with internal stakeholders and external stakeholders?

3. Nike and other dominant brands are faced with the challenge of adding novelty without diluting the existing brand value. What is a specific way the company can tell a truly innovative new story that fits with its core story? (Possibly, be inspired by what Nike did with the development of the SNKRS initiative.)

4. Refereeing to Abratt and Mingione's (2017) main reasons for organizations as needing to change identities, how do you think the Nike brand may be challenged in the coming two years?

Chapter Conclusion

It all starts with brand because without it, an entity is practically invisible. Yet while early efforts may be concerned with basic visibility, visibility is not enough to survive and thrive. The process of branding can take many twists and turns. When all is going well, it can seem so simple. An individual professional or an individual organization is recognized, liked, and engaged. But it can all go wrong for myriad reasons. The need to be vigilant and actively safeguard a brand never lets up. Even for very large and profitable organizations, the foundational importance of brand does not go away.

Whether managing your own brand or that of others, remain clear about what is valued by the brand's stewards, tend to any brand gaps that develop with stakeholders, stay on top of stories of origin and transformation, polish your performances, do not shrink away from addressing crises, and continue to engage, engage, engage.

Key Terms

Brand
Dramaturgy
Identity
Image
Image repair theory

Impression management
Narrative identity
Punctuated equilibrium theory
Reputation

Chapter Discussion Questions

1. Identify an upcoming career-related event that is likely to be highly important to you and in which you will want to engage in impression management. Who is the audience you will be trying to impact? What will you want them to understand about your personal brand? What are two ways you will be communicating verbally and/or nonverbally to leave this impression?

2. 2. What does it mean for your personal brand to be deeply authentic? To what extent are you embodying this authenticity right now? How can you manage your career in the coming years to bring more of your authenticity forward?

3. 3. Since the rise of electronic media, including social media, it has been more difficult for individuals and organizations to control the divide between front and back spaces (because of the leakage of information from back spaces). How, if at all, can back spaces be used effectively to develop and manage personal and organizational brands? What are examples of brands that exemplify your point of view?

4. Origin stories and stories of transformation can be incredibly powerful for creating, building, and repairing brands. From your point of view, which individual and which organization have the best origin stories? Which individual and which organization have the best transformation stories?

Chapter Activities

1. Most organizations have a logo to help represent their brands. Design a logo to represent your personal brand. After developing your logo, explain how it is meaningful to you and would be positive and memorable to one or more of your key stakeholder groups.

2. Brands can be understood as communicating one or more emotions to help make them distinctive. Reflect on your personal brand and select between one and three emotions you want others to feel when they encounter your brand. Explain why these emotions fit your brand. Also, explain how you will communicate these emotions.

3. Give some thought to an organization brand you admire and determine a stakeholder group it does not currently engage but could benefit from engaging. Describe how the brand could most effectively build a relationship with this new stakeholder group.

Recommended Readings and Resources

PricewaterhouseCoopers is a global professional services company best known for the accounting services it offers organizational clients. Although PwC does not have a high proportion of corporate communication professionals in its ranks, its complimentary *Personal Brand Workbook* is largely in line with the personal branding aspect of the chapter you just completed and may be useful to you.

https://www.pwc.com/c1/en/assets/downloads/personal_brand_workbook.pdf

The concept of personal branding is over 25 years old. Read this foundational article on the topic by management consultant Tom Peters writing in the magazine *Fast Company*.

https://www.fastcompany.com/28905/brand-called-you

Read more about Rakia Reynolds, personal branding, and owning her own PR agency.

https://www.elle.com/life-love/interviews/a40808/rakia-reynolds-skai-blue-media/

https://www.phillymag.com/business/2017/11/09/rakia-reynolds-public-relations/

Figure credits

Fig. 2.1: Copyright © 2012 Depositphotos/alphaspirit.

Fig. 2.3: Darren Burton Photography. Copyright © by Skai Blue Media. Reprinted with permission.

COMMUNITIES
Networks of Support and Impact

The chapter will emphasize the idea of community and relationship as critical to strategic communication. We will explore the idea of relationship in terms of social networks, stakeholders, and social capital. You will be asked to consider your personal networks and how you can strategically build networks and social capital related to your personal and professional goals. Finally, we will explore the importance of relationship related to clients through an examination of interorganizational networks and stakeholder networks.

Orienting to the Concept:
Building Relationships for Success

Who do you turn to when you need advice? Money? Information? Chances are it is someone you already know, whom you trust, and with whom you have already exchanged information or other resources. In short, you turn to someone you have a relationship with. Often those relationships are with others in your community. Community can be defined in terms of geography, such as the community in which you live. Or it can be considered in terms of your connections to other people with whom you have something in common. For example, there are online communities for almost every interest, ranging from social support or professional interests to more lighthearted interests, such as gaming or fitness.

The relationships we engage in within our communities are built on communication. Communication repeated over time with the same parties can be conceptualized in terms of networks. Networks are how we come together, connect to others, and build our social structures. As we discussed in Chapter 1, strategic communication is deliberate, and goal-driven communication is designed to achieve desired ends. Depending on our goals, we can strategically choose to communicate with specific people for specific reasons, building our desired networks. An example of such a network could be connecting with others on LinkedIn. When we register for the site, we create a profile that reflects the personal brand we have crafted for ourselves and then connect with others who we think might be professionally advantageous to us.

Individuals aren't the only ones who belong to communities. Organizations are also embedded within larger communities. Again, these can be geographic communities, such as the city or town in which the organization physically resides. Or they can be more specific, such as an industry or lobby. The networks organizations build within their communities are referred to as interorganizational networks. Through interorganizational networks, organizations can leverage communication to gain access to resources, create powerful coalitions, or enact social initiatives, such as CSR (see Chapter 6). In its credo, Johnson & Johnson outlines its responsibility to "the communities in which we live and work and to the world community as well. We must be good citizens—support good works and charities and bear our fair share of taxes. We must encourage civic improvements and better health and education. We must maintain in good order the property we are privileged to use, protecting the environment and natural resources." Such a statement highlights the way that Johnson & Johnson is embedded in the physical communities within which it operates, counts itself as one of the citizens of those communities, and is, therefore, connected to others in those communities. An example of a more strategic interorganizational network is when organizations join a trade association (an organization that is funded by and operates on behalf of the member firms of a specific industry). The relationships in such an organization provide an impetus for competitors to become collaborators who share resources and form coalitions to advance interests that benefit both the individual organization and the industry as a whole.

In short, communities and other types of relationships provide the support to develop our professional offerings and the openings to make a positive difference in our lives as well as the lives of others. In this chapter, we will further define the idea of communities and networks related to strategic communication and look at how you can apply these principles to your own professional development and on behalf of clients.

CENTRAL DEFINITIONS

SOCIAL NETWORKS

A formal definition of networks is "a way of thinking about social systems that focus our attention on relationships among the entities that make up the system, which we call actors or nodes" (Borgatti, Everett, & Johnson 2014, p. 1). Put more simply, they are the connections (ties) that we have with others (actors). These connections are not one-time interactions or people with whom we have a passing interaction. Rather, we are rooted, or embedded, within these connections. Networks can exist on the individual level, as in all of the contacts that one person has, also known as their ego network. Networks can also be conceptualized as whole networks, which consist of all the connections within a specific boundary condition (e.g., a town or an organization). Finally, on the macrolevel, it has been said that we exist within a network society, which is the "organizational arrangement of humans in relationships of production/consumption, experience, and power, as expressed in meaningful interaction framed by culture" (Castells, 2000, p. 5), meaning that rather than being bound by country or other affiliation, we are all interconnected in a variety of overlapping networks of our own communicative making.

INTERORGANIZATIONAL NETWORKS

The networks that connect organizations to other organizations are called interorganizational networks. Interorganizational networks are typically created to manage uncertain environments and gain access to resources (Gulati & Gargiulo, 1999). This, in turn, leads to interorganizational linkages and coordination by networks (Monge & Contractor, 2003). Interorganizational networks can include any organization with whom the organization is interdependent and shares repeated interaction, including suppliers, competitors, other organizations within their industry or community, and more. Members of interorganizational networks are also stakeholders, but here we are distinguishing between the interorganizational networks and stakeholder networks to emphasize the difference between strategic communication with other organizations (interorganizational) and other groups, such as consumers, donors, and others (covered in the next section).

STAKEHOLDERS AND STAKEHOLDER NETWORKS

Stakeholders are "all the groups and individuals that have an affect or are affected by the accomplishment of an organizational purpose" (Freeman, 1984, p. 25). In strategic communication, stakeholders are generally conceptualized as consumers, donors, or other external actors who consume/support the organization's product and contribute to the organization's bottom line. However, by Freeman's definitions, organizational stakeholders are a much more diverse group, including employees, activists, the government, the media, the local community in which the organization operates, the global community that the organization draws from/ contributes to, and more.

Stakeholder networks represent a whole network view of an organization's stakeholder groups (e.g., consumers, shareholders, employees) and how the structure of these relationships affect organizational outcomes (Rowley, 1997). Organizations' interactions with one stakeholder group are often not isolated from their communication with other stakeholder groups. For example, activists are privy to public communication organizations have with their customers, which in turn affects how activists communicate with the organization. Thus stakeholder networks are the web of mutually influenced relationships within which an organization exists, each of which is also connected to each other relative to the organization. The implications of these connections are that stakeholders can band together to exert influence on the organization or even influence each other on behalf of the organization.

Because of the interdependence between organizations and stakeholders, stakeholder communication is one of the most important functions of strategic corporate communication.

SOCIAL CAPITAL

As we create relationships and share resources in our networks, we build social capital, or the collection of resources ingrained in our social structure, which can be activated when needed (Lin, 2001, p. 13). Put simply, social capital can be thought of as the goodwill or access that we gain as we build trust and engage in repeated interactions within the same social circle. Like social networks, social capital can be conceptualized on the individual or collective level and, therefore, can be thought of in terms of one person's participation in a network (e.g., an individual can accumulate social capital that he or she can "cash in" when needed) or the resources embedded in a network as a whole (e.g., a network that is high in participation can be considered a network that is rich in social capital). Thus social capital is tied to strategic communication in that (a) the more we communicate with others in our network, the more social capital we can build, and (b) we can strategically leverage social capital when necessary.

THEORY AND RESEARCH OVERVIEW

Social Network Theory

As we mentioned earlier, networks are created when individuals engage in repeated interactions with the same people or groups of people. Typically, we create networks based on parameters, such as geographic proximity or similarity to others (Powell, 1990). However, individuals can decide to include or leave out certain members of the larger network in order to create smaller, more intimate networks based on more personal values, such as similar interests or beliefs. Or they can choose to engage with others outside of set parameters who have resources that they need, such as information or money. Over time, these choices create communication patterns that change the overall network structure. Again, reflecting on your own network, as you got older and gained more mobility and wider interests, you likely narrowed down your pool of friends in the neighborhood to those you had the most fun with and simultaneously expanded your network to include people at your high school, job, music lessons, or other new activities. Within your ego network, you probably have subgroups of friends (e.g., school, job, clubs) that have some overlapping communication but are also relatively distinct. Those friends that span various subgroups (e.g., your friend from school who also plays the same sport as you and goes to the same religious institution) are probably your closest friends because they are multiplex ties or people with whom you have higher amounts of communication about a variety of interests.

While the original focus of social network theory was on the connections of various actors that make up one's social structure, it is through communication that these connections are made and, hence, social structure is built. While some of these connections happen by chance (e.g., family), as we said earlier, others are made strategically. Thus strategic communication is a tool that we use to build our networks in a way that helps us achieve our goals. It is also through communication that we agree on shared meaning within our networks, such as defining the terms of our relationships. For organizations, this can include defining the parameters of the organization relative to the network, giving shared meaning to the relationships within the network (e.g., a supply chain/customer, corporation/ nonprofit customer), and sharing resources (Shumate & O'Connor, 2010).

The connections that we have with others in our network can be considered in terms of strength and activity. The broadest and most commonly considered ties are strong and weak. Strong ties are those connections with people with whom we share an extended history, more intimate information, and have established norms of reciprocity, such as family and long-term friends. Such ties are useful in times of crisis, offer quick access to commonly held resources, or are available in any other situation in which trust plays a key role. Weak ties are those connections we have with others with whom we have less intimate and frequent communication—for example, a coworker or a classmate. Weak ties generally share a smaller range of information and communication topics. The benefit of weak ties is that they can bring new and novel information into a network, which helps innovation and problem solving. Affiliative ties are those ties we have with other people who are not part of our interpersonal networks but with whom we share a common membership, such as a large club or university. The most effective networks have a combination of strong and weak ties, allowing for both emotional support and trust, while at the same time providing access to innovation and outside resources that keep the network from becoming too stagnant. Ties can also be active, which means there is currently communication flowing through them; latent, which means there is a tie available but not yet activated; or dormant, which means there was once activity, but that activity has ceased.

Actors (people, institutions, etc.) within a network are called nodes and are often considered based on their position within the network. By position we mean how connected they are relative to other members of the network. Think about someone you know who is well connected. That person seems to know everybody and always seems to be in the middle of what is going on. Most likely, he or she is a star or the member of the network with the most direct lines of communication. Are you someone who connects two different groups of friends? If so, you are a bridge in that you connect two different groups that you are part of. Do you have a supervisor who connects your work group with a different work group? That supervisor is a liaison. Do you know someone who pretty much keeps to him or herself? That person is an isolate. If we think of the basis of networks as communication, it is not a leap to infer that communication within networks equates with power. As you can see from these examples, where one is positioned in a network can have implications for access to resources, power, and other important outcomes. For example, stars have access to a lot of information because they are the most direct lines of communication. However, liaisons and bridges have a different kind of power in that they are the only lines of contact between two or more subgroups within a network, which makes them information brokers. They have access to information that others in the network won't have and can serve as gatekeepers for that information, thus determining to a certain extent who knows what. Isolates have very little power because they keep to themselves and neither contribute to nor draw from the network. As we will discuss next, the connections we have, and what flows through those connections, provides access to social capital or the social benefits we draw from being part of a network.

Social Capital

Social capital is built on the communication and participation inherent to networks. Think about a community or institution that you are part of. Now think about how people behave in that community. Is there a lot of communication, time spent together, and working together for the common good? Do you feel that members of that community will help you solve problems, make decisions, or lend you money or other resources? If so, that community is likely high in social capital. Because social capital is intrinsically social, it is strengthened, rather than depleted, through use. Essentially, the more you put into the community, the more you get out of it.

There are three primary kinds of social capital: bonding, bridging, and linking (Putnam, 2000; Szreter & Woolcock, 2004). Because social capital is generated within networks, the types of social capital are related to the types of ties that can be found in networks. Bonding social capital is generally found in networks that are closed and cohesive, which means they do not have a lot of outside links but have many ties and communications within the networks. Bonding social capital is built on, and builds, trust. Bonding social capital creates strong norms, which will likely facilitate coordinated action and sharing of financial or other resources (Chewning, 2016, p. 34). Bridging social capital is related to networks that have structural holes or opportunities for brokerage and input from outside parties. The value of bridging social capital is the fact that it provides access to resources not readily available in the network and relationships with more heterogeneous groups of people. To illustrate the difference between bonding and bridging social capital, think about the difference between the campus network at a small college with primarily local students and one at a large university with students from a variety of U.S. and international locations. While both types of campuses could provide access to both types of social capital, the smaller local campus is more likely to be rich in bonding social capital, while the larger international university is more likely to generate bridging social capital with smaller subgroups of students who share bonding social capital. Finally, linking social capital adapts the idea of bridging social capital specifically to vertical power differentials, primarily looking at interaction across formal or hierarchical relationships (Chewning, 2016, p. 34; Claridge, n.d.). Linking social capital is especially relevant to stakeholder and interorganizational relationships, as it has to do with the power differentials between different parties—for example, stakeholders and organizations or organizations and regulatory agencies. Linking social capital can be critical to community development, as it infuses goodwill and reciprocity into relationships that could otherwise be unbalanced due to power differentials.

Related to strategic communication, social capital is important in both stakeholder and interorganizational networks. Within stakeholder networks, social capital can begin as reputational capital or the goodwill that the organization accumulates through the maintenance of a good reputation (Chewning, 2016, p. 34). Relational capital encourages stakeholder interaction with the organization. When the organization acts in accordance with its perceived reputation, this interaction builds trust, loyalty, and further interaction, which can then be translated into social capital. Once social capital exists in stakeholder networks, stakeholders become more likely to trust and engage with the organization and participate in its initiatives, such as CSR, donation, volunteering, or even purchase.

Within interorganizational networks, social capital facilitates both day-to-day business and special situations that require working together toward a common cause, such as lobbying or crisis recovery. Social capital brings a personal element to business transactions, making both parties more likely to work toward mutual satisfaction rather than simply looking out for their own interests. This, in turn, creates more social capital, which facilitates future interaction. It is worth noting that within organizations, individual social capital and organizational social capital are not mutually exclusive. Research has shown that the social capital that CEOs, business owners, or other employees have via their personal contacts can be leveraged to help their organizations in times of crisis (Doerfel, Lai, & Chewning, 2010). Similarly, employees can benefit from organizational social capital, such as when they use organizational contacts to access resources, including internships for family members. Thus organizations can benefit from the individual-level social capital of their employees and vice versa.

Stakeholder Theories

There are several theoretical approaches that look at the organizational/stakeholder relationship. One of the foundational theories, aptly named stakeholder theory, is a social theory based in the idea of creating value between the stakeholder and the organization and acknowledging the roles of humanity, relationship, and ethics within a capitalist system (Freeman, Harrison, Wicks, Parmar, & DeColle, 2010). Stakeholder theory conceptualizes business as a set of relationships among groups that have a stake in the activities that make up the business. Accordingly, business is about how various stakeholders interact with each other and the organization to create value (Freeman et al., 2010, p. 25). What started out as an idea concerned with understanding and managing stakeholders related to the success of the organization has evolved into a theory that considers the relational and network nature of the organizational/stakeholder relationship and the implications of that relationship for everyone involved.

Within the model of stakeholder theory, there are primary and secondary stakeholders. Primary stakeholders are those who have immediate implications for the survival of the business (e.g., financiers, customers, and employees). Secondary stakeholders are those who directly affect primary stakeholders and, therefore, affect the organization (e.g., media, competitors, and consumer advocate groups) (Freeman et al., 2010). In addition, stakeholders can be conceptualized in terms of power, legitimacy, and urgency (Mitchell, Agle, & Wood, 1997). According to the stakeholder salience model (Table 3.1), stakeholders with power are those who have the ability to influence or "bring about the outcomes they desire" in a relationship (Mitchell et al., 1997, p. 865). Legitimacy is the extent to which the stakeholder group fits within a socially accepted structure or behavior or is perceived "appropriate" within a given belief system (e.g., think about a formal advocacy group versus a fringe group). Finally, urgency is the extent to which a claim or relationship is time sensitive or the claim of the stakeholder is critical. Understanding how to categorize stakeholders in terms of power, legitimacy, and urgency can help organizations figure out which groups to direct communication and resources to at any given time.

Stakeholder categories are transitory and can change as the environment changes, making different groups more or less salient to the organization at any given time. Depending on the situation, stakeholder groups can occupy one, two, or three of these categories at any time. For example, stakeholders are considered latent when they occupy only one category. Latent stakeholders are primarily inactive because they don't have all of the necessary components to impact the organization. For example, an urgent stakeholder, such as a lone protestor, might be able to get some attention, but without power or legitimacy (which could be provided by banding together with other organized protestors in the form of an advocacy group), it is unlikely that they will impact the organization. While the organization does not have to direct a lot of resources at latent stakeholders, they shouldn't completely ignore them either. These stakeholders could acquire another attribute, making them more salient to the organization and moving them to the category of expectant stakeholders.

Expectant stakeholders embody two of the three attributes (power, legitimacy, urgency). Expectant stakeholders are considered "active" as opposed to latent and, therefore, require time and attention from the organization. This can include the government, community officials, consumers, or others who have the resources to directly impact the organization. Finally, definitive stakeholders are those who embody all three attributes. Stakeholder groups often move to the definitive category during a crisis, which automatically injects a sense of urgency into a situation. See Table 3.1 for a breakdown of the various stakeholder categories.

Relative to networks, early iterations of stakeholder theory considered organizational relationships in terms of the organization's ego network (i.e., only in terms of the direct connections an organization had with each of its stakeholder groups). To picture this, imagine a wagon wheel where the organization is the center, and each spoke of the wheel is a connection to a specific stakeholder group. In such a model, everything revolves around the organization, and the organization is the only actor that has direct communication or connection. More recent conceptualizations of stakeholder theory take a more networked approach, acknowledging the fact that no one entity exists in isolation and that stakeholder groups inevitably have some connection to each other, either directly or indirectly (e.g., via the media). These connections between the organization and stakeholders, as well as stakeholder groups, can be referred to as stakeholder networks. Stakeholder networks represent the social structure through which institutions both influence and are influenced by stakeholders.

TABLE 3.1 Stakeholder Classification (Mitchel et al., 1997)

Stakeholder salience model (SSM)

Latent stakeholders	Possess only one of three attributes:
	▪ **Dormant:** power only
	▪ **Discretionary:** legitimacy only
	▪ **Demanding:** urgency only
Expectant stakeholders	Possess two of the three salience attributes:
	▪ **Dominant**: power and legitimacy
	▪ **Dependent**: legitimacy and urgency
	▪ **Dangerous**: power and urgency
Definitive stakeholders	Possess power, legitimacy, and urgency.
Unconcerned lurker	Lacks connections and interest. No power, legitimacy, or urgency. Potential or nonstakeholders
Concerned lurker	Lacks connections, has interest. Legitimacy and urgency. Dependent stakeholder
Concerned influencer	Has connections and interest. Power, legitimacy, and urgency. Definitive stakeholder

At the heart of contemporary stakeholder theories is the idea of relationship. How can organizations build mutually beneficial relationships with their stakeholder groups? Based on work by Grunig and Huang (2000) and Hon and Grunig (1999), Ki (2015) offers six principles of relationship cultivation relative to organizational stakeholder relationships, including access, positivity, openness and disclosure, sharing tasks, networking, and assurances. As a whole, these relationship strategies have to treat the stakeholder as an equal partner in the relationship and build a relationship based on mutuality and respect.

1. **Access.** Providing channels of communication that enable stakeholders to reach an organization

2. **Positivity.** Organizational efforts to make the relationship more enjoyable for stakeholders

3. **Openness and disclosure.** Transparency about the organization's operations and intentions, as well as the expression of opinions and concerns on the part of organizations and stakeholders

4. **Sharing of tasks.** Joint work or problem solving in areas that are of importance to the organization and stakeholders

5. **Networking.** The organization's willingness to work with groups that are important to key stakeholders, such as environmentalists and unions

6. **Assurances.** Organizational efforts to show that they value their stakeholders

STAKEHOLDER NETWORKS AND INFORMATION AND COMMUNICATIONS TECHNOLOGY

The rise of network-based ICT has opened new avenues in relationship building between organizations and stakeholders, notably in terms of stakeholder engagement and dialogic communication. SMS allow organizations to create dedicated pages on which they can share information with stakeholders and engage in one-on-one communication via posts, comments, and messages. They remove barriers of time and space in that a stakeholder from any location can log on at any time and "experience" the organization through pictures, videos, and interaction with both the organization and other stakeholders who have a shared interest in the brand. While the majority of businesses of all sizes have a presence on at least one social media platform, research shows that many organizations use SMS in a more one-way capacity than embodying the true two-way communicative capabilities of the platforms (Bortree & Seltzer, 2009; Waters, Burnett, Lamm, & Lucas, 2009). However, when used correctly, SMS balance the power in the organizational/ stakeholder relationship by giving stakeholders a way to participate with the organization, which can lead to engagement with and loyalty to the organization. It is incumbent upon future strategic communication professionals (YOU!) to create SMS pages that engage stakeholders and honor the relational element of the organizational/stakeholder relationship. We'll discuss this more throughout the book, especially in Chapter 4.

SMS have also supported the creation and activation of stakeholder networks relative to specific brands or brands related to causes that bring stakeholders together (e.g., ethical sourcing). For example, during a crisis in which former Food Network star Paula Deen admitted to using racist language, stakeholders took to her social media pages to both share their support and protest her and her brand (Chewning, 2015). In 2013, activists "hijacked" Kraft's social media page to protest the brand's use of genetically engineered ingredients in macaroni and cheese by inundating Kraft's Facebook page with negative messages about Kraft's use of genetically modified organisms (GMOs) and including links to sites that discussed the negative effects of GMOs (Veil, Reno, Friehaut, & Oldham, 2015). In addition, stakeholders can connect outside of the organization's SMS pages by tagging and hashtagging specific brands or causes or creating their own pages, which forms a loosely coupled network that comes together simply to support or protest the brand (Choi & Lin, 2009). While sometimes beneficial for the organization, this capability can give stakeholders the means to gain both power and legitimacy, thus adding another component in how organizations should assess the salience of their stakeholders.

Acknowledging the power of social media to affect stakeholder reach and salience, Sederevicuite and Valentini (2011) proposed the stakeholder mapping model (SMM), which adds the dimensions of connectivity (position in online stakeholder networks) and content (relevance of posted content to the stakeholder network) to the SSM discussed earlier (Table 3.1). The benefit of integrating the SMM with the SSM is that it helps identify both known and unknown stakeholder groups. By mapping online social networks using web-based software (more on that in Chapter 8), organizations can identify those most central to the network, or those who are central in dense clusters of the network, therefore having real or potential power, depending on their interest in the organization at any given point in time. When these central nodes, also called influencers, are interested and post information about the organization that is relevant to the rest of the network, they are considered *concerned influencers*. When they are relevant to the organizational network, but not interested at a given point in time, they are *unconcerned influencers*. However, even unconcerned influencers are important because they could be influential should they become active. Conversely, *concerned lurkers* are not well connected in the stakeholder network but are posting relevant content and have urgency. They are important because while they may not reach a lot of people, if they reach the right person (i.e., an influencer), their content could go viral.

Think about how you interact with brands via social media. *Do you follow any brands on social media? If so, why? How has this affected your attachment to the brand? Has another poster on social media ever influenced your perception of a brand?*

APPLYING THE CONCEPT TO YOUR OWN SITUATION

At this point in your life, you are likely in a transitional time both socially and professionally. As you approach graduation, you are getting closer to a time when networks matter and knowing who your stakeholders are can make a difference between conveying a solid personal brand and getting lost in a sea of other hopeful professionals. Ideally, your ego network contains a mix of personal contacts that offer personal support and other resources, as well as professional contacts that can provide access to resources and opportunities that can further your career.

As you read the theory section of the chapter, were you thinking about your own networks? Who are the people you turn to for advice? Who influenced your decision on where to apply and attend college? Who might be someone you will turn to when you near graduation and start looking for a job?

The following section lays out how to identify your personal and professional networks and how to (re)build them so that they provide you with support and opportunity. It also covers how to identify your stakeholders so that you can target your communication strategically and, finally, how to build social capital.

IDENTIFYING YOUR STAKEHOLDERS

Who are the people with whom you have a mutual stake in success? That is, which people can affect your success and could also benefit from your success? The number one answer to this question is your potential employer. One of your primary goals at this point in your life is probably to get a job upon graduation. This makes potential employers one of your key stakeholders. Just as organizations have to identify and research their stakeholders in order to be successful, you should do the same. What type of job are you looking for? What types of expectations are those employers likely to have?

Remember that success can be defined in a variety of ways. Because this is an academic textbook, the majority of the topics we talk about are related to your academic and professional opportunities. However, success can also mean happiness. If you frame it in that way, who are your primary stakeholders? Probably parents and friends. But certainly, other groups, such as teachers and coaches, will be interested in your happiness and professional success too.

When you start to consider the different types of people who are your stakeholders, and the variety of ways that they can overlap, you can begin to see the complexity of networks and strategic communication. Different stakeholder groups have different stakes in your success. While their needs and expectations overlap in some ways, they diverge in others. Identifying your stakeholders includes identifying your goals relative to your definition of personal and professional success and then strategically networking and building social capital with existing and potential stakeholders. Message also matters, which we will discuss more in Chapter 4.

BUILDING SOCIAL CAPITAL IN YOUR NETWORKS

Social capital has likely played a role in your life without you even knowing it. Did you get an internship interview because your parents knew someone who needed an intern? You benefited from their social capital. Did you do a favor for someone who then paid it forward to someone else in your community? That's network-level social capital.

Social capital is an intangible resource, which makes it hard to quantify or strategize. However, if you think back to the previous section on social capital theory, you can pick out a few ways that you can build social capital in your networks so that it is there when you need it.

First, *communicate*. This can be hard for some people, especially if you are shy or introverted, but in order to build capital, you have to communicate often and with a variety of people. This will be easier with the strong ties in your network, as you likely have built up trust, have easier access to them, and relate to them on a variety of topics. However, it is important not to take these relationships for granted. Ask them what they are doing. Keep them up to date on what you are doing. This two-way exchange has multiple benefits. One, it builds trust, relationship, and liking. Two, it lets you know if your contacts are working on anything relevant to you or have contacts that may benefit you in the future. Third, it keeps your friends and family aware of what you are doing, so if something relevant comes up for them, they can share it with you. For example, let them know what your major is, what kinds of work you have done, and what kind of job you are looking for. Remember, indirect ties, such as friends of friends, can be very helpful sources of information. Finally, don't forget your weak ties. Sometimes talking to the person you sit next to in class can open up opportunities that you otherwise wouldn't have known about.

Keep in touch. Did you meet someone at a networking event? Connect on LinkedIn and send him or her a message. Your friends from high school? Connect on social media. Comment occasionally on their posts. Get together once in a while. This helps you to build a diverse network of strong and weak ties. In addition, when you use social media, your communication is often visible to others, allowing access to friends of friends and, therefore, indirect ties. However, don't rely only on social media, as face-to-face communication offers the richest kind of feedback and often promotes a greater feeling of closeness.

Reconnect. Research shows that our dormant connections, or connections that were once active and strong, can be rekindled after time, making this contact a strong tie again and reopening pathways. These relationships can sometimes be more valuable than new ties because they bridge the past and the future and are built on a melding of memories and trust from the past and current commonality (Levin, Walter, & Murninghan, 2011).

Build *reciprocity*. Have you heard of the law of reciprocity? The basic idea is that if you do something nice for a person, he or she will feel obligated to return the gesture. Reciprocity is not only a driver of network development but also an underlying principle of social capital. Invest in your network. Don't just take. Give. How can you do this? In addition to the two-way communication described previously, you can be present. Don't turn down invitations. Be available. Give advice. Donate time for a shared cause. Reach out and see how people are doing. Follow up. If people feel that you are invested in them, they are more likely to be willing to invest in you.

QUESTIONS:

- What opportunities do I have to build my networks?

- How can I effectively build and leverage social capital in my networks?

- What obligations do I have to other network members?

Tools and Processes for Self-Action

IDENTIFYING AND BUILDING YOUR NETWORK

As we've already suggested, strategically building your network to include the right types of contacts to offer you both support and access to resources is advantageous at this stage in your life (really, at any stage!). Studies show that roughly 55% of applicants find out about job openings through personal contacts and that those people who find jobs through personal contacts are more likely to be satisfied with their jobs than those people who find jobs through other means (Granovetter, 1995). You want the right mix of strong and weak ties, and some of those ties should be brokers who help you access resources outside of your networks. How do you build such networks?

NETWORKING

You've probably heard the term before. Networking is the communicative process of leveraging your network contacts and strategically seeking out new contacts to add to your network. As we said earlier, who we include in our networks is fluid, changing as our overall circumstances and needs change. As you prepare to enter the workforce, you should start to consider what types of contacts can help you, as well as what types of network contacts represent the personal and professional brand you want to put forward. That person who keeps tagging you in inappropriate pictures on Facebook? Probably not someone you want in your network at this time.

Some people get uncomfortable at the idea of networking. It forces you to put yourself out there, talk to new people, and risk rejection. However, the benefits outweigh the drawbacks. Networking begins with identifying gaps you may have in your networks (more on how to map your networks later in this section) and then identifying *what types of contacts could fill those gaps* and *where you can find them.*

Most likely at this stage in your life, you will need to add professional contacts to your network. Some places you might find those contacts are your campus Career and Professional Development Center, alumni (see if your campus sponsors alumni programs or has an alumni directory and reach out), and professional associations, such as the Public Relations Society of America (PRSA), Public Relations Student Society of America, or other local associations for your chosen field.

Once you've identified the people and places, it is time to communicate. Cheseboro (2014) identifies the following strategies for successful networking:

■ Remember each person's name. If you need help in this area, try repeating the person's name back to him or her as you are introduced or get a business card.

■ Be genuinely curious and ask sincere open-ended questions. This not only shows that you are interested but also helps you and your new contact get to know each other better.

■ Have your personal brand story developed and ready to tell. Have a short (30-second version) and a longer version. Either one could come in handy depending on the situation.

■ Have additional stories relevant to your goals and interests. If the conversation goes longer, it will help you avoid awkward silences.

■ Practice.

PROFILE OF INDIVIDUAL EXPERIENCE:

Jennifer O'Neill

Jennifer O'Neill has been a strategic communicator for over 20 years, beginning with her first job at Ketchum PR agency in New York. Now a vice president of strategic enterprise communications at Realogy, an integrated provider of real estate service that includes brands such as Better Homes and Gardens® Real Estate, Century 21®, and others, Ms. O'Neill credits strategic networking with both personal and professional successes in her life. Networking helped her land her first job out of college, connect with like-minded people to prevent

FIGURE 3.1 **Jennifer O'Neil**

commercial development in her neighborhood, and accelerate the receipt of medical attention that led to early diagnosis and treatment of cancer.

She explained, "Everywhere I go, I tend to meet someone I know or people with whom I have shared acquaintances. For me networking is a combination of natural tendency and effort. One thing is for sure: I would not be where I am today without networking. From landing my first job out of college after networking with an alumnus from my school who spoke at a Public Relations Student Society of America meeting I attended, to landing my current job at a company where my friend worked and hand-delivered my resume to the hiring manager, cultivating and maintaining my personal and professional networks has been one of the most worthwhile investments of my time."

How does she do it? Ms. O'Neill said she keeps in touch with everyone, keeping a collection of old address books, mail return labels, and business cards. She makes it a point to stay in touch with coworkers after she, or they, move on. While her approach was not strategic at first, she quickly realized that staying in touch with people had not only social but also professional benefits. "One of the most important things I've done to build my professional network is to keep apprised of where people are working, what industries they work in and what positions they hold. That way, when I want to tap my network, I can be specific and targeted in my outreach, which usually leads to more fruitful networking."

Technology also plays a role, as Ms. O'Neill primarily keeps connected via a combination of e-mail and LinkedIn. She noted, "Facebook and LinkedIn have only served to further scale what I previously was accomplishing with hand-written letters or phone calls, and then via email. I'm fascinated by how small the world can feel when you learn you have a mutual connection with someone else." LinkedIn helps her connect with a wide variety of people, from the entire executive committee of her company to college students who joined her network after she has guest lectured or spoken to organizations on campus. In this way, she is enhancing both her own social capital and letting others tap into it, filling the role of a network connector. Being a connector has helped her bring together personal and professional contacts to open jobs, freelance gigs, speaking opportunities, new friends, and even spouses.

As someone who has worked in the communication field for 23 years, Ms. O'Neill has developed some tried and true methods for using strategic communication when working with clients. Her tips include the following:

- **Question the premise.** When a client requests a strategic communications plan, first I ask why he or she needs it. Asking why over and over usually gets both of us to a better understanding of the problem so our approach can be more intentional and strategic.

- **Start with the end in mind.** Where are you going? You can't map out a route (strategy) for getting there if you don't know the destination.

- **Get a shared vision.** Discuss up front with your key partners/sponsors what success looks like. Is it a behavior change? A mind-set shift? Both? Without alignment on what success looks like, it is very hard to agree on what trade-offs to make when push comes to shove. What I'm willing to trade off to achieve success might differ from what my partners are willing to trade off. That's why having a shared vision up front is so important. It reduces friction and speeds up decision making.

Questions:

1. How does Ms. O'Neill engage weak and latent ties in her network? How have they helped her be successful?

2. Based on Ms. O'Neill's experience, how might you use technology to build and maintain networks?

3. How has strategic communication helped Ms. O'Neill build and maintain networks? How can you apply some of these principles in your own professional journey?

APPLYING THE CONCEPT TO YOUR WORK WITH CLIENTS

Once you start working in the corporate communication department for an organization, it will be your job not only to know who the organization's stakeholders are but also what the organization's overall networks look like. The following sections lay out how to identify organizational networks and build social capital for your organization in both interorganizational and stakeholder networks.

IDENTIFYING AND BUILDING YOUR CLIENTS' NETWORKS

You may be working in an agency and have several clients, or you may work in-house for an organization, in which case, it is your only client. While we will talk more about how to identify and build your client's networks in the section "Tools and Processes When Acting for Others," the broad view of identifying client networks involves knowing your client in terms of goals, industry, history, geography, and existing contacts. If you identify the relevant stakeholder groups in terms of each of these categories, you will know not only what your network is but also where you want to go. And once you know that, the answer is networking.

Networking on behalf of your client is both similar to, and different from, networking for yourself. You will rely more on trade and professional associations, people in local and state government, community leaders, and suppliers and vendors relative to your client. However, having a mix of strong and weak ties remains an important principle, whether you are building personal or client networks.

BUILDING SOCIAL CAPITAL IN CLIENT NETWORKS

Building social capital in client networks will be similar to building social capital in your individual networks but on an organizational level on behalf of your client(s). It comes down to connecting, communicating, and giving.

1. First, *communicate*. Communicate with internal and external stakeholders. Keep them in the know. For example, employees should never hear about layoffs from an outside source, such as the media. They should hear it first from managers or the CEO. Be sure to maintain good relationships with media contacts by consistently providing them with current and credible information. Be transparent with consumers when something goes wrong; don't hide the truth. Have a strong PA department that liaises with government agencies and advocacy groups that deal in areas relevant to your industry. Don't just reach out when there are problems but engage in maintenance communication so that when a tough decision or crisis arises, the relationships are already well developed, and trust has been established.

2. *Positioning.* Try to position yourself advantageously in important networks. Make connections that matter and support your client and then nurture those connections to create bonding social capital. Create relationships where you connect other parties. This builds bridging social capital and positions you as a broker in the network. Content matters too. If you are a reliable network member who consistently shares reliable information, other network members will likely take notice and seek you out and in turn share information with you. This will increase your centrality, giving you more power and influence in the network.

3. *Give.* Don't be a taker. Be a good citizen in your network. You will notice that this is closely related to communicating and positioning. If you proactively reach out to others, share what you have, and reciprocate when others help you, network members will treat you in kind, and you will have a consistent supply of social capital.

BUILDING SOCIAL CAPITAL IN STAKEHOLDER NETWORKS

While we have defined stakeholders as groups that have a stake in the activities that make up the business, meaning that even members of interorganizational networks are stakeholders, in this section, we are talking about the stakeholders, such customers, donors, and others, who have a direct financial effect on your client (also often referred to as publics). We will discuss stakeholder communication more in Chapter 4 and throughout the text, but the basics of social capital in stakeholder communication comes down to trust, consistency, communication, and transparency.

Stakeholders often begin to build trust in an organization based on a combination of the organization's reputation (e.g., they are known for doing good and being honest) and personal experience. When that personal experience aligns with the reputation, trust is strengthened. When this happens consistently, trust continues to get stronger. Stakeholders begin to expect a good experience; those expectations are met, and trust is perpetuated. Communication from the organization that shows consideration for stakeholder needs and interests furthers trust. Finally, transparency and openness in communication, relational strategies discussed earlier, perpetuate the idea of trustworthiness and openness to stakeholder participation. Participation, in turn, deepens the relationship and strengthens social capital. We will discuss more about how to create content and communication opportunities that lead to social capital in Chapter 4, as well as the ethical imperatives to engender true trust and transparency that come along with strategic communication in Chapter 6.

QUESTIONS:

- What are my client's existing networks?

- Who are my client's stakeholders?

- How can my client's connections to stakeholders be strengthened?

Tools and Processes When Acting for Others

MAPPING YOUR CLIENT'S NETWORKS

Mapping your client's networks might be a bit more difficult than mapping your own at this stage in the game, but it is a worthwhile activity to consider. A good way to do this might be to apply the exercise you did for your own networks, with some modifications. For illustrative purposes, try applying it to your college or university. This will take some adaptation, but the principles remain the same:

- Employees

- Community partners

- Supply chain

- Government contacts

- Partner organizations

- Specialty partners (in the case of universities, this could be students, student families, and alumni)

- Media

Again, when looking at the list, ask yourself the following questions:

- What are the organization's top-three goals?

- Do the people in the organization's network offer it a mix of the support and access to resources/ opportunities that the organization needs to meet those goals right now?

- Do the contacts currently in the organization's network reflect the image I want to present to my client's stakeholders? For organizations, supply chain partners and partner organizations often hold the highest risk.

- If so, how can I communicate the appropriate relationships as part of my client's brand? If not, what role should these relationships play in the organization, and how can we best communicate about them?

- Are the organization's networks capital rich, offering a lot of opportunity and access? If not, how can we begin to include contacts that will help achieve organizational goals?

DETERMINING EXISTING NETWORK AND STAKEHOLDER GAPS

If your network analysis shows that you don't have the right kinds of contacts in your network, you should determine where those gaps are and how you can fill them in a way that relates to your goals. While gaps can indicate a weakness in networks, in that your network is technically missing a contact(s) that provide access to resources you need, these gaps, called structural holes, can also provide ripe opportunities for you to include weak links in the form of brokers. Brokers can connect you to formerly unconnected contacts, therefore providing you access to potentially new and novel resources, infusing your network with diversity and promoting innovation and growth. Sometimes gaps are easily apparent—for example, when an organization launches a new product line and needs to update its supply chain. However, other times, it may not be so apparent, such as when an organization slowly begins to lose a voice in the regulatory areas of its industry, indicating that it might be time to update PA contacts. This is why understanding the larger environment in which the organization exists (more on that in Chapter 5) and routinely reexamining your organization's progress and standing related to its goals is so important.

PLANNING AND EXECUTING ON GAPS

There are multiple ways that organizations can fill gaps with brokers that can help them achieve goals.

Turn to other network members. We talked about the benefits of indirect links earlier. They come with an element of trust and familiarity, therefore making communication and cooperation easier than starting from scratch. Also, existing network members are already likely aware of the needs, capacities, and limitations of your client. This makes them more likely to quickly connect you to useful sources.

Network! It works for your personal network, and you can do it on behalf of your client as well. Join professional associations related to the industry your client is part of. Get to know what is going on in the industry and who is innovating. Join trade associations for your industry and community associations in the community that the organization is located in. Consume news related to your organization, industry, and geographic location daily so that you know who the important players are in this area. Don't be afraid to reach out to them, either in person or on LinkedIn. Similarly, join professional associations related to strategic communication, such as the PRSA or International Association of Business Communication (IABC). This will not only help you personally but also help you tap into contacts who can think outside of your box, providing you with ideas or access to contacts that you wouldn't otherwise have.

PROFILE OF ORGANIZATIONAL EXPERIENCE

Starbucks

Balancing and maximizing network connections and communication is a big part of strategic communication. Many organizations in today's economy are multinational corporations and, subsequently, have complex networks that span countries and time zones. Not only will stakeholders vary in terms of needs and priorities but also those needs and priorities will be dictated by culture and the laws that govern the respective cities, states, towns, provinces, and countries in which they reside. The following case study demonstrates the importance of being aware of, and understanding, organizational networks, as well as the potential power of stakeholder networks.

Starbucks Corporation is a popular and well-known organization. The international coffee shop, founded in Seattle, Washington, in 1971 routinely ranks on the Fortune 500 list, *Fortune* magazine's Most Admired Companies list, *Fortune's* World's Most Valuable Brands list, and *Ethisphere's* World's Most Ethical Companies list. Starbucks is known for its work on ethical sourcing, work with NGOs on community projects, and, of course, good coffee.

Creating and maintaining the contacts that go into sustaining successful operations is a sprawling task that requires attention to building interorganizational networks strategically and an awareness of how each stakeholder within its network is related to other stakeholders. Thus being able to differentiate primary and secondary stakeholders (Freeman et al., 2010) and the salience of

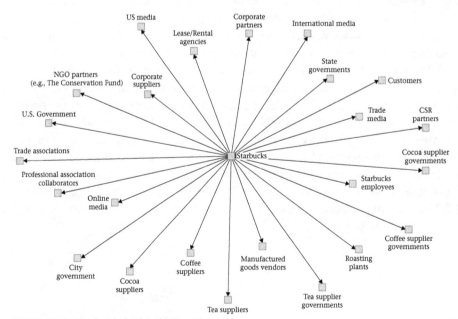

FIGURE 3.2 Starbucks's Simple Ego Network

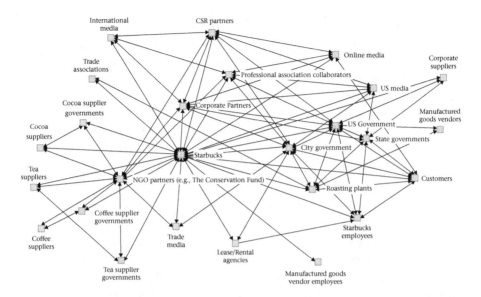

FIGURE 3.3 Starbucks's Connected Ego Network

each group at any given time (Mitchell et al., 1997) are skills required by many people throughout the organization on multiple levels.

Figure 3.2 shows a simplified version of Starbucks's ego network. Each node in the network represents a stakeholder group, as opposed to an individual stakeholder (e.g., CSR partners instead of individual organizations that Starbucks partners with). This figure is a simple spoke-and-hub network that resembles early interpretations of stakeholder theory: the organization is at the center, and the links shown only represent how the organization can affect the stakeholder group and vice versa. Although the links are considered two-way (i.e., looking at the mutual influence of Starbucks and the stakeholder group), because Starbucks is at the center of the network, the main concern is how the relationship affects Starbucks.

Figure 3.3 represents a more complex view of Starbucks's ego network, as it considers the links among the various stakeholder groups. While this view of the network still shows Starbucks as the most central actor (as it should, because it is Starbucks's ego network), you can see that government agencies, vendors, customers, and NGO partners are also quite central. This gives them more power in the relationship simply by virtue of how many other mutual organizations they are connected to. Put simply, they have structural power. For example, the local or federal government is linked to every vendor and customer and has access to multiple media outlets, as well as Starbucks corporate and each Starbucks plant and store. They are also legitimate in that they are culturally recognized formal authorities both in the United States and internationally. For example, city governments set the zoning laws by which each store has to abide; state governments set the minimum wage that Starbucks must pay or exceed; the U.S. federal government establishes trade regulations by which Starbucks has to operate. During routine times, they have relatively little urgency in that laws are already established and there is little change in the organization/government relationship. However, during events such as administration changes (when the various laws governing multinational corporations may come under scrutiny or change) or on a smaller scale when Starbucks wants to open a new store, government stakeholders take on added urgency, potentially moving them from dominant to definitive stakeholders, thus requiring immediate attention and resources according to the SSM.

To give another example based on this figure, certain NGOs, such as Conservation International, are likely to have contacts that include many of Starbucks's coffee, tea, and cocoa suppliers. Conservation International works to make sure farmers' needs are being respected and environmentally friendly practices are in place. Because of their likely contacts with both Starbucks and Starbucks's suppliers, they have structural power. As a respected NGO, they also have legitimacy. However, what is their power and legitimacy relative to the United States and other governments? It likely depends on the situation. While they don't have the power to impose legal sanctions, they do have the power and legitimacy to inflict reputational harm—for example, if they were to report to the media (another shared link) that Starbucks was violating ethical practices.

Finally, Figure 3.4 shows an expanded version of Starbucks's networks, which includes second-degree links, such as the friends and families of employees and customers, as well as latent links, such as advocacy groups, which have the potential to be drawn into the network by one or more stakeholder groups. Relative to the first two figures, Figure 3.4 illustrates how indirect ties can matter,

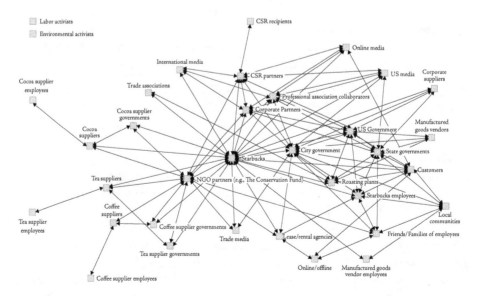

FIGURE 3.4 Starbucks's Whole Network

as well as the importance of considering word-of-mouth promotion and online media. A celebrity well-known for her environmental and human rights concerns can take to Facebook and talk about how much she admires Starbucks's participation with Conservation International, thus leaving a positive impression of Starbucks with her followers, many of whom share her social and environmental concerns and may be Starbucks customers or potential customers. Her structural power, related to the legitimacy of her content relative to her followers' interests, can make her an influencer according to the SMM. This positive post moves her from being a latent influencer to a concerned influencer. While this is potentially a one-time shift in stakeholder status, it points to the importance of keeping powerful and legitimate stakeholders in the organization's line of sight, as well as the potential power of an expectant stakeholder on social media.

Questions:

1. How do the different stakeholder groups in Starbucks's network represent shifts in power? How might this inform your external communication practices if you worked for Starbucks?

2. Looking at Figure 3.4, you can see that second-degree links, such as friends and families of employees, are also part of the network. What does this tell you about the divide between internal and external communication in organizations?

3. Referring to the Starbucks case study in Chapter 6, how do you think its network changed in terms of its crisis? Which stakeholder groups gained more salience during the crisis? How do you think this affected other stakeholder groups? How would this affect Starbucks's communication and priorities?

Chapter Conclusion

This chapter focused on the importance of relationship and community in strategic communication. As we touched on in Chapter 1, organizational stakeholder communication is the focus of the strategic communication process in fields such as corporate communication. This chapter presented social networks as a useful way to conceptualize the organizational stakeholder relationship. Viewing this dynamic from a network lens emphasizes that it is more than just transactional but rather ongoing, flexible, and relational. Applying social network concepts to your own relationships can provide guidance on how to build contacts strategically that will help you achieve professional and personal success. However, structure isn't everything. Without communication and the creation of shared meaning, you will still be unable to achieve your goals, regardless of your networks. In Chapter 4, we will focus on how to create and share messages with and through personal and organizational networks.

Key Terms

Ego network
Embedded
Interorganizational network
Latent ties
Liaison
Networking
Social capital
Social networks

Stakeholder
Stakeholder communication
Stakeholder mapping model
Stakeholder networks
Stakeholder salience model
Stakeholder theory
Whole networks

Chapter Discussion Questions

1. How would you describe the link between networks and social capital? How can you build social capital in your networks?

2. What roles do different types of links (e.g., strong, weak, latent, dormant) play in network dynamics? Why is it important to have a balanced network in terms of types of links?

3. How has stakeholder theory evolved, and how has social media affected that evolution?

4. Name some ways that organizations can use social network sites to build and maintain stakeholder networks. What is the role of social capital in online networking? How do you apply these principles to your own networking?

Chapter Activities

1. Get familiar with LinkedIn. If you don't already have one, create a profile on LinkedIn. Using what you've learned so far about strategic communication and personal branding, create a professional profile that reflects your goals and personal brand, including a photo. Returning to your network assessment from earlier in this chapter, start to build your network on LinkedIn. Read more about building a powerful network on LinkedIn using the tips in the recommended readings and resources section. Use the power of weak ties and indirect ties to build a diverse and useful network.

2. Conduct a self-assessment of your personal and professional networks. It can be overwhelming to try to catalogue all of your contacts. Start listing all of the relationships you have in each of the following categories:

   ▪ Family (don't forget distant family that you may not see often)

- Neighborhood contacts
- School contacts
  - Personal (e.g., friends)
  - Professional (e.g., professors, advisers, coaches)
- Work contacts
  - Personal (e.g., friends)
  - Professional (e.g., supervisors)
- Club/religious institution/sports/personal interest contacts

Next, list two to three people you know secondhand through your contacts (e.g., a friend of a friend, a coworker of your mom's). These are your *indirect ties* and can offer access to resources not available in your primary network.

Now, look at your lists. Here are some questions to ask yourself:

1. What are my current top-three goals?

2. Do the people in my network offer me a mix of the personal support and professional opportunities I need to meet these goals right now?

3. Do the people currently in my network reflect the image I want to present to my stakeholders?

4. If so, how can I communicate these relationships as part of my personal brand? If not, what role should these relationships play in my life, and how should I communicate about them?

5. Are my networks capital rich, offering a lot of opportunity and access? If not, how can I begin to include contacts that will help me achieve my goals?

6. Visit the Johnson & Johnson corporate website: jnj.com. Just by looking at the navigation, can you tell what the company's main stakeholder groups are? Take a while to read through each section. How does Johnson & Johnson target its communication with each stakeholder group while maintaining a cohesive overall brand message (a very important strategic communication principle when communicating within a web of interconnected stakeholders)? Can you identify some ways Johnson & Johnson is strategically building social capital with stakeholders?

Recommended Readings and Resources

How to Build a Powerful Network Using LinkedIn:

https://www.socialmediaexaminer.com/powerful-network-linkedin/

An examination of how social media enables stakeholder networks to take a concrete form and affect organizational outcomes:

Chewning, L. V. (2015). Measuring the enactment of IRT via social media: What are organizations and stakeholders saying during crisis? In J.R. Blaney and L. Alwine (Eds.), *Putting image repair to the test* (pp. 133–156). Lexington Books.

A brief overview of stakeholder theory from R. Edward Freeman:

https://www.youtube.com/watch?v=bIRUaLcvPe8

MESSAGING
Creating Meaning Across Media

While everything in this book relates to strategic communication, *message* is what we most readily identify as communication. Message is the most direct way that you can communicate goals and ideas, as well as build connection. The channel, or the instrument through which you reach out to stakeholders, plays an important role in message reception and comprehension. Thus in strategic communication, message and channel work together. This chapter will review various models and theories of communication, leading up to an examination of how we can use messaging to further our clients' and our own goals.

Orienting to the Concept:
Building Meaning Through Messages

Messages are the basic outputs (and inputs) of strategic communication. They are how we create and share meaning about ourselves. In the field of corporate communication, they are the basis for brand building (Chapter 2) and relationship building and essential to the flow of everyday organizational life. While our networks (Chapter 3) might constitute the skeleton of our communicative structures, messages are the lifeblood that flows through and sustains them.

While original models of communication considered messages simply as something transmitted between a sender and a receiver, a more complex understanding of the role of personal motives and environment, coupled with advances in technology, have led to a better understanding of the complexity of creating messages for both personal and professional purposes.

To tap into that complexity, think about the messages you create to build and support your personal brand (Chapter 2). What choices, both intentional and unintentional, do you make? How are your messages received and possibly (mis) interpreted? Think also about the messages you have received from organizations. What has influenced your understanding of those messages? Are there messages that resonated with you at one point in time that no longer affect you in the same way? As we will explore throughout this chapter, messages are a multifaceted concept affected by both personal and social influences. Learning how to create and share messages that influence and impact specific audiences is a challenging but rewarding process in strategic communication.

CENTRAL DEFINITIONS

MESSAGE

Although we all have an inherent idea of what a message is, actually defining it is more difficult than it may originally seem. We will consider different communication models later in the chapter, each of which defines message differently. However, a good base definition of a message is *the meaning that is assigned to a specific exchange between two or more people or entities* (e.g., organization to stakeholder). Messages can be both verbal and nonverbal and shared through various channels.

CHANNEL

Channels are the vehicles through which we create and share messages. Channels can include face-to-face communication and electronic media, such as the Internet, television, radio, and computer networks. As we will discuss later in the chapter because each type of channel has different affordances, or communicative capabilities, and people have different motives or expectations when using various channels, channel choice can affect how messages are received by our audiences.

PERSUASION

Persuasion can be defined as the process of influencing another actor to adopt the principles or actions that you are advocating. Communication theories, such as the elaboration likelihood model (Petty & Cacioppo, 1986) and theory of planned behavior (Fishbein & Azjen, 1975), consider the connection between beliefs, attitudes, motivations, subjective norms (i.e., what others think about the issue/object of motivation) and perceived behavioral control (i.e., how much one thinks one can control the situation), and subsequent behavior. Such theories posit that creating messages that target attitude, motivation, beliefs, etc., will then create desired behavior change in audiences.

Persuasion plays a big role in strategic corporate communication because the goal of stakeholder communication is often to try to get the stakeholder to buy a product, adopt the organization's point of view, participate in the workplace, donate money, vote in a way that benefits the communicator (e.g., such as a politician), and more. We will discuss the principles of persuasion in much more detail in Chapter 7; however, because of the large role that persuasion plays in strategic corporate communication, it is worth highlighting in this chapter, as well as focusing on the ethical implications of persuasion in strategic communication in Chapter 6.

MEDIA

The plural of medium, media is something that acts as a mediary between or among parties. Thus in communication, it is something that intervenes in the delivery of a message. Within corporate communication, "media" takes on two primary meanings: mediated electronic channels through which messages are communicated and *the media*, which refers collectively to news and information outlets, such as newspapers, television, and Internet news sources, including bloggers. We will cover mediated channels for strategic communication in the next section.

The media consists of journalists who find and create stories, which are typically considered reliable because they go through an editorial process of vetting the background of a story and fact-checking. The media is important to corporate communication, as publication in a third-party media outlet, such as a newspaper, provides far-reaching, free coverage of an organizational story. Coverage in the media also has the benefit of being perceived as more credible than direct "organization to stakeholder communication" because it is fact-checked and published through a third party. Reliance on the media led to the rise of media relations, which is the practice of developing relationships with members of the media and creating materials, such as press releases and media kits, to influence organizational coverage in the media. While media relations are still an integral part of strategic communication, it is worth noting that the rise of social media, combined with the fact that the credibility of the media is continually being called into question, has made media relations less prominent than in previous decades.

THEORY AND RESEARCH OVERVIEW

While communication may seem like something we do naturally, you have probably realized by this point in the book that there is a lot of thought and planning that goes into strategic communication. There are several models and theories or guiding frameworks that describe and predict what types of communication will be most effective in different circumstances. In this section, we will talk about the importance of a proper orientation toward communication, how to create messages, and the importance of the media you use to share your messages.

Communicative Orientation and Messages

Communication orientation is the approach that one or more parties bring to the communication process. It involves the communicators' beliefs about the importance and nature of each interaction. As we will highlight in our discussion of the following theories, communication orientation can also be related to power, and a shift in orientation can have a profound effect on message reception and the relationship among communicators in any given interaction, which can then affect behavioral outcomes related to the communication exchange.

MODELS OF COMMUNICATION

To understand the importance of communicative orientation, it is important to briefly review how we have viewed the communication process since the beginning of modern communication scholarship. Early communication models viewed communication as a simple process whereby a sender created a message, which was encoded, sent through a channel, received, and decoded by a receiver. This type of model is known as the transmission model (Figure 4.1). This approach is considered *linear*, as it positions communication as a sequence that takes place without deviation from beginning to end. Within transmission models, *noise* exists as anything that is a physical hindrance to proper decoding and reception of the message (e.g., static on a phone, background noise). In linear models, the message was treated as a sort of package passed back and forth between sender and receiver.

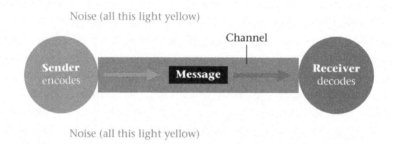

FIGURE 4.1 Transmission Model of Communication

Transactional models of communication (Figure 4.2) built on the transmission models by incorporating the idea of feedback (e.g., Schramm, 1954), which allowed that each person in an interaction could take turns being the sender and receiver. Feedback includes the receiver's interpretation and subsequent reaction to the sender's message, at which point the original receiver becomes the sender. Feedback can be verbal (e.g., a spoken response), nonverbal (e.g., a smile or an eye roll), or both.

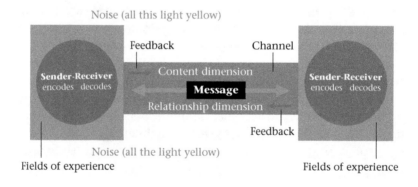

FIGURE 4.2 Transactional Model of Communication

Later models of communication propose a constitutive view of communication. Viewing communication as a constitutive process situates communication as a process of meaning development about social phenomena ranging from self and social structure. Accordingly, from a constitutive point of view, it is through communication that we create shared realities by (re)negotiating meaning through every interaction. Such a point of view takes into account that people come from multiple backgrounds and hold different values and points of view, making communication about more than a simple message but rather the creation of meaning, relationships, identities, and social realities of the communicating parties (Craig, 1999). No message is sent in a vacuum, and a message is neither static nor discrete; all messages are socially created and affected by multiple factors, including environment, situation, timing, parties involved, and more.

ONE-WAY AND TWO-WAY COMMUNICATION

As a forerunner of strategic communication, PR paved the way for many of the contemporary practices used today. Grunig and Hunt (1984) created a model (Table 4.1) that characterized the different ways in which organizations communicate with stakeholders, both historically and at the time of this writing.

TABLE 4.1 **Classic Models of Public Relations**

Press Agentry/Publicity	**Public Information**
▪ One-way communication mass media	▪ One-way communication
▪ Truth isn't valued	▪ Not to persuade but to inform
▪ "Hype"	▪ Truth is valued
Example: Classic: P. T. Barnum	*Example:* Classic: journalists
Example: Modern: Hollywood publicist	*Example:* Modern: government, public institutions
Two-Way Asymmetric	**Two-Way Symmetric**
▪ Scientific persuasion	▪ Mutual understanding, balanced/mutually beneficial
▪ Feedback loop, but only to increase persuasion	▪ Feedback loop to gain insight and galvanize change
Example: Classic: Edward Bernays	*Example:* Classic: relationship building
Example: Modern: marketing and advertising	*Example:* Modern: crisis/risk, social media management, long-term strategic planning

Based on Grunig and Hunt *Classic Models of Public Relations* (1984).

The most important elements to highlight from this model are the different contexts: one- and two-way communication, the difference between symmetry and asymmetry, and the position of the organization relative to the stakeholder in different types of communication. One-way communication is communication pushed out to stakeholders from the organization, with no mechanism for feedback or elaboration. When using one-way communication, the initiator controls the flow of communication and the sending of the message, although there is no way to elaborate on the message or create mutual meaning. Two-way asymmetrical communication allows for feedback, but not in a way that is equal. The feedback is generally used to create greater success for the initiator of the communication rather than for mutuality between the organization and the stakeholder. Two-way symmetrical communication is used to generate mutual understanding and responsiveness. Each of these differences highlight the power and control that the organization is trying to retain relative to the stakeholder.

Although it is tempting to look at the model as a linear historical progression, with all strategic communication now focusing on two-way symmetric communication, that is not the case. There are times when one-way communication is sufficient, such as in some marketing and advertising, or even in media releases. There are also times when two-way symmetrical communication would be the right choice, but organizations take the "easy" way out and tell half-truths or gather feedback simply to persuade stakeholders or better manage a situation. While having a strong, positive reputation is a major goal in strategic corporate communication, current thinking highlights the benefits of two-way symmetrical communication that values the needs of both the organization and the stakeholder. This concept is embodied in a dialogic theory of communication (Kent & Taylor, 2002).

BUILDING MUTUALITY AND SHARED MEANING THROUGH MESSAGING

A dialogic theory of communication (Kent & Taylor, 1998; Kent & Taylor, 2002) emphasizes the importance of a mutual orientation to all communication enacted by the organization. What does this mean? Basically, it moves away from the idea that communication should not only benefit the organization but also focus on the needs and goals of the stakeholders with whom the organization is communicating. Dialogue, in communication-based fields, is tied to the ethical imperative of the organization to build relationships with stakeholders, which can involve communicating about issues, opportunity for debate, and advocacy with an open and mutual orientation (Kent & Taylor, 2002). Employing a dialogic orientation in strategic communication fields has been an important part of the shift away from *communication management* to *communicating to build relationships*. This shift may require a change in organizational thinking to position the stakeholder as equal to the organization, particularly when, as a communication practitioner, it is your job to communicate in the best interest of the organization. A dialogic orientation guides the practitioner to see this very power shift *as* what is best for the organization, as it can create trust and social capital between organizations and stakeholders, which goes far beyond the benefits of pushing out one-way, asymmetrical communication. While there is no standard for specific messages or strategies that constitute dialogue in professional communication, maintaining a dialogic orientation will provide a guide for maintaining an ethical stance toward stakeholder communication.

Creating Effective Messages: Communication Strategy and Storytelling

Messages are the meat (or Tofurky®) of the strategic communication sandwich. While there are many different kinds of writing in corporate communication, such as media releases, advertisements, featured stories, and social media content, there are some common elements that make for good messaging. Perhaps more than anything, messages are best when they *reflect the goals, mission, and vision of the organization.* Always start with what you know to be true and genuine about the organization and work from there. Related, good messages stem from the goals you have for any given communication endeavor, whether it is a full campaign or a one-off media release. Knowing what you want to accomplish with the material you are writing keeps your messages relevant and on point. After that, you can divide effective messaging into three areas: content, word choice, and mechanics. Content is your message, word choice relates to the specific words you choose to share your message, and mechanics refers to the grammar, punctuation, and formatting of the writing.

- **Do your research.** We will talk much more about research in Chapter 8, but for now, it is important to realize that after setting your goals, research should be the first step you take before writing. It is important to know more about the topic you are writing about, what your organization (or others) has said about it before, related topics in the media that might influence the way people read your content, and more.

- **Know your stakeholders.** Know who you are writing for. What do they like, what are they interested in, and what will they respond to? Make sure you keep your stakeholders in mind for the entirety of the writing process.

- **Engage stakeholder interests.** Would you be more interested in content that was catered to you or only focused on the organization? We tend to engage much more if something is interesting to us. For example, social media posts that push information, sell something, or extol the benefits of an organization often get very little engagement and can turn people away. However, content that gives us interesting news or requests our participation is much more likely to draw us into individual interactions, as well as the overall brand.

- **Tell a story, share an idea, or solve a problem.** Good content will rarely overtly sell but rather draws the stakeholder in by building a connection through story. Sometimes this means conveying the identity and values of the organization in anecdotal form or by sharing the positive experiences of other stakeholders. It can also involve showing stakeholders *why* they need to engage with the company by sharing the benefits of doing so, including the fact that it could solve a problem for stakeholders. Scott (2013) calls this thought leadership. Whole Foods Market® does a great job with this. Their web content (including a robust platform of website, blog, and social media) often includes recipes, holiday cooking ideas, and healthy eating tips. For example, one of their articles is titled "10 Tips for Helping Kids Try New Foods." This is a problem that almost every parent (one of their key stakeholder groups) faces. Thus it is engaging content that does not specifically reference the brand, but you can bet that every tip can be fulfilled at Whole Foods.

- **Know your grammar and proofread.** Take online grammar quizzes, brush up on when to use its versus it's, and where to add your commas.

Although, arguably, content is the most important part of creating messages, without the proper grammar, punctuation, or format, your meaning could get lost or misunderstood. Always work in drafts, and always have a second and third set of eyes check your content.

- **Use proper formatting.** External communication spans a wide variety of materials, including media releases and alerts, web content, social media content, brochures, and more. As you can imagine, and have probably seen to some extent, each of these types of materials has a different purpose, tone, and format. In order to be read appropriately, each must follow the proper conventions and formats. For example, media releases follow very strict formatting so that editors can find all needed information with just a glance. Knowing how people scan web pages so that you can use the right balance of text and imagery is as much a part of the message as is what you write. The *AP Stylebook* is a comprehensive source for formatting, grammar, and word usage that can help you with your writing in several areas.

- **Use small words and short sentences.** Writing between the fourth- and seventh-grade levels is recommended for all strategic communication materials. This ensures that most of your audience will be able to read, understand, and recall your message.

- **Be consistent and different.** Although we tend to think about messages in the short term—that is, as a single element of communication—it is worth noting that each message we send out contributes to the overall organizational message. As you work to build an overall brand through ongoing smaller communication, you are creating larger messages that tell the story of the organization. To that end, it is important to have a sense of cohesiveness, or synergy, among your messages. This can be accomplished by using consistent wording, themes, and/or imagery across instances of communication. While messages will vary according to which medium you use to publish them, your stakeholder should be able to recognize the message as *yours*. That said, it is important not to get stagnant. Think of different ways to tell your story over time. Innovate. Pay attention to what is going on in popular culture, your industry, and with your key stakeholder groups to figure out how to change up your messaging without changing your overall capital "M" Message. Or, if it is time to change your Message because of changes to the rebranding, new innovations, or other changes, you can accomplish that too.

Media Channels for Strategic Communication

As we mentioned earlier, the choice of channel and media can play a large role in message exchange related to exchange, comprehension, and overall involvement. The following theories look at what types of media might be best for specific types of messages, as well as why different people will receive and react to messages differently across types of media. Understanding these principles can play a large role in choosing how to share your messages with stakeholders and why stakeholders may or may not engage with your message.

TYPES OF MEDIA

The contemporary media climate provides many choices for communication for both individuals and organizations. They can be classified into three primary categories: mass media, online/social media, and mobile media. While these three categories have some distinct features, there is also considerable overlap. For example, social media and mass media, such as commercials or advertisements, can often be viewed via mobile devices.

Mass media typically communicates one-to-many and includes television, news, radio, and billboards. Mass media was traditionally the only way organizations could reach stakeholders outside of interpersonal interaction in physical locations (e.g., interaction in organizational locations, customer service via phone, or organizational events, such as openings or annual meetings). Mass media was, and still is, either *earned* or *paid*. Paid media is media that is paid for—most commonly advertising. Paid advertising gives you complete control over the content and timing of your message but can often be very expensive. Earned media is coverage that shows up in media, such as newspapers or television/radio shows. It is accomplished through media relations, including press releases, media alerts, and developing relationships with journalists. With earned media, you have little to moderate control over the message, as it is typically the journalist or editor who decides if, when, and how to give you coverage. A good media release and consistent relationships with reporters give you more control, but at the end of the day, the media gatekeepers decide. In terms of financial cost, earned media is technically free. *Are you aware of organizational messages you have received through mass media lately? How much weight do they carry in your decision making about a brand?*

Online/Social media is tied to the Internet and enables both one-to-many and one-to-one communication. For example, organizational websites are one-way communication aimed at several audiences, while social media is more interactive, allowing people to post one-to-many but with the opportunity to interact one-to-one within apps, such as a messenger, or in responses to posts. Organizational use of social media is growing rapidly, with upward of 88% of organizations using social media (Bennett, 2014). *Do you use social media to follow brands? How does the platform you use affect your expectations and interpretations of organizational messages?*

Mobile media is unique in that it allows the user to make mediated communication portable. Think about your mobile phone and the types of communication you most often engage with on the phone. Information seeking, communication via social media and other apps, interpersonal communication via the audio or video calling functions, and more. *How does communicating mobily change your goals and orientation toward an act of communication?*

So how do these different forms of media work together? Think PESO: paid, earned, shared, owned (Dietrich, 2014). Paid media is, as the name implies, media that you pay to create and/or share. Think advertising (print, television, radio, online, sponsored posts/tweets). The benefits of paid media are that you have complete control over the message content, timing, and placement of the message. Earned media is what you would traditionally think of as publicity. Publicity is often gained through media relations or the cultivation of relationships between the organization and various media outlet using tools, such as interpersonal communication, media releases, media kits, and online media rooms. The benefit of earned media is that you get wide coverage (think of a story about your organization in a media outlet such as the *New York Times*). However, you don't get as much control over your message, timing, or placement with earned media. Shared media is essentially social media in which content and messages are often cocreated and shared by users. Finally, owned media is media that the company owns, such as a website, blog, podcast, or newsletter. Owned media is often used to build and solidify organizational branding. Think about organizational websites. They are a 24/7 one-stop shop for just about any information about an organization. Most people across age groups will visit a website first for organizational information. As with paid media, the organization has complete control over content in owned media.

CHOOSING THE RIGHT MEDIA FOR YOUR MESSAGE

Would you break up with someone over text? What difference do you think it would make if an organization announced layoffs via e-mail versus a face-to-face meeting? Media richness theory (MRT) (Daft & Lengel, 1986) considers the effect media choice has on our comprehension of, and reaction to, messages in relation to the degree to which each type of media helps us reduce uncertainty. MRT considers uncertainty to be the absence of information and states that uncertainty is reduced as information increases. *Rich media* allow for the conveyance of the most verbal and nonverbal clues and most closely approximate face-to-face communication. Rich media are typically considered best for relational messages, sensitive information, or complicated or debatable concepts, as they provide the capacity to process complex messages (Daft & Lengel, 1986, p. 560). The richest medium is face-to-face (although not typically considered a medium in the sense we have discussed it thus far in this chapter), video conferencing or calling, and telephone. *Lean media*, or those media that allow for more concise communication with less feedback, typically through written documents, are most useful for concise, easy-to-understand information. Examples of lean media (in descending order) are e-mail and messaging, social media, discussion forums, websites and blogs, personal written documents, generic written documents, and numeric documents. Inherently, we know that richer media generally provide a better understanding of messages and have created message enhancers, such as emoticons, smiling/winking/frowning faces using text, memes, and other hybrid written visual cues to enhance message comprehension and infuse intimacy into written communication. Interestingly, some online studies have shown some exceptions to the preference of rich media for equivocal situations. In particular, studies show that e-mail is often preferred over richer communication channels, even in situations high in uncertainty. Maybe this is because we can take our time to craft messages via e-mail, which might be preferable for detailed or even emotionally charged messages.

Closely related, ICT succession theory tells us that using complementary media in sequence can increase the likelihood that communicators will reach their intended audiences (Stephens, 2007, p. 486). Complementary medium go together because each media has capabilities that the other doesn't have, which allows for expanded communication cues (Stephens, Sornes, Rice, Browning, & Saetre, 2008). For example, to share an important message with internal stakeholders, you might use face-to-face communication and then follow up with an e-mail (Stephens, 2007). Because face-to-face has visual and auditory cues and e-mail has textual cues, using the two together can increase comprehension or persuasion. Other research shows that we not only use ICT successively, or one after the other, but also simultaneously, or at the same time (Brito, 2013). An example of simultaneous media use would be using your computer to do homework while you chat with someone about the assignment on the phone. Or, more closely related to corporate communication, a stakeholder may read about a new product and then visit the product website for more information or post on Facebook asking opinions about the new product.

There are several implications of MRT and image restoration theory (IRT) succession theory research for strategic communication.

- Medium choice matters. While this is, to a certain extent, obvious, it is worth stating. Consider what your message is when you are choosing which channel(s) will best convey it to your chosen audience.

- In general, more equivocal, sensitive, or relational messages are better suited for rich media. For example, messages about layoffs in a company are best given face-to-face, with an opportunity for Q&A. Information about an organizational crisis is best addressed face-to-face with employees and media, transmitted over live stream or television.

- For easy to understand, nondebatable information, such as straightforward marketing of a product's features or the announcement of a new hire within an organization, lean media is a sufficient, and sometimes preferred, mode of communication.

- Communication redundancy via a combination of rich and lean media can increase reception and comprehension of messages across situations and is a best practice in strategic communication.

- Complementary channels (e.g., written and visual) can enhance attention to, and comprehension of, messages.

- Cultivating online platforms that create a sense of social presence can help increase message attention and retention.

- The average stakeholder receives multiple messages through multiple channels on a daily, or even hourly, basis. Creating messages that stand out on each medium is important for capturing and keeping stakeholder attention.

APPLYING THE CONCEPT
TO YOUR OWN SITUATION

MAKING MESSAGE GOALS AND CHOICES

Message choices, whether personal or professional, are rooted in several factors, including audience, context, timing, and goals. Audience refers to who you are creating messages for; context is what is going on in the larger environment that is creating the need for or prompting your message; timing is when you are sharing your message; goals are what you want to achieve through this act of communication. In this section, we are not talking about single instances of speech but rather communication sequences that convey a big message or idea—for example, applying for a job, presenting yourself during a networking event, or pitching an idea to your boss or client. You will likely be building these messages around your personal brand (Chapter 2) and in your professional voice (later in this chapter).

The first thing to do when making message choices is to take inventory of what is prompting you to create a message. What do you want to communicate about and why?

Next, think about your audience. Who you are trying to reach? Why do you want to communicate with them? What do you want them to know, believe, or act on? What is your relationship to this audience (individual or group), and how will this affect their communication with you? It is also important to consider secondary audiences. Who might overhear or see your message? These secondary audiences could affect message reception if they are influential to your primary audience and may share your message with other audiences.

Now, consider the macrolevel context in which you will be creating and sharing your message. What cultural factors (organizational or societal) might affect message creation and reception?

With all of these factors in consideration, decide what you hope to get out of the message. Just as communication does not exist in a vacuum, communication goals cannot be created in a vacuum. Goals should always relate to what you want your audience to think, believe, know, feel, or do relative to your message.

Arguably, timing can be part of context and goals, but it can also stand alone. When to initiate your message is relative to what you are trying to achieve, as well as what is going on in the larger context. Issues such as follow-up messages are important, as waiting too long or following up too soon can affect the overall outcome.

MAKING MEDIUM CHOICES:
CHOICES FOR PROFESSIONAL PRESENTATION

The theories covered in this chapter provide great direction for choosing the appropriate media to convey your messages. The media that you choose should consider *what you want to say, the context in which you are saying it,* and *who you are saying it to.*

As you move out into the career world, you will have to choose which messages to display on which media and for whom. Some of the common tools that you will use include the following:

▪ **Face-to-face.** No matter which career route you take, face-to-face communication will be an important part of how you get a job, develop relationships with clients and coworkers, network, share your ideas, and more. Face-to-face communication is considered the richest medium and, therefore, provides the greatest possibilities for making personal impressions on the people with whom you are communicating. How can you enhance your face-to-face communication?

  ● **Be prepared.** Whether you are interviewing or networking, it is important to be able to concisely tell your audience *who you are, what your goals are, and what makes you unique/right for the job/the best candidate*, etc. Have a 20- to 30-second elevator pitch prepared to convey these ideas and generate interest with your audience. Having a pre-prepared pitch allows you to make a positive impression on the spot without having to think about what you are going to say if time is limited.

  ● **Be positive. Be gracious.** Take turns talking and show interest in the people you are talking to. Don't complain or badmouth others.

  ● **Be aware of your nonverbal communication.** As we discussed earlier, nonverbal communication is any communication that is not spoken, including appearance, gestures, and tone of voice. Nonverbals either reinforce or undermine a message. For example, if you go on a job interview and say that you are qualified for the job but don't make eye contact, you are undermining your message of competency.

▪ **Social media.** Whether or not you intend to use social media for professional communication, the fact is that you are. Prospective and current employers can (and many will) Google you, with the potential of pulling up any information about you that was ever published on the web. However, this doesn't have to work against you. Rather, you can proactively create social media content that highlights your assets rather than simply trying to hide what you don't want future professional contacts to see. How can you enhance your social media communication?

  ● **Create professional content.** Create a professional page on Facebook or Twitter where you share information that shows you are up to date in what is going on in the communication field. If you have a special area of interest, highlight it here. Connect with other professionals on your page, see who they follow, and connect with them too. Or start a blog on which you write about current communication trends and your thoughts and experiences. Basically, move your professional voice online and connect with other professionals.

  ● **Show your personality.** While your professional media isn't your personal media, you can still show your personality. Highlight one or two hobbies or unique characteristics that you have and post about them once in a while too. It shows that you are well-rounded and multidimensional.

- **Be interactive.** Because social media sites come with the expectation of interaction, you would be remiss not to comment on the posts of the professionals you follow and respond to them if they comment to you.

- **Use the "networking" in social network sites.** It is a good idea to create a profile on a professional networking site, such as LinkedIn. This gives you a place to develop your professional voice, connect with other people in fields relevant to the field you want to enter, and connect with friends of friends. Remember the importance of weak ties for finding a job (Chapter 3)? Professional networking sites are developed to help you tap into weak ties in a context that is designed to help you maximize professional connections.

- **Written documents.** While you will use a variety of documents over the course of your career, some of the most important documents in your near future will be your resume and cover letter. Written documents are a medium where message function meets form. That is, grammar, punctuation, sentence structure, and flow become part of your message. How can you enhance your written communication, such as resumes and cover letters?

  - **Be specific.** Because written documents represent a leaner media, you can't rely on visuals or nonverbal to convey your message. Thus you have to create a clear and understandable message. Use descriptive and active words to depict your previous work experience. For example, instead of saying that you "created social media content" at your internship, you could say that you "curated targeted and timely content across Facebook, Twitter, and Instagram. Created messages that promoted synergy while staying true to the capabilities of each platform."

  - **Address your audience.** Just as you have to create stakeholder-specific content in corporate communication, you should do the same in your resume and cover letter. Explain why you are interested in, and how you are qualified for, *this particular position*. Say what you like about the company and why you want to work there. Tweak your resume goals so that they align with what the job offers. Make sure your readers know that you are talking to them.

  - **Break your message into discrete chunks.** Just as we would zone out if we were talking to someone who droned on in a monotone voice, resumes and cover letters can be overwhelming without proper formatting to enhance readability. In your cover letter, start and end with a paragraph, but use bullet points to list your qualifications relative to the job. Follow the appropriate formatting for resumes, and use bold, italics, and tabs to clarify and break up the different parts of your resume. Improving readability will improve the reception of your message.

QUESTIONS:

- How do I represent myself?

- How can I improve my messaging?

- What are some important messages I want to send to my stakeholders?

- What medium or mix of mediums are most advantageous for each of these messages?

- How can my messaging process be more dialogic?

Tools and Processes for Self-Action

CREATING YOUR PROFESSIONAL VOICE

Your professional voice should be an extension of your personal voice, influenced by your personal brand (Chapter 2). That is, your professional voice should reflect who you want to be perceived as in professional settings, such as your workplace, talking with clients, and at networking events, to name a few places. While your professional voice will be influenced by a number of personal characteristics, there are some qualities that should be consistent across individuals.

- **Credible.** How credible we are has to do with how believable others perceive us to be (Richmond & McCroskey, 2009), and it can be broken down into the dimensions of competence, character, and goodwill (McCroskey & Young, 1981). Competence has to do with our knowledge and ability; character is tied to the degree to which we can be counted on to act in a certain way; goodwill is holding and acting in the best interests of others. We have to speak and act in a way that is credible to be taken seriously in an organizational context.

- **Context appropriate.** Your professional voice should, to some extent, reflect the context in which you are working. Each organization and industry has its own culture, norms, and assumptions. For example, some organizations require formal business wear and likely follow a more formal protocol when addressing leaders and other coworkers. This is very different from a company in which everyone is on a first-name basis and socializes frequently outside of work. Your professional voice should account for these factors and match the setting in which you work.

- **Competent.** Although competence is considered a dimension of credibility, it also serves as a stand-alone quality that is important for developing a professional voice. Simply, to be competent is to be efficient and capable. Both your tone of voice and what you say should reflect your knowledge of your job requirements and the skills necessary to effectively do your job.

- **Confident.** Your professional voice should reflect the fact that you believe in yourself and your ability to get the job done.

- **Positive.** Be civil at least, friendly at best. Be interested in others and avoid gossiping, complaining, or getting too personal with people you don't know well enough to trust.

- **Proactive.** Speak in a way that is energetic and indicates that you are interested in what is going on, solution oriented, and ready to take action. Don't be afraid to propose ideas and inject your point of view into a conversation.

PROFILE OF INDIVIDUAL EXPERIENCE:

Brandi Boatner

Brandi Boatner, social and influencer communications lead and global markets, brand communications manager for IBM Corporate Communications, uses media daily when crafting messages for internal and external stakeholders. Her responsibilities include developing a consistent coordinated approach to identify top external influencers in each global market and how internal IBM influencers drive engagement around strategic communications narratives, such as blockchain, artificial intelligence, hybrid cloud, and cybersecurity. In addition, Boatner has extended responsibilities as the brand communications manager for IBM marketing, supporting external engagements, including press, events, and social media for IBM's senior vice president of digital sales and chief marketing officer.

FIGURE 4.3 **Brandi Boatner**

In terms of both voice and strategic messaging, Ms. Boatner emphasized that authenticity is key: "My 'professional voice' and my 'personal voice' is all one voice—BRANDI. As my skill set and expertise developed throughout my nearly decade in my organization, I did not really have to cultivate it but simply continue to grow and remain true to myself, gaining a little more wisdom and knowledge with each passing year. In turn, this provides value and both ROI (return on investment) and ROE (return on engagement) to the communications function or business unit."

Embracing authenticity and transparency is a perfect fit for working in social media, which has changed expectations for stakeholder communication. Social media demands open and genuine connections among organizations, content, and stakeholders. Working in social media allows Ms. Boatner to develop a voice that is consistent across the personal/professional spectrum. Ms. Boatner explained, "Social media plays such a large role in my life both personally and professionally. I am what I share. I am a social strategist, a digital communicator, a social media maven." In terms of building the organizational voice on social media, Ms. Boatner focuses on four primary platforms: Slack, LinkedIn, Twitter, and blogs. Boatner said, "Professionally, I use Twitter daily which is the best news aggregator for my day to day tasks serving in a global role in corporate communications. I can get snackable headlines that keep me in the know across topics I care about like business, technology and culture. Personally, my go to platform is Instagram because I feel as if I have a relationship with the people, places and things that pop up on my feed."

Having both the confidence and competence to be authentic has allowed Ms. Boatner to maintain a strong professional brand throughout her career. Although she has evolved, she said, "My professional voice and personal voice have remained the same. I was hired into my company because I had a unique skill set around social media and that still holds true today. Who I am and what I can bring to the organization hold true to my day to day interactions at work, so the voice of Brandi is still going strong for nearly a decade."

For students looking to work in social media, Ms. Boatner had the following advice: "Practice authenticity and consistency in your social and digital communications. Consistency which is key in driving message effectiveness. Social media should not be an ad hoc approach or execution. It needs to be consistent driving value for both brands/organizations and the audiences who consume their messages."

Questions:

1. What do you think it means to have one combined personal and professional voice? How do you decide which elements of yourself to emphasize in your personal brand?

2. What do you think it looks like to be authentic and consistent but also to evolve over the course of your career? How might you achieve that balance?

3. What role can social media play in developing your professional voice?

APPLYING THE CONCEPT
TO YOUR WORK WITH CLIENTS

CREATING STAKEHOLDER-APPROPRIATE MESSAGES

As a point of review, stakeholders are members of any group that affects, or is affected by, the organization. Common stakeholder groups include employees, consumers, donors, activists, and the government. As we discussed in Chapters 1 and 3, building relationships with stakeholders is one of the most important tasks of strategic corporate communication. Defining and knowing your stakeholders is also one of the most important elements of messaging. Even if you have already defined your goals for any instance of messaging, if you don't know (a) who you are writing for and (b) what your audience's motives and interests are, how can you create an effective message?

Creating *buyer personas* is one way to segment and define your stakeholders (Scott, 2013). Buyer personas are profiles that communication professionals create in order to develop a nuanced understanding of their various stakeholder groups. Creating a fake "person" that represents each stakeholder segment can lead to a better understanding of how to most effectively communicate with each group.

The first step is to break a stakeholder group, such as employees, into smaller groups. Although employees constitute a single stakeholder group, there is likely to be variation in employees, meaning that one message may not fit the entire stakeholder group. Depending on the organization, "employees" can be broken down by work groups or divisions (e.g., office workers, warehouse workers, and drivers) or possibly by union status (e.g., union or nonunion).

Next, research your groups. Find out their goals, aspirations, needs, wants, media choices, way of talking (e.g., more or less formal), hobbies, cultural references, and more. We'll talk more research in Chapter 8, but some of the ways you can find out this information is through focus groups, interviews, and third-party research, such as Pew Research Center, or hiring a market research firm. Once you know what their interests are, immerse yourself in them so you understand them and can "speak" the language of each specific stakeholder (Scott, 2013).

Finally, create a two- to three-paragraph profile that describes a typical person for that segment. Give the person a first name and write a description of that person using the language and writing style that your research indicated might be adopted by that person (Scott, 2013). Reference your buyer's profile when you have to create messages for that stakeholder group.

CREATING PERSUASIVE MESSAGES

As we discussed earlier, persuasion is part of strategic corporate communication, as organizations are often trying to engage stakeholders to adopt a certain type of attitude or behavior relative to the organization, such as purchasing a product or donating time or money. While several different theories and strategies have been pulled in from many disciplines, this section highlights an easy-to-understand and implement theory of messaging: heuristic or central route processing.

The principle of heuristic versus central route processing is tied to the elaboration likelihood model (Petty & Cacioppo, 1986), which posits that people follow one of two routes to persuasion based on factors such as motivation and ability to process the message. Those people who have high interest or personal relevance related to a subject and/or time to attend to the message and level of distraction will rely on *central route processing* in which they attend to message factors, such as credibility and strength of argument. *Peripheral route processing* is used when people don't have a high level of interest in the issue or time or focus to concentrate on the message. Peripheral route processing relies on *heuristics*, or mental shortcuts, to persuade people to adopt an attitude or behavior. Heuristics include repetition (think of all the lawn signs you see for political candidates around election time), celebrity (we have emotional connections to celebrities and often grant them an air of credibility), or attractiveness (we often respond more positively to attractive people). For example, PETA (People for the Ethical Treatment of Animals) creates materials that address both routes of processing: campaign materials that talk about the abuse/mistreatment of animals, often using vivid language and pictures, as well as celebrity spokespeople and campaigns, such as their "I'd Rather Go Naked than Wear Fur" campaign, which featured famous, attractive, mostly naked people. These links demonstrate examples of materials targeting central route processing:

- https://www.peta.org/media/psa/

- https://www.peta.org/features/elisabetta-canalis-rather-go-naked-wear-fur/

While both routes can affect attitude and behavior, messages processed through the central route create longer lasting change and more likely affect behavior, whereas messages processed through the peripheral route enact a temporary attitude change that is susceptible to change and not as predictive of actual behavior change. While this suggests that central route processing is always desirable, because communicators often have to reach both more and less interested audiences, and there is so much noise in our contemporary media climate, peripheral route processing can be an effective way to reach fringe or overloaded audiences and begin the process of drawing them into the organizational message.

MEDIA RELATIONS:
EXTENDING CONTROL OVER THE ORGANIZATIONAL MESSAGE

While organizations have full control over messaging on paid media, such as brochures or the organizational website, they don't have control over what the media prints about them. Media coverage can be great because it reaches a wide audience and doesn't cost the organization anything. However, it can also be dangerous because journalists can frame the facts of the story however it suits them, portraying the organization in either a positive or negative way.

Communication specialists can extend control over media messages through the practice of media relations, which is essentially developing long-term relationships with journalists by providing truthful, timely, and interesting material on a consistent basis. Media releases follow a specific format in order to pitch a story to journalists, providing all of the information that a journalist needs to write a story covering the organization. Although the media release is written in an objective format, it still presents the news from the organization's point of view, extending at least some control over how the story will eventually read when it is printed in the newspaper. While news releases traditionally went only to journalists, they now also reside in the newsroom on an organization's website. The following are best practices for creating a news release:

- The headline is one of the most important parts of a media release because it is the first thing people read and will likely determine whether they read the rest of the release. It should be centered, bold, and written in a way that is both creative and portrays the bottom line of the story. Occasionally, subheads, or summary statements that provide more detail, are included in italics directly below the headline.

- The first paragraph includes a dateline, which is the city and state in which the news originated, as well as the date of the release.

- The first paragraph, or *lead*, should consist of two sentences and tell *who*, *what*, *when*, *where*, *why*, and *how*. Essentially, the reader should get everything he or she needs to know from the lead. This is useful for journalists, who often scan only the title and first paragraph to see if they want to pursue the story. Ultimately, the lead is the most important part of the news release.

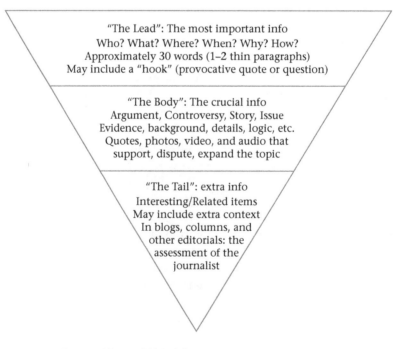

FIGURE 4.4 Inverted Pyramid Model

▪ The rest of the release should be anywhere from four to six paragraphs and follow the inverted pyramid format (Figure 4.4), which involves putting the high level, need-to-know information toward the beginning and then drilling down in level of detail as the release goes on.

▪ While releases are written in objective, third-person language (i.e., no using "I" or "we" to refer to the organization) quotes from the highest ranking organizational member related to what is being discussed in the release offer an opportunity to use superlative first-person language.

▪ A *boilerplate* closes the news release and provides basic information about the company, such as when it was founded, its mission, how many locations it has, and contact information for the organizational media representative. Boilerplates are designed to provide readily available background information to journalists so that they don't have to call the organization to follow up but rather have it at hand.

Visit the website of your favorite organization and look through its media room (this can often be found in the "News" section of a website). How does the organization write its media releases? What are some best practices or commonalities that you can find?

QUESTIONS:

▪ What are my client's goals and objectives?

▪ How do I create messages for different stakeholder groups?

▪ How do I know which media to use to get the right message to the appropriate stakeholder group?

Tools and Processes When Acting for Others

CREATING MESSAGE MAPS ACROSS MEDIA

A message map is a tool for distilling an organization's core message and then coordinating other messages around that main message. Similar to a concept map, which is a visual representation of the relationship among concepts that are used to structure knowledge, message maps are visual tools in which the main message is visually connected to submessages and supporting points. They serve not only as a way to organize messages for synchronicity but also provide a way to organize the core message in short, medium, and long formats. While message maps are an internal tool that only practitioners see, they can be used as the springboard to organize and create more extensive messaging.

PROFILE OF ORGANIZATIONAL EXPERIENCE:

United Airlines

One area in which the importance of messaging is paramount is during a crisis. Crisis has been defined as "a fundamental threat to the very stability of a system, a questioning of core assumptions and beliefs, and risk to high priority goals, including organizational image, legitimacy, profitability, and ultimately, survival" (Seeger & Ulmer, 2002, p. 126). Within crisis communication, there are several important turning points for communication, including the golden hour, or the first 60 minutes following the organizational incident. Messages sent during that time can set the tone for the rest of the crisis response. While this is still true, the crisis narrative, which used to rest squarely on the shoulders of the organization and traditional media, is now a polyvocal narrative. Social and mobile media have changed the way that crisis communication unfolds, transitioning power from the organization and putting it in the hands of anyone with a mobile phone and a social media account.

On April 9, 2017, 69-year-old David Dao, a Vietnamese American passenger on a United Airlines flight originating from Chicago, was forcibly removed from the airplane when he failed to give up his seat to accommodate United crew members from a different flight. Mr. Dao was dragged down the airplane aisle by aviation security offers, suffering a concussion, broken nose, and two lost teeth. Stunned passengers looked on, some of them filming the incident and posting it to social media.

The social media reaction was swift and viral. By the following day, the story was trending on Twitter and other social media platforms, and it received repeated international coverage in traditional media outlets. As the crisis unfolded over the next few days, through a series of mixed and somewhat contradictory messages from United chief executive Oscar Munoz, United became the recipient of scorn and ridicule as hashtags such as #United and #NewUnitedAirlinesMottos started trending on Twitter, allegations of racism were leveled against United as observers in China called for a boycott of the airline, and late-night comedians incorporated the incident into their monologues (Czarnecki, 2017; Temin, 2017). Shares of United fell 6.3% in premarket trading and were down 4% by the Tuesday following the incident (Farber, 2017). In short, United suffered both reputational and material damage.

The first response from United came Monday morning, via a statement from United chief executive Oscar Munoz, who apologized for the "overbook situation" without mentioning what happened to Dr. Dao (McCann, 2017). Later that day, Munoz offered a second apology, saying, "This is an upsetting event to all of us here at United. I apologize for having to re-accommodate these customers. Our team is moving with a sense of urgency to work with the authorities and conduct our own detailed review of what happened. We are also reaching out to this passenger to talk directly to him and further address and resolve this situation" (McCann, 2017).

Separately, on Monday evening, Munoz sent a letter to United employees in which he framed the situation so that Dao was blamed. Excerpts of the letter include: "as you will read, this situation was unfortunately compounded when one of the passengers we politely asked to deplane refused and it became necessary to contact Chicago Aviation Security Officers to help. Our employees followed established procedures for dealing with situations like this. While I deeply regret this situation arose, I also emphatically stand behind all of you, and I want to commend you for continuing to go above and beyond to ensure we fly right." Separately, he called Dr. Dao "disruptive and belligerent" (McCann, 2017). The letter went public, causing more outrage and undercutting Monoz's original apology.

On Tuesday morning, United changed its message, taking a more remorseful tone. Munoz said, "The truly horrific event that occurred on this flight has elicited many responses from all of us: outrage, anger, disappointment. I share all of those sentiments, and one above all: my deepest apologies for what happened. Like you, I continue to be deeply disturbed by what happened on this flight and I deeply apologize to the customer forcibly removed and to all the customers aboard. No one should ever be mistreated this way." He then took full responsibility for the incident and followed up with a commitment to customers and employees to "fix what's broken so this never happens again," stating "it's never too late to do the right thing."

Munoz also appeared on the ABC News show *Good Morning, America* and repeated his remorse and commitment to do better.

Over the next week, new and old voices entered the narrative as Dao's lawyer held a press conference and accused United of treating passengers like cattle. Dao's daughter said she was "shocked and horrified," and the United Master Executive Council issued a statement expressing anger and separating itself from United and the incident (Czarnecki, 2017). All the while, voices from social and traditional media kept the story alive and trending.

There are several theories that provide guidance as to how an organization should respond during a crisis, including IRT (Benoit, 1997). We discussed IRT briefly in Chapter 2 as a typology of responses that can be used during a brand crisis. Message strategies include denial, evading responsibility, reducing offensiveness, corrective action, and mortification (i.e., apology). Within these strategies, there are substrategies. While Munoz did express *mortification* in his original statement, it was arguably over the *wrong* thing, as he apologized for overbooking (which was not the case) and failed to mention the assault on Dr. Dao. In his internal documents, he switched tactics to *attacking the accuser*, which is a strategy associated with *reducing offensiveness*. This made him seem both out of touch and disingenuous, as the event was so offensive that any attempt to minimize the offense only highlighted the disconnect between Munoz's statement (and by extension United's point of view) and the reality of the situation. Finally, he shifted to mortification about the actual incident, as well as *corrective action*, in his repeated claims to make things better.

While mortification and corrective action are generally considered successful reactions to a crisis (Benoit, 1997), they came too late, as his first and second messages so clearly expressed different sentiments.

Arguably, this could have been avoided with clearer organizational policies, better crisis planning, and more sensitive and consistent messaging. While the action was so offensive that it is likely United would have suffered some reputational and financial damage no matter what message strategies it enacted, this is a clear case in which poor messaging set a trajectory that became impossible to recover from.

Questions:

1. As this crisis unfolded, there were several turning points where United could have changed the course of the crisis. Can you identify some of these turning points? What would you have done differently?

2. Based on what you learned about messages in this chapter, construct a different initial response from United chief executive Oscar Munoz.

3. What medium, or combination of media, do you think is most effective for crisis communication? Why?

4. What role does media, new and old, play in crisis response?

Chapter Conclusion

Message and media, two elements of strategic corporate communication that seem straightforward, are actually complex variables affected by a number of personal and social factors. While you have been creating and receiving messages all of your life, it is unlikely that you've ever considered the effect of medium on how we understand and share messages. The theory introduced in this chapter can guide you not only as you move through college and into the professional world but also as you take on the responsibility for organizational messaging.

Key Terms

Constitutive communication
Dialogic theory of communication
Elaboration likelihood model
ICT succession theory
Mass media
Media
Media relations
Media richness theory
Message

Message map
Mobile media
One-way communication
Online/social media
Persuasion
PESO model
Synergy
Theory
Transactional model of communication

Transmission model of communication   Two-way symmetrical communication
Two-way asymmetrical communication

Chapter Discussion Questions

1. Using public organizational communication, such as advertisements or web content, find examples of each of the persuasive message types discussed in this chapter. Which do you think is most effective and why? What other factors (e.g., type of organization, topic) affected the efficacy of message choice?

2. How might the tenets of MRT and ICT succession theory affect the way you communicate with employees about an upcoming change to company insurance plans? How might those same theories affect the way you communicate with external stakeholders during an organizational crisis?

3. Which of the strategies from the "Creating Effective Messages" section do you feel you have mastered best? Which do you need to work on?

4. Visit an organizational website and evaluate it in terms of a dialogic theory of communication. Does it have a dialogic orientation? Can you find evidence of the dialogic web principles discussed in this chapter?

Chapter Activities

1. Think about something newsworthy that is going on in your school or town and create a media release about it. Start with a strong lead and follow the inverted pyramid format. Check prnewswire.com for examples of media releases.

2. Whether or not you have a LinkedIn page, practice developing your professional voice be creating your profile description. Using the steps for developing professional voice in this chapter, create a two- to three-paragraph description that will make you stand out among other young communication professionals.

3. Choose a favorite organization (one you haven't used in previous exercises or questions) and conduct an internet search of them. What comes up in terms of paid, earned, shared, and owned content? Reviewing the PESO model as described in this chapter, how do you think these different elements work together as part of this organization's strategic communication strategy? Is it effective, or would you recommend changes? For more information about the PESO model, check out this explanation from PESO model creator, Gini Dietrich: https://www.obicreative.com/gini-dietrich-peso/

Recommended Readings and Resources

For up-to-date examples of multiple styles of media releases:

https://www.prnewswire.com/

An example of successful crisis responses by an airline:

Dosoqi, M. (2016, August 4). 5 digital PR lessons to learn from Emirates Airlines crisis management. LinkedIn. https://www.linkedin.com/pulse/5-digital-pr-lessons-learn-from-emirates-airlines-crisis-maher-dosoqi/

More on message maps:

Gallo, C. (2012, July 17). How to pitch anything in 15 seconds. *Forbes.* https://www.forbes.com/sites/carminegallo/2012/07/17/how-to-pitch-anything-in-15-seconds/#31235c591dd9

Figure credits

Fig. 4.1: Source: https://commons.wikimedia.org/wiki/File:Linear_model_of_comm.JPG.

Fig. 4.2: Source: https://commons.wikimedia.org/wiki/File:Transactional_model_of_comm.JPG.

Fig. 4.4: Copyright © by Christopher Schwartz (CC BY-SA 3.0) at https://commons.wikimedia.org/wiki/File:Inverted_pyramid_in_comprehensive_form.jpg.

5

CONTEXTS

The Broad Spaces in Which People and Work Are Situated

This chapter explains context as functioning at all levels of human interaction and as vital to determining meaning. The theory of the coordinated management of meaning is a view of contexts competitively or cooperatively positioned and repositioned. Intercultural communication competence is explained as including the concept of context as one of its three main features. The situational theory of publics is shared because it illuminates problems as a function of stakeholder awareness of context. Situational crisis communication theory brings context to bear in several ways in the development and remediation of difficult situations. Structuration theory is helpful for grasping the effect of individuals on contexts and vice versa. Systems theory, although originating in the hard sciences, offers a perspective analogous to a contextual approach.

For the individual professional and the client organization, context will primarily be considered for how it continually shapes the meaning of messages, how it offers individuals and organizations opportunities to be proactive, and how it sometimes forces individuals and organizations to react. The depth and breadth of contextual change will be highlighted in terms of ongoing social, political, and economic changes. You will become more aware of the contextual drivers in your life and be encouraged to be more deliberate in your exposure to contextual information that can support your professional goals. You will also be supported in exploring how changing contexts can affect organizations you may represent.

Orienting to the Concept: The Importance of Context

David Foster Wallace was an American writer who is perhaps best remembered for a graduation speech titled "This Is Water" that he gave in 2005 at Kenyon College (Kenyon Bulletin Archive, 2005; Krajeski, 2008). He started that speech by sharing a short parable about an older fish who happens upon two younger fish in the ocean one morning. The older fish greets and then asks the younger fish, "[H]ow's the water?" With the older fish swimming away, one of the young fish says to the other young fish, "What the hell is water?" (Kenyon Bulletin Archive, 2005). While Wallace primarily intended this parable as a call to awareness of that which is fundamental but can easily be overlooked (Kenyon Bulletin Archive, 2005; Krajeski,

2008), it can also be interpreted more narrowly as an exhortation to recognize the life-and-death importance of context.

The nature of human consciousness combined with the fast pace of our world means we tend to be consumed by what exists in the foreground, most often what is literally in front of us in the moment. Unless we have had specialized education or training or other specialized acculturation, we may not have considered the interrelations between foreground and background, including the capacity of the two to swap functions. Context is background, and its value is much greater than its potential to become foreground because it creates meaning in the foreground, even while remaining set back or set off to one side. And whatever you attempt to explore in detail, concentrate on, or thoroughly isolate, context remains relevant. Nothing exists apart from it.

In a far less esoteric respect and to switch from a spatial metaphor to an aural one, corporate communication professionals are composers and conductors of context. Many times, wanting to break out and get noticed, clients rely on us to be heard in their solo capacities rather than blend into an undifferentiated chorus. Yet, other times, wanting to escape embarrassment or worse, our clients may find themselves forced to stand at the main microphone and yearn to once again blend into the background.

Describing context is inherently challenging since it is a concept that refers to the "out there," and yet we are addressing it "right here." In that respect, any metaphor for it will fall short. But the significance of the concept to our field requires that we try our best. From the conceptual to the applied, and whether working with context as spatial, temporal, and/or virtual, we must sharpen our understanding of it and actively engage it in our work. We corporate communication professionals need to always be aware of the waters in which we swim.

CENTRAL DEFINITIONS

CONTEXT

Context is the setting for anything or anyone that is considered the focus. Alternatively, context is what is outside a frame, and the process is complicated by the fact that frames exist within other frames (Goffman, 1974).

CULTURE

Culture is a complex concept with many different meanings. In terms of this chapter, culture is defined as a relatively unique blend of communication behaviors shared by a group of people.

MICROSTRUCTURE

Microstructure refers to the avenues and constraints that are created in small-scale social interactions, such as single conversational turns spoken in relation to previous conversational turns.

MACROSTRUCTURE

Macrostructure refers to easily identifiable, large-scale social structures, such as organizations and nations. It also refers to somewhat less defined yet large-scale social systems, such as patriarchy (van Dijk, 1980).

SYSTEM

A system is a complex organism composed of many parts that interact with the environment around it.

ENVIRONMENT

The environment frequently refers to the natural world (i.e., the land, oceans, and atmosphere) in which humans live. Humans interact with, affect, and are affected by this so-called natural environment. Humans are a part of the natural environment. The term can also be used to refer to the social setting of particular human activities and, therefore, can function as a synonym for context.

THEORY AND RESEARCH OVERVIEW

Coordinated Management of Meaning

The theory of the coordinated management of meaning (CMM) is based on the idea that we create our social worlds in communication with one another, and we, in turn, are shaped by them (Pearce & Cronen, 1980). CMM is closely related to the social constructionist perspective (Gergen, 2015) that assumes no objective communicative reality. Rather, communications exist in shifting contextual relationships. At a narrow level, CMM posits that even a seemingly straightforward conversation between two people can become complex as the conversational partners differently prioritize the contexts of culture, episode, identity, and relationship that surround any speech act (Pearce, 1994) and possibly also disagree about the nature of one or more of these contexts, even when the ordering is not in dispute. To overcome destructive differences, CMM promotes dialogic communication (Buber, 1971) when individuals share their own perspectives and remain open to appreciating the perspectives of others. CMM can be challenging to grasp but offers rich insights and practical models, including the idea that we are always attempting to coordinate the tensions among the stories we individually tell and the stories we live with others (Pearce & Pearce, 1998). At the center of any CMM analysis or application is the issue of what context is taking priority.

Context as a Main Feature of
Intercultural Communication Competence

Upon considering various conceptualizations of intercultural competence by a diverse group of leading scholars, Deardorff (2009) suggested the following three themes were apparent: (1) importance of relationship, (2) importance of identity, and (3) importance of context. Although some Western scholars ignored context in their definitions of intercultural competence, others from the West and many of those from elsewhere recognized its vital role (Deardorff, 2009). For instance, some thought it imperative to recognize historical, social, and political/power contexts (e.g., Medina-López-Portillo & Sinnigen, 2009; Moosmüller & Schönhuth, 2009). Others emphasized a holistic context, including a principle of oneness (Manian & Naidu, 2009) and interconnected and multidimensional global citizens (Ashwill & Du'o'ng, 2009).

Situational Theory of Publics

The situational theory of publics explains how the perception of problems and the likelihood of related action is dependent on the contexts in which a stakeholder group is embedded (Grunig & Hunt, 1984). A situation is unlikely to attract sustained attention unless there is a feeling of there being a problem that needs fixing. Variables include the following: (a) constraint recognition—the degree to which individuals feel limited, (b) level of involvement—the degree to which the situation is perceived as relevant, (c) information seeking—the degree to which individuals are pursuing information, and (d) information processing—the degree to which individuals are engaging information to which they are passively exposed.

Situational Crisis Communication Theory

Situational crisis communication theory (SCCT) was developed to protect and repair organizational reputations during a crisis (Coombs, 2007). It can also be applied to individuals. SCCT is based on attribution theory (e.g., Weiner, 2006), which is concerned with explanations for the cause of an event, along with corresponding emotions of either anger or sympathy among onlookers (Coombs, 2007). If a crisis occurs and the organization is positioned as a victim, stakeholders are likely to feel sympathy for it, and reputational damage is unlikely. If a crisis takes place and the organization is positioned as making an honest mistake, stakeholders are unlikely to get too angry, and reputational damage is typically more of a moderate concern. If a crisis takes place and the organization is positioned as having acted purposefully, it should be expected that stakeholders will get very angry, and the risk of reputational damage is high.

SCCT is relevant to the exploration of context because attributions of responsibility are affected by the larger context of the crisis—namely, perceptions of initial crisis responsibility, crisis history, and relational reputation (Coombs, 2007). The issue of context also hovers over crisis communication for other reasons, including whether an organization is positioned as understandably not knowing about a changing context, being negligent in not staying on top of a changing context, or inappropriately taking advantage of a changing context.

Structuration as Contexts That Shape Us and Contexts We Reinforce and Rebel Against

Anthony Giddens is a social theorist who is well known across disciplines for making sense of the way we are both constrained and empowered as human beings. His theory of structuration (Giddens, 1986) explains that we are limited by the social structures in which we live and work. These structures include long-standing and far-reaching conventions, such as capitalism and formal policies, as well as less formal social norms within particular organizations. But who made these structures, and who keeps them stable or changes them? Giddens noted that it was and is individuals who are responsible

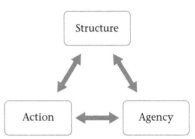

FIGURE 5.1 Structuration Theory

for enacting structures. Although we always face some structural constraints, we also have some degree of agency or ability to exert free will. The theory of structuration can be interpreted to mean that contexts are a strong force on individual actions, but they do not fully explain or dictate human actions. There are opportunities to reinforce and rebel against the present state of the contexts in which we find ourselves.

Systems Theory

The close study of systems—rooted in what is known as systems theory—originated in biology and engineering, most notably with the work of the biologist von Bertalanffy (1968). Systems theory has been explored in many other fields, including communication (e.g., Katz & Kahn, 1978). Key principles of systems theory include the following: (a) holism—the system is more than the sum of its parts, (b) interdependence—any single part of the system depends on other parts of the system, (c) openness—the system interacts with its environment, (d) equifinality—a system allows for many paths to the same outcome, (e) negative entropy—an open system adapts and grows, and (f) requisite variety—to survive, a system must have internal diversity to account for diversity-related demands in its environment (Miller, 2015). As part of a system, the organization exists in a reciprocal relationship with the environment in which it takes in inputs, such as information and capital, and, subsequently puts outputs into the environment in the form of products, services, information, or more. Inputs influence the organizational processes, which influence organizational outputs, which in turn influence the environment, which continues to happen as part of a continual process. Systems theory is particularly relevant to corporate communication, as it explains communication networks (e.g., Shumate, Fulk, & Monge, 2005) and sensemaking (e.g., Weick, 1995). The notion of a part or process embedded in a larger whole is translatable to a contextual understanding. See Chapter 10 for more information about systems and their effect on corporate communication.

APPLYING THE CONCEPT TO YOUR OWN SITUATION

*RECOGNITION OF THE CONTEXTS AND
CULTURAL FORCES THAT SHAPED YOU AS A PERSON*

Your professional self is a subset of your personal self. Worded slightly differ-ently, your personal self provides context for your professional self—and is worth exploring here in that respect. A concern with context and culture can seem like an attack on the notion of you as unique, but that does not need to be the case. By seeing yourself at the confluence of various contextual and cultural streams, you may deepen your appreciation of how you are truly one of a kind. The bigger point here is that the contextual and cultural experiences of your life in many ways explain who you are as a professional or emerging professional. Get insight into your professional passions, talents, abilities, and potentials by examining the contexts and cultures to which you have been exposed since the earliest years of your life and, especially, to which you continue to feel strong resonance.

*RECOGNITION OF THE CONTEXTS AND
CULTURAL FORCES THAT SHAPED YOU PROFESSIONALLY*

Obviously, surveying your life experience for contexts and cultures that have directly shaped you professionally is a much more focused activity and probably easier to do than considering these influences across your life for who you are as an overall person. Did you seek out this professional area, or did the professional area seem to find you? In either case, who was around you, where were you, and what, if anything, does this mean for the professional you are or intend to be? Are you motivated to enrich yourself and/or enrich others with your work? What are your past experi-ences, past relational webs, and past sources for making sense of your chosen field that shaped your understanding of your capabilities and clarified your goals, as well as clarified your sense of appropriate strategies and tactics for meeting those goals?

*CONSIDERATION OF ESSENTIAL CURRENTS
AFFECTING ALL PROFESSIONALS (INCLUDING YOU) RIGHT NOW*

Context is constant; it is about more than history. One of the ways to increase the likelihood of realizing success in what you do today and in the weeks and months ahead is to make sure you are taking in the conversation on important topics con-cerning all professionals today. These topics are getting attention in virtually all types of media, but that does not mean you should automatically parrot the line from a random source. Look to well-recognized and well-respected sources. Topics of general importance to all professionals include not engaging in any behaviors possibly constituting sexual harassment and assault, using inclusive language, and otherwise demonstrating respect, particularly to those with a long history of being disrespected, such as women, ethnic and racial minorities, and those identifying with the lesbian, gay, bisexual, transgender, queer (LGBTQ) community.

CONSIDERATION OF ESSENTIAL CURRENTS IN YOUR SPECIALTY AREA
Strategic communication is a broad and fast-moving field, in part, because the field is evolving on many fronts. For every professional in the field, there is a burden of responsibility to stay current in terms of new and changing topics and approaches. To make the burden more manageable, generally track developments but also try to commit to a deeper level of tracking by identifying and following developments in one or two specialty areas as soon as possible.

QUESTIONS:

▪ What contexts and cultures are most relevant to how I see myself as a professional?

▪ What contexts and cultures are most relevant to my key stakeholders (i.e., those who might hire me professionally and others I might serve professionally)?

▪ How might emerging social, political, economic, and technological developments alter the meaning and value of my work?

Tools and Processes for Self-Action

COMPLETING A PERSONALITY PROFILE SUCH AS
MYERS-BRIGGS TYPE INDICATOR OR THE VALS SURVEY
Delving into your personality can seem antithetical to the concept of context, but personality insights can inform contextual insights. Personality is shaped by a complex interplay of genetics and lived experience. Therefore, contexts have played a role in shaping your personality. Completing a well-regarded personality profile may provide you with insights that move you to reflect on the contexts that have shaped your personality. The results of a personality assessment can also be helpful in pointing you toward the professional contexts that will be most appealing to you and otherwise rewarding. Two such personality assessments are the Myers-Briggs Type Indicator and the VALS Survey.

GETTING SYSTEMATIC ABOUT IDENTIFYING
NEWS SOURCES AND CONSUMING NEWS
Most people take in a great deal of information each day, but it is not always done in a mindful manner. For instance, who has not lost an hour or more by intentionally watching one short YouTube video before getting pulled into other recommended videos, becoming a zombie entranced by clickbait. Staying on top of developments in the wider world helps keep corporate communication professionals informed, as well as fueled with new ideas. Deliberately selecting your main sources of news and entertainment is a smart way to stay connected to changing contexts and maintain your ability to be innovative in your career. Strongly consider regularly reading one or more of the following respected newspapers to stay on top of developments in

the United States and in the world: the *Guardian*, the *New York Times*, the *Wall Street Journal*, and the *Washington Post*. Digital versions of these publications are usually the most convenient and cost-effective. (Note that all the publications in the list except the *Guardian* require payment.) For those publications that charge, considerable discounts are given if you can use an educational (i.e., .edu) e-mail address.

Committing to consuming high-quality general news is necessary but insufficient for staying up to date professionally. You are also encouraged to identify and read or listen to more specialized sources of information. This information could relate to a subarea of corporate communication or reflect the kinds of clients for which you work. You could access information in books, articles, podcasts, videos, or other formats.

RESEARCHING AND SELECTING A
RELEVANT PROFESSIONAL ASSOCIATION

A professional association is an organization that exists to develop and advance the interests of individual professionals in a specific field. Sometimes professional associations also directly represent the interests of their members' respective companies, etc. Professional associations are typically national or international. Each usually has an annual conference. Large professional associations also frequently have local chapters where members meet monthly. Many who belong to professional associations find their involvement with their local chapter to be the most valuable and meaningful part of their overall association experience. Associations are perhaps best known for the opportunities they offer members to interact face-to-face. However, many also provide mediated networking and learning opportunities, as well as publish practical resources for their members. One or more association memberships can provide you with a way of staying current in your field. They are especially important to consider if you are not taking courses at a university. Note that signing up with a professional association prior to graduating often results in you receiving a greatly discounted membership rate. If you are interested in internal communication, consider joining the IABC. If you are interested in external communication, consider joining the PRSA. If you are academically oriented, consider joining the National Communication Association (NCA) or the International Communication Association (ICA).

SELECTING AND VENTURING INTO A NEW CONTEXT OR
CULTURE OUTSIDE OF YOUR MAIN PROFESSIONAL INTERESTS

While exploring new contexts that directly relate to your professional focus makes immediate sense to most of us, the career value of doing so in other areas may not be so obvious. And yet such a move can be transformative. Committed involvement in the arts, culture, athletics, or volunteering can broaden our perspectives, teach us new skills, and positively affect the quality of our professional pursuits. A good way to start is by assessing your needs and interests. For example, if you are experiencing stress or burnout, you could look into local athletics. If you live near a city, exploring opportunities to participate in local arts or culture could be a great way to connect with others and develop new skills. Many larger organizations partner with nonprofits to provide volunteers as part of their CSR program. You could check with your organization to see if it has any such connections.

PROFILE OF INDIVIDUAL EXPERIENCE:

David Goosen

David Goosen is the director of streaming strategy and marketing at Sony Music Entertainment Inc. Legacy Recordings. His job includes identifying opportunities and creating marketing campaigns to increase catalogue streaming revenue for Sony artists.

David is currently based in New York City, but his first full-time professional position was as a customer relationship management and social media assistant with Sony Music in London. He did not know anyone at the organization and had no prior experience at a record label, so he had to learn a lot just to make it through the initial interview. "I was already reading publications such as *Music Business Worldwide* and *Music Week* to keep me in the loop with the industry in general, but I also began researching other articles online specific to this area of the business, such as *Social Media Examiner* and *Digital Music News*. I used Sony Music's own websites to familiarize myself with the roster across their record labels, so I could easily reference my favorite artists at each label, if asked—which I was."

FIGURE 5.2 David Goosen

Once hired, David made a point of learning from his Sony colleagues. "I made a conscious effort to learn from everyone, from interns to the CEO, finding value in digital marketing experts on my team and gaining new perspectives from colleagues in completely different fields." He was deliberate about seeking viewpoints beyond his own organization. "I spoke with university friends who worked in other areas of business. I kept creativity fresh by acknowledging our own standout marketing campaigns and keeping an eye on our competitors' successes. I attended music industry talks and events such as *Adweek*, that weren't always directly applicable to my job but supplied inspiration for how I could innovate to improve my work."

To be optimally positioned in his career and in his work for Sony, David believes in the value of understanding the past and the future. "Being an early adopter and specializing in an emerging area can be very worthwhile, but it holds much more value if you also have strong knowledge of what has traditionally worked. Of course, if you only bet on what worked in the past, you can't expect to maintain your value. I recommend always being aware of cultural trends and new technologies and their potential impact on your business." David's list of must-access sources to inform him in his day-to-day responsibilities and over-all career include the following: Music Business Worldwide, *Music Week*, Digital Music News, Tech Crunch, Music Ally, MIDiA, *Wired*, *DigiDay*, Social Media Today, LinkedIn, and industry Facebook Groups.

David emphasized how achieving progress in his work for Sony artists and his own development often involves scanning for trends identifiable in hard data. For example, the current dominance of streaming was evident in early numer-ical data. "It became very clear that the streaming space was the future of the industry. This reflected in the numbers. Year-over-year streaming revenue continued to increase and therefore the business put more resources toward this area to ensure we stayed ahead of the game." Quantitative data is also useful as Sony representatives like David generate new strategies for artists. "We often compile deep dive reports for our artists so we can analyze the num-bers to better understand their audiences. We also look at streaming specific reports so we can determine how their audiences interact with their music across platforms and devices." Voice-based search and streaming is an exam-ple of a larger, data-supported issue driving David's thinking, including around search engine optimization (SEO). "We are seeing increasing music consumption coming from users streaming from voice devices so this is a key area of focus for me as a streaming marketer, particularly how we can develop and utilize SEO best practices in the space to increase our music consumption over our competitors."

When asked how to not get overwhelmed by the seemingly infinite task of stay-ing on top of trends, David offers the following insights: "It's not possible to be an expert in every single evolving area of the business, but it is possible to have a basic understanding across areas, particularly ones that directly impact your day-to-day work. You don't have to be an early adopter of every technology, but you should be able to identify the newest technologies that are potentially impactful on your business. I personally do this by reading articles, talking with friends and colleagues and looking at what jobs other companies are hiring for and what areas the industry is investing in. If companies are investing in people with expertise in voice SEO or augmented reality, then perhaps it is worthwhile learning about these new technologies."

David offers a simple yet profound analysis of how he has seen artists maintain longevity, and it is advice that could apply to corporate communication profes-sionals in their own careers too. "I have worked with various established artists who already sold millions of records and amassed huge followings. For these artists, it can become challenging to stay at the forefront of the scene. I think the artists that achieve true longevity are the ones that (a) truly know their core audience and (b) identify potential new audiences and are prepared to experiment and evolve to reach these new audiences. This doesn't necessarily mean changing their creative vision. It can be something as simple as being prepared to jump on an emerging social media platform or collaborating with a new media partner to engage with a different demographic. It is imperative to do this while still acknowledging and speaking to their core audience."

A big part of what motivates his openness to new ideas and the effort this process entails is David's intention of moving up. "I would like to lead a larger team of highly skilled professionals across differing areas of the business. I would like to be in a position where I am making more impactful decisions that shape the future of our business. Being aware of cutting-edge culture will always stay a goal as I need to stay valuable."

Questions:

1. In your opinion, did David overdo it in preparing for his initial interview at Sony? Might he have still secured the position just by describing his good character and experience in classic college student jobs like restaurant server or retail sales representative?

2. Do you think it is possible for someone in a role like David's to have a long career without being as committed to staying on top of changing contexts and cultures? Explain your answer.

3. What are two or three ways David could be more empowered or alternately empowered in terms of his knowledge of and comfort with contexts and cultures beyond what was mentioned in the case?

4. How might the reflections on contexts and culture of an early career corporate communications professional in another industry be similar to and different from David's? Be specific in your response.

APPLYING THE CONCEPT TO YOUR WORK WITH CLIENTS

UNDERSTANDING THE OVERALL ORGANIZATION
(ALTHOUGH YOU MAY ONLY BE WORKING IN ONE SEGMENT OF IT)

Even relatively small organizations can be surprisingly segmented. Whether working as a contractor or an employee, take time to become familiar with the overall entity. This process can keep you from working at cross-purposes with others. It can also unlock previously unrealized capabilities.

PLACING THE CURRENT ORGANIZATION IN HISTORICAL CONTEXT

Just as seeing the organization's current breadth can help you better understand your narrower core job responsibilities, so you can also benefit from learning the organization's history. In all but the youngest organizations, there will be plenty that has changed and plenty that has not changed. This will give you cultural insights to guide your work in, for example, creating messages that are new and resonant with the historical brand.

UNDERSTANDING THE ORGANIZATION'S POSITION IN ITS INDUSTRY

A vital context for any organization is its positioning in relation to partner and competitor organizations. This will reveal distinct differences and sometimes easily overlooked norms functioning in an industry or smaller economic niche. By thoroughly exploring the situation, you will hopefully be able to determine opportunities for effectively breaking norms in the corporate communication work that you perform and, consequently, make your organization stand out in a positive way.

EXPLORING WIDER OPPORTUNITIES
AND CONSTRAINTS IN THE ORGANIZATION

Not infrequently, professional communicators are the individuals tasked directly or by default with scanning the organization's broader operating environment for essential information and helping the organization integrate it. This is especially the case for social, cultural, and technological shifts that may be outside the core focus of the organization but are too important to ignore as time marches on. Is the organization referring to people in ways that are contemporary and thoroughly respectful? Is the organization making effective use of the latest social media platforms, even if its main competitors are not yet on board?

USING AN APPRECIATION OF
CONTEXT TO INSPIRE INNOVATIVE MESSAGING

To be an effective strategic communicator for your clients, you need to be able to offer credible and fresh perspectives on their situations. The capacity to balance these requirements in many ways rests with your willingness to put yourself in new spaces, whether physical or virtual. Grasping the limits and the limitless and turning that knowledge into practical strategy and messaging means putting yourself out there—literally and figuratively. There is no running out of ideas for the organizations you represent if you do not stop challenging yourself by learning about others and experiencing different social worlds. Fragments of those varied experiences will almost assuredly enhance the day-to-day communication work you need to accomplish.

QUESTIONS:

- Does my client have any history of misreading contextual changes?

- What is my client's history of seizing opportunities (or even creating opportunities) in terms of making contextual adaptations?

- What are the essential demands of my client's current context?

- What actions does my client most need to take to succeed in its current context?

Tools and Processes When Acting for Others

PERFORM AN ORGANIZATIONAL STRENGTHS, WEAKNESSES, OPPORTUNITIES, AND THREATS ANALYSIS

A strengths, weaknesses, opportunities, and threats (SWOT) analysis is a straightforward and time-tested framework for determining whether and how to move forward with a project. Each of the four quadrants is differentiated by their location on a two-by-two grid with one axis delineating internal or external focus and the other axis delineating helpfulness or harmfulness. Strengths are those aspects of the project that are internal to the organization and helpful. Weaknesses are those aspects that are internal to the organization and harmful. Opportunities are those aspects that are external and helpful. Threats are those aspects that are external and harmful. A SWOT analysis is an easy-to-remember and efficient way of assessing internal organizational context and external organizational context for executing a plan, including implementing a communication strategy or tactic.

PERFORM A COMMUNICATION AUDIT

A communication audit is typically an extensive attempt to document all communication activities in an organization. It involves identifying all noteworthy communication topics, channels, senders, and receivers and usually combines this with an assessment of what is and is not working. When finalized, communication audits can provide structures for systematically monitoring communications on an ongoing basis and for initiating communication rollouts. A communication audit is a thorough attempt to determine the internal and at least near-external context for an organization's communication efforts.

INITIATE A PROCESS FOR ONGOING COMPETITIVE ANALYSIS

A communication-focused competitive analysis is useful for thoroughly assessing and tracking the broader external context for an organization. These analyses can be aided with specialized software that makes it easier to aggregate and analyze the organization's media coverage, competitor information, industry information, and general news relevant to the organization.

MAXIMIZING INVOLVEMENT IN INDUSTRY
ASSOCIATIONS AND INDUSTRY TRADE GROUPS

Although most corporate communication associations are oriented to the needs and interests of individual professionals rather than the organizations that employ them, these associations do at times directly advance organizational interests. This can take the form of providing industry statistics or strategic guidance directed at overall organizations more so than individual professionals. It can also take the form of lobbying. It is important to point out that many, if not most, corporate communication professionals specialize in industries that are aligned with trade organizations more heavily committed to meeting the needs of institutions, most notably lobbying government for favorable laws and a favorable regulatory environment.

PROFILE OF ORGANIZATIONAL EXPERIENCE:

Apple

Steve Jobs, Steve Wozniak, and Ron Wayne started Apple Inc. in 1976. (Ron Wayne sold his stake to his other founding partners very early on.) Steve Wozniak was the technical mind, and Steve Jobs handled the user interface and marketing aspects. Successes in those first 10 years included the development of the first Macintosh computer—the first commercially successful personal computer featuring a graphic interface—and an acclaimed corresponding marketing campaign. Apple then went through a difficult transition period due in part to turbulence involving the founders and other leadership challenges at the company. Jobs left Apple to start the hardware and software company NeXT and become the majority shareholder in the animation company Pixar (Telegraph, 2011).

In 1997, Apple negotiated with Steve Jobs to acquire NeXT and have him rejoin a then-struggling Apple. That same year, Jobs became interim CEO, and the company has thrived ever since. Apple under Jobs transformed music with the introduction of the iPod. It transformed the phone with the introduction of the iPhone. It created a whole new technology category with the launch of the iPad. In the years prior to Jobs's death in 2011, Jobs elevated Jony Ive, widely recognized as a design savant and someone who has carried on Jobs's Apple design trajectory (9to5mac.com, n.d.; Telegraph, 2011).

Apple Inc. is one of the highest revenue-generating and highest valued companies in the world (Bary, 2018). In 2018, it was the first to achieve the trillion-dollar market capitalization level (Bary, 2018). It remains among the largest companies in the world based on gross earnings (Bary, 2018). Apple is also one of the most highly recognizable brands in the world. It stood out from the start and continues to stand out because it brings innovative design to all that it makes and, more broadly, in how it communicates—from product launch events, to store design, to product packaging, to product advertising, and more. What is the Apple design sensibility, and where does it come from?

Shortly after Jobs rejoined Apple, he made a bold decision that, in retrospect, seemed pivotal for the company's success in the decades that followed. Jobs insisted that Apple's primary goal would not be to make money but to focus instead on creative design (Baig, 2017). Apple design is distinctive because of its quality, minimalism, humanism, delightfulness, and intuitiveness. In terms of quality, Jobs famously insisted on the excellence of the inner construction of his computers, although most users never see them (Isaacson, 2011). In terms of minimalism, Ive has described the lack of clutter as not only an aesthetic decision but also an understanding of complexity. "You have to deeply understand the essence of a product to be able to get rid of the parts that are not essential" (Isaacson, 2011, p. 343). In terms of humanism, Jobs once shared the following: "There's lots of ways to be as a person. People express their deep appreciation in different ways. But one of the ways that I believe people express their appreciation to the rest of humanity is to make something wonderful and put it out there. And you never meet the people, you never shake their hands. You never hear their story or tell yours but somehow, in the act of making something with a great deal of care and love, something is transmitted there. And it's a way of expressing to the rest of our species our deep appreciation" (Owen, 2018). In terms of delightfulness, so many Apple products consumers can recall the thrill of unpackaging an Apple product and just enjoying it in their hands the first time. As Bob Messerschmidt, a key figure in the development of the Apple Watch, explained, "It's not so much the technology. It's the design of the product that creates that sense of happiness in the user" (Sullivan, 2016). In terms of intuitiveness, it's remarkable how Apple products, even when completely new, just work the way you would expect them to. Apple changed the broader expectation about needing a thick user manual when launching a new piece of technology.

It is apparent that the two most important figures in the design history at Apple are Steve Jobs and Jony Ive. Yet they were not just born with their design ideas. Steve Jobs was inspired and drew practical insights for his work at Apple from a calligraphy course he took in college, his explorations in Zen Buddhism, the look and feel of driving a Porsche and older Mercedes cars, and the design of such disparate items as Henckel knives, Braun electronic products, and the Bosendorfer piano (Carlson, 2011; Isaacson, 2011). Jon Ive's design sensibility has been shaped by experiences such as growing up the son of a silversmith, traveling to a remote part of Japan to learn about thinly shaping metals and working with candy makers to explore colors (Etherington, 2014; Tetzeli, 2017). The case of Apple under the design leadership of Jobs and Ive (Baig, 2017; Isaacson, 2011) suggests the following equation: Success with context is a function of caring, valuing creativity and innovation, following curiosity, and accepting a high degree of failure.

Questions:

1. Given your knowledge of Apple from this case and possibly beyond it, make an argument for one contextual influence rising above the rest at Apple or make an argument that a blend of contextual influences should be credited.

2. An appreciation for far-flung contextual influences at Apple is strongly connected to a culture of caring, as well as innovation and other progressive values. Does it also make sense for a more conservatively styled organization to be open to possible influences from contexts far beyond the immediate organization, or would this be misguided?

3. This case emphasized the effect of contextual influences on design thinking. Identify an example at Apple or another organization where contextual influences affected other types of business decisions.

4. This case was about a large company, and yet it focused on the role of context for just two individuals. Is it desirable to expect openness to new ideas to just be championed by a few, or should there be an effort to have everyone in an organization on board? Make an argument using Apple or another organization.

Chapter Conclusion

Hopefully, this chapter has impressed upon you how inextricably you are connected to the environment in which you live and work. We are simultaneously enabled and constrained by our context, and at the same time, we have the ability to exert agency, or our own internal power, over our circumstances. Choosing to ignore context and forge ahead without accounting for what is going on around you can have catastrophic consequences, both individually and for organizations. Conversely, looking out into the world with a combination of discipline, curiosity, and wonder can yield incredible rewards. Such a practice can help you understand your stakeholders' needs, the demands and opportunities for your organization, and even how to execute your strategies and messaging.

Key Terms

Attribution theory
Context
Coordinated management of meaning
  theory
Culture
Dialogic communication
Environment
Intercultural communication
Intercultural communication
  competence

Macrostructure
Microstructure
Situational crisis communication theory
Situational theory of publics
Structuration theory
SWOT analysis
System
Systems theory

Chapter Discussion Questions

1. The David Foster Wallace "This Is Water" story can be read as a cautionary tale both for relatively younger and relatively older professionals who take essential context for granted. What might the average younger corporate communication professional possibly take for granted about his or her professional context? What might the average older corporate communication professional possibly take for granted about his or her professional context?

2. To what degree does it make sense for you professionally to expose yourself to contexts and cultures that run counter to your personality? Explain your response.

3. Does the exploration of a contextual, cultural, and/or systems view make you feel more or less empowered as an individual in the field of corporate communication? Why is that the case?

4. What is one context shift you can think of that is not described in the chapter that has the potential to make your career prospects brighter or dimmer in the coming 2 years?

Chapter Activities

1. Create a "context sources" menu for yourself so you can keep up to date and powered with ideas in your career. Arrange it in terms of the following sections: (a) context sources to keep me updated on general news, (b) context sources to keep me updated in my general field, (c) context sources to keep me updated in my professional specialization, (d) context sources relating to my personal interests outside of work, and (e) context sources that truly challenge me.

2. Create a "context sources" list identifying at least five likely founts of information for a demographically distinct group that represents a key constituency for a particular organization. Describe how each source tends to affect the group in relation to the single organization you selected. (This activity is intended to help the organization and its communicators better understand one of its constituencies.)

3. Find news coverage of a recent organizational crisis. What role did context play in this crisis? Based on SCCT, did the organization take the correct approach in its crisis messaging? If not, create an alternate crisis narrative that could have helped the organization move through the crisis more effectively.

Recommended Readings and Resources

Context can be a difficult concept to wrap your head around or apply. The following book was authored by a social psychologist and is written in an accessible style. It does a good job of explaining context and showing its importance in different areas of life.

Sommers, S. (2012). *Situations matter: Understanding how context transforms your world*. Riverhead Books.

Bill Gates is one of the wealthiest individuals in the world. He was a founder of Microsoft and filled the roles of chairman, CEO, and chief software architect. Along with his wife, he now co-leads the Bill and Melinda Gates Foundation. Gates has a blog at the following site. It is perhaps most relevant to this chapter on context because Gates frequently recommends books that address major issues in the world.

https://www.gatesnotes.com/

Fast Company is a business magazine and website with a strong emphasis on leadership, innovation, and design. The Fast Company website is a great source of information for the shifting contexts of our world.

https://www.fastcompany.com/

ETHICS

The Right and Wrong of
Actions Taken (and Not Taken)

This chapter explores ethics as a concept that is variously complex and straightforward, theoretical and practical. The major approaches of virtue ethics, rational ethics, and postmodern ethics are introduced as distinct frameworks that can help us determine the correct pathway or merely acceptable pathways through present-day issues. CSR is explained as a central ethical construct for corporate communication professionals. In a world that is in many ways fractured in its values, CSR is a practically universal expectation for organizations. Professional association ethical codes, likewise, offer guidance for how to work with ethics affirmatively.

This chapter emphasizes the distinction between statements of values and values evidenced in day-to-day interactions. Individual professionals can benefit from forethought as to which organizations and topics may be the best fit. Considerable ethical pressure can exist on professionals since they are often hired to manage or comanage ethical challenges. Advanced attention to supporting decision making under stress may be beneficial for organizations too. The subject of ethics is not all difficult and threatening news. Clarity and fortitude around the practice of ethics can make for a more meaningful career and add greatly to the positive visibility and overall brands of individuals and organizations.

Orienting to the Concept: Ethics in a Post-Truth World

The 2016 Brexit vote—the vote by the citizens of the United Kingdom to leave the European Union—and the 2016 election of President Donald Trump in the United States marked a shift in how ethics are understood in much of the world. For the prior 70 years, since the end of World War II, the horrors and widespread devastation of that war led to a conservative-liberal consensus in democratic nations about there being right and wrong in most high-stakes situations of public relevance. Further, there was general trust that right and wrong could be discerned by elites, such as academics, journalists, and government officials, working on behalf of the public. That has shattered, even though there are different explanations as to why and whether it is a positive or negative development. There is a feeling that ethics are more narrowly defined now. And ethical decisions affecting the masses are decided not by dialogue and debate but by the power games, if not sheer dominance, of narrower stakeholder groups. The application and meaning of ethics can seem up for grabs.

Somewhat ironically, given that the strength of a new conservatism launched Brexit and the Trump administration, this new moment for ethics was preceded, perhaps foreshadowed, by the rise of postmodernism, a largely left-wing intellectual movement. The roots of postmodernism extend back over 100 years, but the philosophy accelerated along with the rise and passing of World War I and II in the first half of the 20th century. Postmodernism is the view that humans may not be best understood in strictly logical terms and that there really is no such thing as the possibility of attaining a singularly rational or objective point of view. The positionality of an individual or community must be taken into consideration when making sense of its view of the world, including its view of ethics.

The result of postmodernism, Brexit-Trump, and the larger flow of history means we find ourselves in a time of contested truths and contested ethics. Yet this does not mean that ethics have lost meaning in the corporate communication field.

Corporate Communication: A Field of Soft and Hard Ethical Boundaries

The complexities of ethics, including the high-stakes ethical situations in which many individuals and organizations find themselves, open incredible work opportunities for corporate communication professionals. The murkiness of our ethical world means that organizations need more help than ever with ethics-related communications. Every act of communication has an ethical component and must be managed accordingly since having a brand stand out in a positive way means being seen as good and true in an ethical sense. The topic may not be as commonly defined across society as it once was but that does not mean it has lost importance.

Some widely shared hard ethical lines certainly still exist, especially where ethics meet legal limits and policy requirements. Hard ethical lines also exist within the specialized stakeholder milieus in which most brands are situated. Wherever ethical positioning can be negotiated, including around the repair of hard ethical violations, corporate communication professionals can play a key role. Of course, the presence of hard and soft ethical boundaries also applies to corporate communication professionals themselves. Stepping over a hard line can threaten to do serious damage or even end your career in this field. Acting ethically and otherwise mastering positive ethical positioning can make you stand out above the competition and be rewarding in various ways. For all organizations beyond small start-ups, participation in CSR is nearly mandatory. However, it is far more than a box to check. CSR efforts need to be thoughtfully designed and executed so as not to backfire on their sponsors.

CENTRAL DEFINITIONS

ETHICS

Ethics is a major area of philosophy that is concerned with the thinking behind what is right and wrong. Ethics can also refer to any instance of deciding right and wrong (e.g., "that is a matter of ethics"). The term can also be used to refer to one school of thought on the subject of right and wrong (e.g., "their ethics are such that the ends justify the means") (Deigh, 2015).

APPLIED OR PROFESSIONAL ETHICS

Applied ethics are concerned with ethical behaviors in the day-to-day world versus the theoretical study of ethics. Applied ethics are also known as professional ethics. There can be interprofessional differences about appropriate ethics, as in different professions can have different ethical norms and codes (Gert, 2015a).

MORALITY

Morality can be a synonym for ethics (Blackburn, 2016a), but Gert (2015b) offers a definition that sets it apart and is helpful in this regard. In this view, morality is an informal system for guiding behavior, and it is shared by rational members of a community (for Gert, the public). It minimizes behavior with the potential to harm others. The system is informal, in part, because there are too many scenarios for which to formally account in terms of direct teaching and enforcement. The system functions because most people value the metaphorical game, most rules are shared, and most follow the rules, at least most of the time.

VALUES

Qualities desired as means or ends and/or qualities apparent in the communications or other actions of individuals or organizations.

BELIEFS

Confidence in the existence of something not rigorously provable.

CSR

CSR, also known as social marketing or corporate citizenship, is the concept that organizations need to be sensitive to social issues to be successful (Carroll, 2008).

THEORY AND RESEARCH OVERVIEW

Ethics is an age-old topic, a major area of philosophy since its beginning in ancient Greece. A great deal has been written about this complex and important subject. This section attempts to provide an overview of ethics in general, as well as how ethics has been addressed in the communication field and, specifically, in corporate communication.

Three major categories of ethical thinking are virtue ethics, rational ethics, and postmodern ethics. Each of these categories and the many approaches that fall within each may be adopted by corporate communication scholars and practitioners. The framework used to explore these three categories is modified from the work of Lipari (2009). The ethical codes put forth by professional associations can also be helpful as a guide to ethical analysis and everyday action in our field. And the rise and prominence of CSR needs to be explored because its role is difficult to overstate when considering the role of ethics in contemporary corporate communication work.

Virtue Ethics

Virtue ethics were one of the first approaches to ethics and remain a type of ethics still used by some scholars, practitioners, and people in the world. The summary of virtue ethics provided by Hursthouse and Pettigrove (2016) is relied upon here. Virtue ethics involve identifying and developing desirable character traits to make good ethical decisions. The history of virtue ethics can be traced back to Plato and Aristotle in the West and Mencius and Confucius in the East. A virtue, such as honesty, is seen as something someone is born with, something fundamental to a person's character but also something to be cultivated. Practical wisdom, largely coming from life experience, is seen as necessary for effectively bringing the virtue forward given the complexities of the world. To subscribe to ancient Greek virtue ethics (and most other types of virtue ethics) is to seek *eudaimon* or a deep (i.e., not superficial) happiness.

Rational Approaches to Ethics

Rational approaches to ethics are derived from attempts to use logic to determine qualities or principles that can be applied to all kinds of situations. Rational approaches are universal, meaning they are intended to apply to all people in all circumstances. Two major types of rational approaches are deontological ethics and consequentialist ethics. These types of ethics grew out of the Greek tradition of using logical arguments to hone thinking but developed in the post-Renaissance or post-Enlightenment period after the Middle Ages, when religious thinking dominated.

DEONTOLOGICAL ETHICS

Deontological ethics are a major branch of post-Enlightenment ethics that continue to have considerable influence on discussions of ethics. The summary provided by Alexander and Moore (2016) is drawn upon here. The word deontological is a combination of the Greek words for duty *deon* and science *ology*. Deontological ethics are principles for taking action that are not tied to the consequences of action. They are ethics that focus on means versus ends, including valuing the treatment of humans versus using humans in whatever way necessary to get a desired outcome. Deontological ethics have their foundation in the writings of Kant (1780/1965; 1785/1964). He emphasized acting in goodwill. He also stressed that there were no exceptions to living in a principled manner, so, for example, lying in any circumstances, even if it meant saving someone from death, was not ethically sound.

CONSEQUENTIALIST ETHICS

Consequentialism is the second major branch of ethics emerging in the last few hundred years and very much a part of many current ethical analyses. The summary by Sinnott-Armstrong (2015) informs the description of it given here. Consequentialism is a type of ethics concerned with outcomes. It is also known as teleologic ethics and as utilitarianism, the latter a philosophy whose originators include Bentham (1789/1961) and Mill (1861). Consequentialist ethics can take different forms but are primarily focused on maximizing net good. This means that the right course of action is the one that produces the most positivity in terms of outcomes while subtracting any negativity of outcomes. Consequentialist ethical approaches can vary according to factors such as emphasis on actual versus expected consequences, as well as consideration of outcomes for narrowly defined versus broadly defined stakeholders.

TABLE 6.1 Comparison of Ethical Approaches

ETHICAL APPROACH	KEY ELEMENT
Virtue Ethics	Emphasizes character traits, such as honesty or benevolence, as a key aspect of ethical behavior.
Deontological Ethics	Focuses on our more duty to take action. Emphasizes that principles for taking action that are not tied to the consequences of action, and is, therefore, focused on means versus ends.
Consequentialist Ethics	Focuses on maximizing net good. States that the right course of action is the one that produces the most positivity in terms of outcomes while subtracting any negativity of outcomes.
Feminist Ethics	Accounts for the role of morality of compassion and care, as well as rights-based moral reasoning.
Dialogic Ethics	Emphasizes that humans are necessarily engaged with the world and exist in deep relation to other humans through actual and metaphorical conversation. A major goal of dialogic ethics is to create shared ground.

Postmodern Approaches to Ethics

Postmodernism is a highly notable critique of the fundamental premises underlying the approaches to the nature of reality, being, meaning, and ethics that came before it. Postmodernism rejects the claim that the world is objectively knowable, that a universal rationality exists or should be sought out, let alone that language can capture universal truths. Therefore, postmodernist ethics do not pursue the identification and advancement of universal traits, rules, and principles. Any postmodern approach to ethics assumes that an understanding of context is required for exploring matters of right and wrong, that the individual is inextricably connected to others, and that the very language of ethics only has meaning as it is socially situated. Basically, from this perspective, the whole notion of ethics is something communicatively created and communicatively ongoing.

The preceding description of postmodern ethics is broad, and there are different schools of thought in this area, sometimes based on different origins. Two specific types of postmodern ethics are feminist ethics and dialogic ethics.

FEMINIST ETHICS

Carol Gilligan began her career as a research assistant to Lawrence Kohlberg (1973), a major figure in providing a rationalist explanation of the moral development of young people but initially only studying boys. Gilligan (1982) critiqued Kohlberg's work and demonstrated that he was pushing a limited view of morality—one that valued the ethics of justice and fairness over the ethics of compassion and caring. In her groundbreaking book titled *In a Different Voice*, Gilligan made the case that, because of girls' socialization, they viewed themselves interdependently and made moral decisions with sensitivity to taking care of others. Boys, on the other hand, tended to view themselves individualistically and use rights-based moral reasoning. Gilligan called for an expanded view of moral development that accounted for both moralities. Arguably, the larger legacy of Gilligan's work is that it supported the empowerment of women, demonstrated the subjectivity behind so-called objectivist approaches to ethics, and emphasized the role that social interaction plays in shaping our ideas of what counts as ethical and how conceptions of ethics flow out of our personal, including gendered, identities.

DIALOGIC ETHICS

Dialogic ethics is rooted in the writings of Buber (1970) and Levinas (1998) who emphasized that humans are necessarily engaged with the world and exist in deep relation to other humans through actual and metaphorical conversation (Lipari, 2009). Dialogic ethics is advanced by those who recognize our postmodern society involves different people making good-faith claims to different ethical viewpoints and, therefore, a meta-ethical and communication-based process is necessary for bridging the divides (Arnett, Arneson, & Bell, 2007). Given the diversity of views in our time, proponents of dialogic ethics suggest a past focus on ethical judgment be replaced with a focus on ethical learning while acknowledging an important limit in the inability for dialogue to be forced (Arnett, Fritz, & Bell, 2009). A major goal of dialogic ethics is to create shared ground, often modest when achieved in practice, where proponents of differing maximalist views can coordinate their activities and continue their conversation (Arnett et al. 2009). To participate in dialogic ethics is to listen without demand, to be attentive to the moment, and to be willing to negotiate new possibilities (Arnett et al., 2009).

Corporate Social Responsibility

Milton Friedman was a Nobel Prize–winning economist who had considerable effect on corporate thinking in the 20th century. He famously presented the view—a kind of rationalist ethics—that a corporation's only obligation was to its shareholders (Friedman, 1970). Except for engaging in deception or fraud, a company had the ethical obligation to focus solely on creating wealth for its owners. For Friedman, the idea that a corporation would take on social responsibility was not even an option; it was plainly unethical.

The idea that corporations should ignore making a positive difference beyond profit-making is naïve in the current world, even if the corporation or those acting on its behalf are unapologetically self-interested. Somewhat oddly, since the world seems more splintered in terms of ideological differences than it has been for many decades, there is a widely shared view that organizations simply must support the greater good. However, the concept of the "greater good" is certainly understood differently depending on one's politics and overall worldview.

CSR, or an organization's efforts to positively contribute to social issues, has long been analyzed in terms of four rationales: economic responsibility (i.e., use it to drive profits), legal responsibility (i.e., use it to comply with the law), ethical responsibility (i.e., use it to meet stakeholder expectations of what is right), and discretionary responsibility (i.e., use it make a distinctly positive difference) (Carroll, 1979). CSR efforts can focus on topics such as basic resources for those in need, education, healthcare innovations, the environment, and employee supports. The effectiveness of these efforts can differ according to an organization's stakeholder groups and the overall sociocultural setting in which the organization is operating. For instance, the CSR concerns of companies in the United States and China have been shown to be converging yet remain different (Tang, Gallagher, & Bie, 2015). As Morsing (2017) has explained, the practice of CSR has generally developed from an instrumental and one-way approach to a more dialogic and network-oriented approach, yet still very much under the control of organizational managers. As Figure 6.1 shows, there are several levels to CSR that range from protecting organizational interests to spearheading social change.

Professional Associations' Ethical Codes

Many corporate communication professionals and most corporate communication leaders belong to one or more professional associations. These associations tend to be organized at the national or international level and often have regional chapters in major economic centers. Professional associations are a great way to network, stay on top of knowledge in your field, learn skills, earn certifications, contribute to your field, and generally enhance your professional credibility. They also play an important role in setting ethical expectations and enforcing ethical standards for their members with the direct promotion of ethics.

An example of a national-level (United States of America) communication professional association ethical statement is the NCA Credo for Ethical

Value	**Where should big corporations be spending their CSR resources?**		
	Purpose	**Impact**	**Benefits**
CSR as value creation ★★★★★	Innovative and promotes sustainable business model	Fundamental strategic and operational impact	• Shared value (business–institutions and communities) • Promotes competitiveness and innovation • Promotes a sustainable business model • Integrates business into the community • Develops Human Capital (key in developing countries) • Incorporated into the business strategy
CSR as risk management ★★★	Compliance	Medium to high strategic and operational impact	• Mitigates operational impact • Mitigates operational risks • Supports external relationships
CSR as corporate philanthropy ★★	Providing funding and skills	Little strategic and operational impact	• Corporate philanthropy and sponsorships • Short-term benefits; not always sustainable • Limited funds available • Impact diluted because limited budget is allocated to many charities • Corporate competencies and other business assets not fully utilized • Misalignment between business and social responsibility strategies and functions • Result in minimal social and business impact of social programs

FIGURE 6.1 **Levels of CSR**

Communication. NCA welcomes scholars and practitioners but is primarily scholarly in its orientation.

https://www.natcom.org/sites/default/files/Public_Statement_Credo_for_Ethical_Communication_2017.pdf

An example of an international-level communication professional association ethical statement is the ICA General Statement on Standards. ICA is like NCA in welcoming practitioners while mainly attracting scholars with its offerings. ICA is notable in its handling of ethics because it directly acknowledges that ethical guidelines are often best delineated at the national or regional levels.

https://www.icahdq.org/page/MissionStatement

Another notable international-level communication professional association, and one with a robust network of local chapters and a predominantly practitioner membership, is the IABC. The main IABC ethical statement is IABC's Code of Ethics. The IABC approach to ethics is noteworthy because it plainly states that membership can be terminated for those found to be in violation. The IABC is also an outlier in openly offering its members assistance with ethical issues.

https://www.iabc.com/about-us/purpose/code-of-ethics/

APPLYING THE CONCEPT TO YOUR OWN SITUATION

CLARIFYING PERSONAL ETHICS

The academic study of ethics has challenged some of the brightest minds across the ages. There are many instances of nuanced or otherwise challenging ethical situations. And yet every one of us can also point to lived examples of people and organizations plainly doing the right thing or the wrong thing. Ethics can be complex, but it can also be crystal clear. To generally guide ourselves in doing the right thing, especially in complicated and stressful circumstances, it can help to be proactive in defining our ethics.

Perhaps there are one or more virtues you particularly value. Perhaps there are ends you are especially motivated to achieve, even feel a responsibility to achieve. Regardless of whether you have goals that should or must be reached, perhaps there are things you would almost certainly not do or definitely not do to get you there, even if it meant falling short of your desired destination. Inversely, perhaps there are ways of being you are proud to embrace and to which you are ethically committed. When it comes to encountering diverse others, especially those who have different ethical standpoints than you, perhaps you would find it helpful to proactively determine how you would proceed.

As established earlier in this chapter, the topic of professional ethics, as typically understood, flows out of the larger category of ethics which, in turn, flows out of the discipline of philosophy. Philosophy is notable for its use of reasoned argumentation to establish credible concepts and related ideas. While philosophy and philosophy-related ethics and professional ethics are nonreligious in nature, it may be that you hold religious or spiritual beliefs that work in tandem with secular professional ethics. If so, it may be helpful for you to acknowledge this blending and consider how it might best work for you and others in practice.

ALIGNING PERSONAL ETHICS WITH ORGANIZATIONAL ETHICS

Ethics can be the openly stated high ideals for which individuals and organizations claim to stand. Ethics can also be the implicit value orientations we take in our regular lived activities with others. Sometimes stated ethics align with ethics in practice. Sometimes they do not. Serious conflicts can arise when outside parties disagree with the stated ethics of individuals or organizations or, more often, when there are different interpretations of the ethics implicit in day-to-day actions.

As someone new to or otherwise seeking to advance as a corporate communication professional, it may be worthwhile for you to research organizations to determine whether they are a good fit ethically before you commit to working with them. The easiest and most obvious way to do an ethics check on an organization is to search out and consider its own ethical statements. While many organizations take a middle-of-the-road approach by stating, for example, a commitment to treating people well and giving back to the community, others make bolder ethical statements. For example, Patagonia, a manufacturer and retailer of outdoor wear and gear, is a world leader in advancing environmental protection. It is probably not advisable to join the organization if you do not care deeply about the environment and accept the science establishing humans' role in climate change. The CEO and cofounder of Chick-fil-A, a fast-food restaurant, is a conservative Christian who speaks openly against gay marriage. It is probably not advisable to seek to join that organization if you are committed to equal rights for those who are LGBTQ. It is a good general rule to assume that an organization making a stronger or nonmainstream ethical statement is an organization relatively more committed to putting that statement into practice. Therefore, take this as an important opportunity to check for alignment between your values and the organization's values.

Another relatively easy way to check for whether an organization's ethics are in sync with your own is to search for articles, blogs, and social media posts created by unofficial organizational sources. See if the message themes from these sources match the messaging from official sources and, of course, see if you continue to have a sense that this organization continues to be one that you could proudly associate yourself.

Although tougher to access, insights from those working in and with the organization and your ability to directly experience the organization in action can be very clarifying when it comes to determining your likely ethical comfort as a possible future insider. Keep in mind that you are looking for more than the possibility of uncovering a blatantly unethical environment that you, of course, should avoid becoming dependent on or actively perpetuating.

Ideally, you are looking to find a particularly good or great ethical fit for yourself. For instance, some organizations have more nurturing or more competitive internal cultures. Neither is necessarily more or less ethical than the other from a general point of view, but they can feel that way to different individuals. If you do well in a nurturing space, you will probably feel like it treats you ethically because it recognizes the humanity in you and others. However, if you do well in a competitive space, you may come to judge the nurturing space as unethical because, for example, it may seem to you like people are not held properly accountable for their actions and inactions. The opposite can also occur. Someone who prefers a nurturing climate may feel a competitive climate is ridiculously cut throat, while someone who likes a competitive climate appreciates the straightforward communication and reward system that can be experienced as honest and fair.

Remember that ethics is a factor in everything an individual or organization says and otherwise does. It could wear on you to be with people or in an organization that is ethically inconsistent with who you are. On the flip side, putting yourself in the right ethical environment could be affirming and energizing.

QUESTIONS:

- Who do I admire as an ethical professional communicator and why?

- What is my ethical framework?

- When has my ethical framework helped me make the right decision in a difficult situation?

- How does my ethical framework make it likely or unlikely that I could work for certain organizations or on certain issues?

Tools and Processes for Self-Action

PERSONAL STATEMENT OF VALUES

For many, right and wrong can seem self-evident and, therefore, we may have never given thought to developing our own ethical statement or values statement in writing. It can be a useful process, though. It can help make our ethical thinking more precise in terms of getting us to decide on specific values, elaborate on specific values, and, perhaps, prioritize our chosen values. You may find that your statement falls squarely within one ethical tradition (e.g., virtue ethics, deontological ethics, consequentialist ethics, feminist ethics, or dialogic ethics) or that it draws from two or more. Consider the ethical statements of professional associations to which you belong or may join. Feel free to include values you hold dear that come from other sources (e.g., religious or spiritual affiliations). Feel free to make your statement specific to your professional life or broadly encompassing of who you are as a person.

STATEMENT OF VALUES-LINKED COMMUNICATION BEHAVIORS

Values are most impactful when they are communicated with others in everyday interactions. Values can be clarified through behavioral delineation. This process is worth examining, as two or more people can claim to hold the same value, and yet their deliberate performances of the value may be similar or vary greatly, sometimes being entirely divergent. Increase your own likelihood of embodying the values you hold dear by taking the time to write down specific ways that each of your values can come through in communication with other people. Be sure to share examples that apply to the professional settings you are likely to find yourself in during the months and years ahead. You are encouraged to articulate nonverbal as well as verbal behaviors.

CONTINGENCY PLAN IF FACING AN ETHICAL DILEMMA OR CRISIS

When exploring ethics in a scholarly setting, it is easy to be idealistic and think about ourselves acting our best at the best and worst of times. Of course, most of us have encountered and will again encounter difficult circumstances, including in our professional lives. At such times, we could feel considerable stress in acting ethically or even in discerning the right thing to do. Lived ethical dilemmas and crises have real stakes with much higher mental, emotional, and overall physical demands than hypothetical scenarios. To prepare for what is likely ahead, it can be helpful to create a written plan for self-care, as well as for what resources you might access and who you might ask for assistance so that you can navigate the central challenge in a manner that is ethically sound.

PROFILE OF INDIVIDUAL EXPERIENCE:

Angela Balduzzi's

Angela Balduzzi earned a master's degree in organizational communication and has spent much of her career in positions that directly address ethics in major organizations. She was senior manager of talent and organization development at Johnson & Johnson, director of organization development, and, later, senior director of global values and strategy at GSK, as well as global vice president of talent, leadership, and organization development at SAP. She now operates her own communication consulting firm. Although there is much that Ms. Balduzzi can share about advising, co-leading,

FIGURE 6.2 **Angela Balduzzi**

and leading as a professional communicator directly and indirectly managing ethical issues for her organizations, her experience handling ethics in her own career is an important basis for her work for others and is worth studying on its own.

Ms. Balduzzi takes a deliberately humanistic approach to communication. This includes respecting every person, incorporating recognition, looking out for the team, and taking responsibility, especially as a leader. Here is Ms. Balduzzi in her own words:

"Every person deserves to be treated like a valuable human being. I believe in transparency and sharing information. Honesty and authenticity are critical principles for me. It's not about being perfect in your relationships, but it is about having the humility to admit when you are wrong or have made a misstep in behavior and recover and mend. Share the success with the team—we all win together. Take a 'buck stops with me' leadership approach if something goes wrong. Never distribute blame at the expense of others—be a buffer for your team. Give appreciation freely and publicly. Lead with love and concern for the whole person."

For Ms. Balduzzi, personal reputation is generally important and a motivator to do the right thing as a professional communicator but acting with ethical consistency is of primary importance. "Doing the right thing regardless of anyone watching is so critical. If you are true to your values, then people's perception of your reputation will naturally fall into place."

It was the experience of growing up watching her father and grandfather run a small-town restaurant that helped shape Ms. Balduzzi's ethical outlook and actions. "My dad was giving to the community. He served the community not only with food but with his generosity. He ran the business to make a living, not to gouge his customers, all of whom were his neighbors and fellow community members." This experience watching her father and working in the restaurant taught her to work hard, be honest, and give wholeheartedly to her community.

Ms. Balduzzi is also aware of being influenced by a few role models she has had the good fortune of working under as a professional. She pointed out that these "real human beings" were not perfect, and yet she respected them for their honesty and transparency. They were "authentic about their decisions and how they reached them." It is noteworthy how Ms. Balduzzi was impacted by these leaders' willingness and ability to share their decision-making processes with her and others. "They cared for their people as whole people. We had open discussions about tough decisions and how to handle them. They sought my advice on dilemmas, and we worked through an open decision-making process."

Ms. Balduzzi is aware of sometimes having made a deep impression on others by making sure a sensitive situation was navigated properly. For instance, she once co-led a remote meeting where one of the participants, a very dedicated individual, was calling in as he was driving to an out-of-state family funeral. The main call lead was senior to Ms. Balduzzi and had requested that the person call in. This did not sit well with Ms. Balduzzi or others who were participating. "I was very uncomfortable with this decision, as we should not ask this person to call in given the bereavement. I could tell from the body language of others in the room that it made them uncomfortable that he called into the meeting given his circumstances."

Ms. Balduzzi spotted an opportunity to intervene when the connection to the man's mobile phone began breaking up. The senior leader was actively brainstorming ways for the man to stay active on the call, but Ms. Balduzzi felt compelled to speak up. "I think this is a sign that you should be with your family during this time of grief. We are all very sorry for your loss and want you to focus on your family. I am closing the telephone connection and not reopening it. We can loop you back in when you are back."

Afterward, a few people approached Ms. Balduzzi and thanked her for "being so human" and boldly freeing up their colleague. Ms. Balduzzi described it succinctly, "It was just the right thing to do." She also added that, ideally, the situation would never have progressed as far as it did. "If my co-leader would have asked me about it beforehand, I would not have allowed him to participate in the call in the first place. This was about respect for boundaries." Ms. Balduzzi's boss (not the main person managing the call) was also in the meeting and acknowledged her for taking such a bold and caring action.

There have been other times when Ms. Balduzzi made difficult but appropriate choices despite the fact it was almost certain that no one with the power to reward or punish would ever know. There was one scenario with a long-standing vendor that did not seem quite right. Ms. Balduzzi's group had a lot of ongoing work with them—multiple purchase orders and invoices. There was an instance in which the vendor invoiced twice for the same work by mistake and informed Ms. Balduzzi. The vendor requested that Ms. Balduzzi count the second invoice for payment of other upcoming work versus dealing with the bureaucratic procurement process to void one of the invoices. As Ms. Balduzzi admitted, "This was a tempting solution. The procurement process was so arduous and painful, it would have been the easiest thing to do and no one would have known otherwise." Ms. Balduzzi, however, declined the request and asked them to process the void of the second invoice. An audit would be unlikely, but should one occur, there would not be proper records for the second invoice and that did not sit right with Ms. Balduzzi. What Ms. Balduzzi did was a potential risk to the long-standing relationship with the vendor, but in the end, the vendor understood the decision to do it the right way. And Ms. Balduzzi certainly did the right thing as far as expectations from her company and tax authorities.

Ms. Balduzzi sees how representing an employer on the most highly charged corporate communication matters is closely linked to personal reputational matters. Difficult reputational challenges facing leaders and organizations place the corporate communication professional at the center of the storm. There can be an ethical dilemma in deciding whether a situation should be spun. As Ms. Balduzzi explains, "I think corporate communication professionals can be put in situations where they will be asked to help tell a different story and they will have to search their souls to stand with what is ethical, even if what they are being asked to do is unethical. It is important to not get sucked into providing rationalizations for bad choices or bad behaviors."

Ms. Balduzzi acknowledges these can be wrenching predicaments. Her advice for making these situations easier is to develop relationships in advance and seek the input of others when charting your course. "The most successful strategy in ethical dilemmas is to connect with others and seek advice and counsel. It is important to build trusting relationships, so you have the support you need when the going gets tough and there is an ethical issue to be confronted."

As someone who has worked in complex national and global business environments and frequently had the responsibility of creating company-wide communication processes and end-point communications bridging diverse groups and different ethical perspectives, Ms. Balduzzi offers the following advice: "Ethics can be in the eye of the beholder. I think it is the Corporate Communicator's role to create the forums to have the meaningful debate, if there are varying ethical principles at play. Be bold in bringing in the different views and looking for ways to bridge cultural gaps in ways that keep the brand intact but allow for localization so that people can connect with the messaging."

Finally, while the big projects legitimately demand close ethical attention, the ethical significance of everyday tasks and more modest projects should not be taken for granted. "The opportunities to be ethical and values-driven can be both big and small. And in many cases the small examples are where you really show the values that drive you."

Questions:

1. Review the "Theory and Research Overview" section in this chapter and identify the various types of ethics that you see Angela Balduzzi demonstrating. Also, which single type of ethics seems most evident in her actions?

2. Notice how Ms. Balduzzi's stories of acting ethically rely on her using her communication skills to appropriately and effectively navigate interactions with others. For one of these instances, identify at least two specific communication skills she demonstrated.

3. Given what you know about Ms. Balduzzi's ethics, her communication skills, and her professional status, brainstorm an ethical situation not included in this case study, which she could probably directly navigate well despite its potential pitfalls.

4. What is a potential ethical situation that might be beyond Ms. Balduzzi's ability to directly manage in an appropriate and effective manner, and what would be her best course of action? Also, what would be your own course of action in this scenario?

APPLYING THE CONCEPT
TO YOUR WORK WITH CLIENTS

LEARNING AT THE OUTSET THE ETHICAL IDEALS OF THOSE YOU REPRESENT

Most organizations have ethical statements available on their websites. Clear value statements can often be found in mission and vision statements. A mission statement explains an organization's reason for existing. A vision statement explains what an organization wants to become. Most larger organizations have formal onboarding processes for salaried employees that include at least some direct mention of ethical expectations. Ethical expectations are also communicated in less direct ways, including in terms of work norms or expectations that are shared with you in the process of setting up and managing your working relationships. Pay attention to how the overall organization and your direct organizational contacts define and take pride in doing the right things, at least how they define those things. Generally, new entrants into an organizational culture need to show some level of adaptation, but, of course, do not lose sight of your own personal ethics and what is generally expected in society. Being knowledgeable of the organization's own view of itself ethically, including its ethical ideals, is necessary to represent it effectively in any aspect of its stakeholder communications.

MAKING SURE YOUR COLLEAGUES AND CLIENTS
KNOW THE IMPORTANCE OF MANAGING ETHICAL ISSUES

Just because your client organization expresses ethical ideals, it does not mean that those individuals you are working with and for have uniformly high levels of knowledge, skill, and motivation in this area. Educate those around you and advocate for the importance of the work that you do. Get them to realize the CSR expectations faced by all organizations. Help your colleagues and those paying your salary or contracting for your services to understand some of the main ways trust can be broken through an ineffective communication function. For instance, breaking trust can occur by cutting corners on basic social expectations or the organization's brand promise. Breaking trust can occur by delaying, attempting to cover up, or otherwise inappropriately and ineffectively managing a crisis. Breaking trust can occur by breaking the law.

MAINTAINING YOUR ETHICAL
WATCHFULNESS AND TAKING APPROPRIATE ACTION

Weeks and months may click by without you and your colleagues or you and your clients directly talking about the topic of ethics, but it is an element in everything you do as a professional communicator. Be vigilant about what is going on ethically, even if things are going well. When working in an environment that is following ethical norms, your main responsibility can be summed up as "steaming ahead" or continuing along and even gaining positive ethical momentum. If you see an ethical problem possibly emerging at a distance, you might think of your responsibility as "raising your hand" or asking questions or otherwise politely but firmly voicing your concerns to one or more people who can address the matter. If you uncover an urgent ethical problem, you might think of your responsibility as "blowing your whistle" or insisting on immediate action with those with the power to act, even if your insistence is on the strong side. As you go about your professional work and particularly as you progress in your career and assume more status, scan for opportunities, urgent or entirely nonurgent, when you and others can directly take charge and set an example of ethical excellence or focus on "reaching for and grasping the brass ring." This variegated but constant approach to acting ethically as you serve others is good general advice for advancing the interests of your employer or clients and for protecting your own reputation.

QUESTIONS:

▪ What is my client's ethical stance from the perspective of its leaders and the perspectives of other stakeholders?

▪ What are the most likely ethics-related threats and opportunities for my client?

▪ What steps are being taken to optimize the ethical standing of the organization?

Tools and Processes When Acting for Others

SWOT ETHICS ANALYSIS

SWOT is a tool that is over 50 years old yet remains widely used across a broad array of fields (Helms & Nixon, 2010). SWOT is an abbreviation for strengths, weaknesses, opportunities, and threats. The SWOT strengths and weakness areas apply to the internal organization while the opportunities and threats areas apply to the external organization. The SWOT analysis is a planning tool. It was not developed specifically for the topic of ethics, but it can be applied in that way. A comprehensive SWOT ethics analysis might very well try to account for virtually all ethics-related issues relevant to an organization. A narrower SWOT analysis could focus on the handling of one ethics-related issue. Just as communication professionals can play an important role in immediate ethics messaging, so too can they play an important role in assessing what is already in place and planning for the future.

▪ Clarify your charge.
▪ Assemble your team.
▪ Gather relevant data.
▪ Analyze the data.
▪ Generate findings and recommendations.
▪ Report findings and recommendations.
▪ Execute on recommendations.

DEVELOPING AND EXECUTING CSR STRATEGY

CSR activity is common for organizations and expected by many internal and external stakeholders. While not engaging in CSR is risky, so too is executing a CSR strategy. Communication professionals can play a central role in many aspects of CSR work. Primary areas include the crafting of the organization's CSR statement, the development and management of a CSR campaign, and the sending and receiving of CSR communications to and from stakeholders. The CSR statement is a statement of commitment that is clear, positive, and distinctive. A CSR campaign is an attempt to advance that commitment with a specific initiative. A CSR campaign is often uniquely named, focuses on making a difference with a specific population and/or in a specific geographic location, has a time frame, and is measurable in terms of its effects. CSR communications can take different forms, including one-way communications, basic two-way communications, and cocreated communications.

ETHICS TESTING NOTABLE COMMUNICATIONS

Ethics testing notable communications means taking the time to consider all nonroutine communication efforts for ethical suitability prior to launching them. Ethics testing may work best when ethics criteria tailored to the organization are first identified. These criteria can be compiled by examining the mission statement, vision statement, and CSR statement, as well as by considering the sensitivities and opportunities associated with all of the organization's stakeholder groups.

PROFILE OF ORGANIZATIONAL EXPERIENCE:

Starbucks

On April 12, 2018, Rashon Nelson and Donte Robinson, two African American men, waited to meet Andrew Yaffe, a White business acquaintance, in a Starbucks in Center City Philadelphia. They came to the attention of a manager because they had asked to use the restroom but, according to store policy of only allowing restroom use for those making purchases, were refused access. The Starbucks manager then called 911 because Mr. Nelson and Mr. Robinson were refusing to buy anything or leave. Shortly afterward, two officers arrived and called for backup. Cell phone video recorded six officers instructing the seated men to leave. Mr. Nelson and Mr. Robinson were subsequently arrested for trespassing and disturbing the peace and were held in custody for close to nine hours. By the end of the day, a video of the event had over 10 million views. The two men were not charged with a crime because Starbucks did not want to press charges (Bacon, 2018; Siegel, 2018; Siegel & Horton, 2018).

In the days that followed, the story continued to unfold and draw considerable attention. Starbucks posted a short statement of apology to Mr. Nelson and Mr. Robinson and their customers; the company expressed disappointment that the two men were arrested (Starbucks, 2018, April 14). Protests were held at the

Starbucks store and at other sites in Philadelphia (Boren, 2018), and a #boy-cottstarbucks campaign was launched (Fortin, 2018, May 2). Philadelphia Police Commissioner Richard Ross initially fully defended the actions of the police officers but then later apologized (Siegel & Horton, 2018). The actions of Starbucks and the Philadelphia Police Department were described as demonstrating implicit racial bias (Morial, 2018), and the incident was connected to a history of using loitering laws to target minorities (Goluboff, 2018) and the pervasive racial profiling of African Americans in daily life (Owens, 2018). Mayor James Kenney made statements, including an apology and an acknowledgment of racism playing a role in the incident (Bacon, 2018; City of Philadelphia, 2018). Mr. Nelson and Mr. Robinson appeared on the TV show *Good Morning America* to share their version of the event with the public (Winsor & McCarthy, 2018, April 19). The mayor entered into a settlement with Mr. Nelson and Mr. Robinson on behalf of the City of Philadelphia that involved the city giving a symbolic payment of $1.00 to each man and committing $200,000.00 to a program to help young entrepreneurs (Fortin, 2018, May 2).

Starbucks CEO Kevin Johnson responded to the situation by putting out two statements through his organization (Johnson, April 14; Johnson, April 15) in the days closely following the incident and by providing statements to Philadelphia newspapers (Tornoe, 2018, April 16). He traveled to Philadelphia to apologize to Mr. Nelson and Mr. Robinson in person and to meet with the mayor, the police commissioner, and other community leaders (Silva, Chuck, & Radford, 2018, April 17). He also appeared on *Good Morning America* (Winsor & McCarthy, 2018, April 19). On the same day, the city and Mr. Nelson and Mr. Robinson announced a settlement, Starbucks and Mr. Nelson and Mr. Robinson announced a settlement too (Fortin, May 2, 2018). It consisted of an undisclosed financial payment to each of the men, the opportunity to provide further input on issues related to the incident, and the opportunity for each of them to complete their degrees with full financial support from the Starbucks College Achievement Plan, a partnership with Arizona State University.

Starbucks also responded by instituting a new bathroom policy and by carrying out a company-wide training involving store closures. The new policy affecting the use of Starbucks bathrooms was announced on May 19 and made all Starbucks customer spaces available to individuals regardless of whether a purchase was being made (Fortin, 2018, May 20). The policy was criticized by some and, as a result, clarified by Starbucks (Kelnhofer, 2018, May 22), but it was also argued to be in alignment with its founding credo (Roberts, 2018, May 23). The company-wide training initiative was announced on April 17 and took place on May 29 (Starbucks, 2018, April 17). The training was designed in conjunction with national leaders and involved almost 175,000 employees at over 8,000 U.S. stores. The training addressed implicit bias, conscious inclusion, preventing discrimination, and making people feel safe and welcome. Some questioned the effectiveness of the training effort (e.g., Koerth-Baker, 2018), and others suggested that Starbucks was really pursuing the larger goal of maintaining its brand as a so-called third space, or safe and welcoming space outside home and work (e.g., McGregor & Siegel, 2018).

All in all, Starbucks faced a major communication crisis when they got on the wrong side of one of the major ethical issues of our time. By Starbucks's own admission, the incident represented a betrayal of its core ethics. Howard Schultz, Starbucks founder and executive chairman at the time of the incident, commented that he was "embarrassed" (CBS/AP, 2018), that "[t]he company's founding values are based on humanity and inclusion," and that the company would "reaffirm our commitment" (Starbucks, 2018, April 17). There is no question that the organization mobilized considerable resources both internally and externally. While not all communication experts favorably evaluated Starbucks's overall handling of the situation, some were impressed with how the company and CEO Johnson mounted a noteworthy effort, particularly with the all-company training and Mr. Johnson's direct and seemingly sincere involvement (McGregor, 2018).

Questions:

1. What, if anything, could Starbucks have done in advance of this ethical crisis to have prevented it from happening or that would have minimized damages for those affected?

2. Once the crisis broke, how, if at all, could Starbucks have better managed the situation?

3. Compare Starbucks's stated and lived values to your own (referring to one or more types of ethics in the "Theory and Research Overview" section) and explain why you would be willing or unwilling to work for them as a corporate communication professional.

4. Even before this incident took place, Starbucks was a company that was well-known for attempting to highlight its ethics to advance its brand. To what extent, if any, did Starbucks's self-promotion as an ethical organization make the Philadelphia story more or less of a crisis for them? Explain.

Chapter Conclusion

Looking at the present-day world, it can sometimes seem that ethics do not matter since some powerful individuals and organizations seem to do whatever they please without negative effects. For most individuals and organizations, though, right and wrong actions have consequences, even if the negative consequences associated with negative actions end up being delayed. While the threat of unethical actions can be a motivator for some of us, others of us are inspired to do the right thing so that we can sleep better at night and to leave a proud legacy. And, perhaps, the best among us do the right thing even if it comes at a great personal cost and without obvious personal benefit.

Getting informed about major ethical schools of thought can be helpful for building and protecting a personal brand, deciding which organizations to represent, and how best to represent those who have put their trust in you. Statements of ethics, affirmative supports, and punitive actions by professional associations can help steer us and our field.

Many corporate communicators will manage CSR efforts for organizations. In doing so, there is a lot to consider in getting it right. Be clear about the ethics of those you represent and the many affected stakeholders.

No matter your stated ethical position or the meaning of your ethics in practice, remember that ethics are not just what we encounter on a tough day; they are part of everything we do. Whether you act as a lead ethics communicator or not, it will be important for you to handle the issue thoughtfully and strategically to protect your own reputation as well as the reputations of the organizations you represent.

Key Terms

Applied ethics
Beliefs
Campaign
Consequentialism
Consequentialist ethics
Corporate social responsibility
CSR campaign
Deontological ethics
Dialogic ethics
Ethics
Feminist ethics

Inclusion
Morality
Postmodern ethics
Professional ethics
Rational ethics
SWOT analysis
Teleologic ethics
Utilitarianism
Values
Virtue ethics

Chapter Discussion Questions

1. What is the single value to which you are most committed as a corporate communication professional? What ethical school of thought does this most exemplify (e.g., virtue ethics, deontological ethics, consequentialist ethics, feminist ethics, or dialogic ethics)? Explain.

2. In your personal life, do you expect more of organizations that expect more of themselves? For instance, are you more likely to get angry or upset with an organization that takes a strong ethical stand but then seems to transgress versus an organization that is imperfect but never really strived to be so?

3. Which of the three professional association approaches to ethics would you most want to work under and why?

4. To what extent is it ideal for a corporate communication professional to follow one type of ethics versus a hybrid of ethics types? To what extent is it possible to do so in practice?

Chapter Activities

1. Go on the web and locate an association for communication professionals (not already listed in this chapter) and explain how its approach to ethics is similar to or different from the three professional associations listed earlier.

2. Research a diversity-related Starbucks story covered in the media prior to or after the Philadelphia racism incident and consider whether it was effectively managed in terms of internal and external communication.

3. Find a CSR campaign active in the past year and launched by an organization other than Starbucks that positively positioned the launch organization from an ethical point of view. Explain why it was successful by analyzing the specific values that were advanced and why these mattered to stakeholder groups.

Recommended Readings and Resources

Glassdoor.com is a site where current and former employees can post about their experiences working for particular organizations. It can be a good resource for learning about internal organizational cultures, often implicitly addressing ethical matters and, occasionally, explicitly doing so.

https://glassdoor.com

Read the following articles to delve further into the Starbucks racism case. Consider what was at stake and what was effective and ineffective about the company's reaction.

McGregor, J. (2018, April 19). Anatomy of a PR response: How Starbucks is handling its Philadelphia crisis. *The Washington Post*. https://www. washingtonpost.com/news/on-leadership/wp/2018/04/19/anatomy-of-a-pr-response-how-starbucks-is-handling-its-philadelphia-crisis/?utm_term=. e2070578c68c

Salmon, F. (2018, April 19). Why the Starbucks racial bias training is more than just good PR. *Slate*. https://slate.com/business/2018/04/why-the-starbucks-ra-cial-bias-training-is-more-than-just-good-pr.html

Figure credits

Fig. 6.1: Source: https://commons.wikimedia.org/wiki/File:CSR_framework_-_value1.jpg.
Fig. 6.2: Copyright © by GlaxoSmithKline plc. Reprinted with permission.

INFLUENCE
The Tools for Making a Difference

This chapter clarifies influence and allied terms. It also offers various major mechanisms of influence that are applicable to internal and external corporate communication and potentially useful for individuals' self-representations. The elaboration likelihood model is introduced to acknowledge that influence is sometimes rational and sometimes not. Framing in general and narrative framing (or storytelling) are acknowledged as regularly used influence tools for corporate communicators. Coverage of stakeholder theory serves as notice that even professional influencers will themselves be influenced. Image restoration theory is valuable when needing to influence while under attack. Compliance techniques and popular influence models offer a plethora of influence tools from which to select for almost any occasion.

The application of the theory and research will help you make gains in winning the confidence of others to secure and maintain positions of trust and influence. The various theories and models of influence will also open opportunities to further the positions of clients for whom you work.

Orienting to the Concept: The Art of Ethical Influence

To work in the corporate communication field is to work in the "influence business." It is very difficult to conceive of a role in our field that does not involve trying to shape the thoughts, feelings, and/or actions of others. To be appropriately and effectively influential involves several things. It means feeling comfortable with the idea of being an influential person. It means being knowledgeable and skilled in influence processes. It means feeling simpatico with the positions you are representing. The overarching point is that to be a strategic communicator is to set goals deliberately and work on achieving them with considerable emphasis on influence for getting the job done.

In terms of feeling comfortable as an influencer, you need to believe that, in the abstract, exerting influence can be a positive endeavor. And you need to believe that you can influence for good in the world. Furthermore, it is ideal if you are more than comfortable shaping the actions of others. Hopefully, you are highly motivated to influence.

Feeling charged up about influencing others does not mean you are fully capable of doing so. Knowledge and skill in different influence processes are essential elements of being successful. Learning mental models and related verbal and nonverbal skills is going to add to your confidence and your effectiveness.

A consequential issue facing competent influencers is the matter of ensuring that you are personally and professionally okay with the clients, clients' goals, and clients' tactics you are committed to advancing. This matter circles back to comfort but less so as a matter of competence and more so as a matter of ethics and credibility.

CENTRAL DEFINITIONS

INFLUENCE

Influence is the ability to affect others' thoughts and/or behaviors. Influence also refers to the process or processes of changing the thoughts and/or behaviors of others. Influence processes can be subtle or obvious. They can be rational or non-rational. They can take various forms, including verbal and nonverbal. The use of influence and susceptibility to it can be intentional or unintentional.

PERSUASION

Persuasion is the deliberate use of spoken or written language to get others to adopt a position and/or behavior. Persuasion typically involves making rational arguments. Persuasion can be understood as a subset of influence.

COMPLIANCE

Compliance refers to whether a targeted person will positively respond to a request.

POWER

Power is the ability to achieve a particular outcome without needing to rely on influence. To have power in a situation means to have full control.

THEORY AND RESEARCH OVERVIEW

The Elaboration Likelihood Model

Influence is a complex process and one that sometimes uses rational processes and sometimes does not. The elaboration likelihood model (ELM) (Petty & Cacioppo, 1986) was developed to account for this disparity. ELM describes influence occurring on the central route in the case of reason-oriented influence while it describes influence occurring on the peripheral route in the case of more impressionistic influence. An example of an influence situation using the central route is buying a cell phone plan since it is typically a calculated decision based on metrics like data rates, data limits, and network reach. An example of an influence situation using the peripheral route is buying a piece of jewelry since in this instance people are mainly swayed by "what speaks to them" in terms of style and symbolism. Corporate communicators are wise to determine if a central route or a peripheral route is more likely to be relevant in each situation and structure influence communications accordingly.

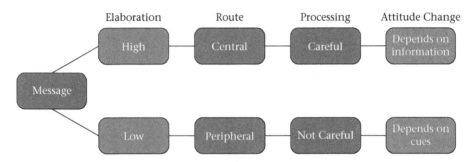

FIGURE 7.1 Elaboration Likelihood Model

ATTITUDE CHANGE PROCESS VIA CENTRAL AND PERIPHERAL ROUTES.

FRAMING

Framing in corporate communication is a metaphor for defining meaning in a situation. Within our everyday life, there is more information than we can possibly process and to have what might be called total meaning. Further, data does not exist without some frame; even if no one is deliberately framing, some kind of frame is still in effect. Therefore, framing is a basic processing necessity.

Framing clarifies which information is relevant and irrelevant. What is inside the frame and what is outside the frame? Information inside the frame is frequently further structured into foreground, midground, and background thereby implying degrees of importance based on context.

Framing becomes a strategic factor as two or more factions actively compete to establish a definitive frame—the very definition of a shared reality. Corporate communicators often find themselves assessing situations and determining how to frame a person, service, product, etc., in the most effective way. Sometimes they act in an innovative manner, positioning someone or something new. Sometimes they act in a reactive manner, repositioning someone or something, frequently within a competitive environment, meaning an environment in which there are frames in tension with each other.

NARRATIVE FRAMING OR STRATEGIC STORYTELLING

Narrative framing means using the structure of stories to influence. The story structure makes it easier for people to remember information, and that alone makes it a tool of influence. The story structure works in part because it involves simplifying sometimes complex topics to make them more vivid and accessible. Standard story elements, such as conflict and resolution, make stories not only memorable but also often highly enjoyable for those exposed to them. Effective stories not only explain the trials and tribulations of the characters inside the stories but also position the audience.

The use of strategic storytelling has gained widespread attention over the last 20 years. There are several reasons why. The explosive growth in information sources, decline of a common culture, declining significance of rational argumentation, greater understanding of the principles of effective storytelling, and visibility and impact of notable storytellers and their stories have all played a part. In a complicated and tribalized world, stories are often a go-to approach to influencing others, as stories make things straightforward and connect with people emotionally. The revolutionary product pitches of Apple cofounder Steve Jobs, the rise of TED Talks, and the general interest in storytelling in efforts such as Story Corps all demonstrate the appeal of this influence mechanism.

STAKEHOLDER INFLUENCE

Stakeholder theory (Freeman, 1984) was introduced in detail in an earlier chapter. Stakeholder theory developed in part because the prevailing view of managers simply needing to be successful at meeting shareholders' interests was proving to be limited (Zakhem, Palmer, & Stoll, 2008). This was a time when influence toward and from constituencies external to the organization was becoming more and more apparent (Zakhem et al., 2008). With the passage of time, the further development of stakeholder theory, and the unfolding of numerous actual cases demonstrating its importance, the opportunity for the organization to influence both internal and external constituencies, and the opportunity for the opposite is now well established. Organizations can seek to influence one or more specific stakeholder groups. And one or more specific stakeholder groups, even external groups, can sometimes transform whole organizations. Whatever the influence direction, these dynamics reflect the sometimes-tremendous effect of focused messaging based on group identity and group interests. Of course, those championing a stakeholder influence strategy need to be mindful of the potential of other stakeholder groups to support or counter the originating influence attempt.

IMAGE RESTORATION THEORY

Image restoration theory (Benoit, 1995) is based on an examination of what individuals and organizations have done when facing reputational crisis situations. It also provides guidance as to what they should do to influence others to accept their image rehabilitation efforts. When an entity is accused of being responsible for an offensive act, it has five basic choices: (a) deny responsibility for the offensive act, (b) evade responsibility, (c) downplay the offensiveness, (d) take corrective action, or (e) take responsibility and ask for forgiveness (Benoit, 2015). When formulating a response, the entity should consider the nature of the accusations, the target audience, and the known facts (Benoit, 2015). The originator of the theory generally recommends that wrongdoers take responsibility and ask for forgiveness in a timely manner (Benoit, 2015). Corrective action is also generally recommended (Coombs,

2006). However, in some cases, an effort to simply bolster the previously positive image of the accused may be a better course of action (Coombs, 2006). A false denial is a dangerous influence strategy, as it can be revealed and end up both reinforcing the original transgression and creating a new transgression (Benoit, 2015).

TABLE 7.1 Image Restoration Typology

Denying Responsibility	Rejects the idea of organizational responsibility for the crisis of offense
Evading Responsibility	Admits committing the offense, but not fault (e.g., offense was provoked or accidental)
Reducing Offensiveness	Seeks to diminish the offense (e.g., emphasizing previous good acts of the accused, framing the offense as less serious than it is being perceived by others)
Corrective Action	Admits responsibility and offers a plan to solve the problem/ address the offense so it does not happen again
Mortification	Accepts responsibility and apologizes

COMPLIANCE TECHNIQUES

As stated earlier, compliance refers to whether a targeted person will positively respond to a request. The use of compliance techniques can increase the likelihood of achieving a desired "yes" from another person. Researchers from many different disciplines have contributed to our knowledge of compliance processes and techniques, including the communication scholar Ryan Goei, who has sharpened our understanding of the roles of liking and reciprocity (Goei & Massi Lindsey, Boster, Skalski, & Bowman, 2003) as well as gratitude-based reciprocity versus obligation-based reciprocity (Goei & Boster, 2005).

The list of compliance techniques is quite lengthy. Psychology professor Robert B. Cialdini (2009) provides a helpful selection of the main ones.

- **Reciprocation.** Humans often feel compelled to give back to others who have given to them. Corporate communicators can use this mechanism by giving something of perceived value to a target before requesting something of value.
- **Commitment and consistency.** Humans generally want to feel that they are stable in their beliefs and behaviors. Corporate communicators will frequently design an early low-stakes way for a target to commit to a desired course of action and then structure subsequent commitment opportunities to fall in line with it and advance beyond it.
- **Social proof.** Humans feel better about believing something or acting a certain way when others are doing the same, especially when the situation is uncertain and those with whom they are interacting are similar to them.

Corporate communicators seek to demonstrate how others are already on board with the belief or behavior they are advocating.

- **Liking.** Humans are more likely to comply with people they like, and they tend to like people who are attractive, similar to them, and familiar. Corporate communicators often work hard to look their best, find common ground with targets, and have many points of contact with targets.
- **Authority.** Humans generally respect authority figures. Titles, clothing, and other material goods, such as cars, are perceived markers of authority to which others often accede. Corporate communicators frequently take the opportunity to display authority markers of themselves and of their clients, where appropriate.
- **Scarcity.** Humans are more highly motivated to act when resources are perceived to be in short supply. Corporate communicators are aware of using time limits and otherwise controlling the availability of goods and services to trigger compliance in others.

POPULAR INFLUENCE MODELS

Several popular models of influence have emerged in recent decades. Some are noteworthy because they are credible efforts to translate theory and research into everyday applications. In *The Tipping Point*, Gladwell (2000) made the case that transformative influence is possible with the involvement of key people, the quality of the concept, and sensitivity to context. Key people to mobilize are mavens (i.e., experts, although Gladwell dislikes that term), connectors (i.e., highly networked individuals), and salespeople (i.e., effective and bold advocates). He used the word "stickiness" to describe how a concept should have positive and memorable features built into it. Context sensitivity means time and place prime people for receptivity to the concept.

Heath and Heath (2006) openly embraced Gladwell's "stickiness" idea and developed it in their book *Made to Stick*. They presented the acronym SUCCES to explain why certain ideas spread: simple, unexpected, concrete, credible, emotional, and stories.

Designed as a critique of *The Tipping Point*, Berger's (2012) *Contagious* incorporated the author's own quantitative research and attempted to argue against the role of connectors or influential individuals in spreading ideas. Berger offered the acronym STEPPS to explain effective influence: social currency, triggers, emotion, public, practical value, and stories.

APPLYING THE CONCEPT TO YOUR OWN SITUATION

ACKNOWLEDGE THAT INFLUENCE IS AN UNAVOIDABLE PART OF PROFESSIONAL LIFE

Yes, some people embrace the idea of influencing others. Maybe it is because these individuals feel confident about their abilities to do so. Maybe it is because these individuals are very aware of having successfully influenced others in the past.

Maybe it is because they were socialized in a way that normalized influence. If this describes you, then great!

There are other people who are uncomfortable or at least lacking confidence when it comes to strategically influencing others. If this is you, then, well, there is bad news and good news! The bad news is that strategically influencing others is an essential part of the corporate communication field. While the field is vast, there are virtually no roles in it that do not involve changing the hearts, minds, and behaviors of others. There is no avoiding strategic influence. The good news is that different areas of the field and different roles demand and reward different influence competencies based on different causes. So, if you are drawn to the field but worked up about the idea of influencing others, know that there is very likely still a place for you. This is especially the case because—more good news here—the ability to influence can be learned. For starters, though, it is important to see that strategic influence is something that corporate communication professionals simply must engage.

RECOGNIZE HOW YOU ARE ALREADY INFLUENTIAL

Whether you are an influencing pro right now or someone who feels skittish about it, a great thing to do is to take stock of how you have already influenced those around you. This normalizes strategic influence, builds confidence, clarifies key factors making influence comfortable for you, and starts the process of seeing how you can deepen and expand your skills. No doubt there are one or more people in your personal life who you have influenced to make a change. Maybe these individuals even asked for your help. When you give it some thought, you realize help is often a form of influence. No doubt you have also influenced those around in your academic and work settings. Sometimes our most deeply rewarding influence successes are hidden because we think about them as just being instances of acting as a good friend, a good student, or a good employee. When you uncover these influence achievements, sift through them for what made you effective, as you will likely find themes as well as seeds of influence that can grow.

UNDERSTAND INFLUENCE DYNAMICS IN
YOUR DESIRED SPECIALTY AREAS AND ROLES

Corporate communication is a broad field with many specialized areas and roles. Anyone should feel overwhelmed in trying to somehow master influence across it all. It is probably impossible. Mastery in a particular area and with a particular role is much more realistic. To begin the journey toward this kind of influence mastery, draw the line between the influencer you are and the influencer needed in a particular location in our field. Very possibly, you already bring some essential influencing talents. Regardless, this way of thinking leaves you with a more manageable influencing to-do list.

SEEK TO EXPAND YOUR INFLUENCE STRATEGY AND TACTIC REPERTOIRE

No matter where you want to start and finish in our field, a good general goal when it comes to influence is to expand the influence strategies and tactics you can use. This is a matter of motivation, knowledge building, and skill building. While it is normal for a person to have his or her favorite strategies and tactics that flow out of the person's personality, habits, and comfort zone, a wide repertoire of possibilities is going to be helpful for dealing with the diversity of job demands and inevitable changes in our field and the wider culture.

QUESTIONS:

- What is the best frame in which I can describe myself professionally in as few words as possible, and what is the potentially competing frame that I most want to avoid?

- How can I incorporate three or more persuasion cues into a specific career-related proposal that I am likely to make in the near future?

- How will I be most prone to negative and positive influence as I develop my career?

Tools and Processes for Self-Action

CREATING YOUR ELEVATOR PITCH

An elevator pitch is a roughly 30-second self-introduction that you can use with a prospective employer or other networking target. It is so brief that you could share it in a typical elevator ride. Many individuals start their personal pitches by sharing their names before sharing information such as key past accomplishments, key current activities, key talents, select professional goals, and/or the professional value they can provide. An alternate format is to share one distinctive story that indirectly communicates credibility and value. The purpose of a personal pitch is to make a positive and memorable impression so that the person you are engaging, at a minimum, wants to learn more about you. To succeed, it is important to be honest, professional, audience centered, and polished in all aspects of the delivery. Some find it appropriate and effective to include personal details, but make sure this information is relevant to your professional message. Some routinely end their personal pitches with a request or proposal in an attempt to win the listener's commitment, especially to a more in-depth, follow-up conversation. The inclusion of a request or proposal is a direct attempt at influence and almost certainly increases your chances of achieving your goals, although there are never guarantees.

WRITING YOUR COVER LETTER

Although the online submission of resumes is generally increasing, along with the use of artificial intelligence to screen for key words and other key data, the traditional approach of submitting a cover letter with a resume remains relevant for many positions. Cover letters may play a greater role for corporate communication professionals because they are an easy test of some of the influencing skills needed in much of our field. A cover letter immediately precedes a resume. While a resume is assumed to be a stable document in terms of stating a person's professional qualifications in an objective manner, a cover letter connects the dots between the resume and the prospective employer's needs and wants. It can be highly influential. Cover letters should always be customized.

CREATING A PORTFOLIO THAT TELLS YOUR STORY

A portfolio is a collection of past work. While portfolios are a standard part of some fields, such as photography, they are somewhat less common in corporate communication. You will probably not be asked to bring one to your next interview. However, you should share access to one whenever you are interviewing, as they are a great way to tell your professional story and otherwise influence a prospective employer. Many use web-based portfolios, but some still prefer old school, hard-copy portfolios. A portfolio can make it easier for you to explain yourself and highlight your value.

PRESENTING YOURSELF IN AN INTERVIEW

If you have been invited to interview for a position, chances are you already outcompeted many other candidates and are part of a select group of finalists. It is normal to feel at least a little bit nervous but, hopefully, you also feel excited about making it to this stage. One way to feel more comfortable is to be fully prepared. Do what you can to find out about the structure of the interview process in advance. Particularly as you progress in your career, you will find that many interview processes consist of multiple one-on-one or group-based question-and-answer sessions, a chance for you to present on a relevant topic, a shared meal, and even the request that you tackle a problem that you would face in your new position. Think through and even practice how you would verbally and nonverbally handle these experiences. Recognize that you can make a positive impression even after the interview is over by following up with thank you e-mails or hard-copy notes to each of the people who took time to meet with you. Customize these messages by referring to a particular topic you addressed with each person. You may even want to share an insight or recommend a resource to address a problem that each person shared.

PROFILE OF INDIVIDUAL EXPERIENCE:

Nicole Tirado

Nicole Tirado is a recent graduate of a corporate communication program and an advertising account executive at Univision Communications, a company that started as the Spanish International Network but has grown into a large multimedia company. Ms. Tirado represents the TV station Univision 65, giving voice to the Latino community in the greater Philadelphia area, a top-five media market in the United States. She is responsible for new business development, creating strategic marketing campaigns, and managing accounts.

Univision is an established brand, and account executive positions are not typically awarded to newly minted graduates, so in seeking the position, Tirado realized she had to do something out of the box. "I went on LinkedIn and added almost everyone in the Philadelphia and New York City markets. I messaged each person and asked about their experience, their position, and even set up a few calls." She found herself getting some great advice and participating in enjoyable conversations. One contact was impressed by Ms. Tirado's experience working in a support position in an immigration law firm. Tirado used this topic to pivot the conversation to asking for the person's help in spotting any opportunities to serve the Latino community by working at Univision. The woman to whom Ms. Tirado was speaking asked if she had sales experience. Tirado shared that she had once worked in sales at a jewelry store and had more minor retail experience as well, and she was open to being challenged and growing. Ms. Tirado was about to encounter a pleasant surprise. "The contact then sent me an application. Little did I know she was the hiring manager for the Philly market!"

FIGURE 7.2 Nicole Tirado

Tirado did not sit back at this point. "I studied for a week—literally a week! I made sure I was more than prepared." Ms. Tirado made sure she had a firm grasp on the company and more. "I knew how to carry myself; I knew why I wanted to work at Univision, how I wanted to grow, and how I was going to handle objections." She was definitely nervous at the start of this process but simply did so much homework that her anxiety went away. "I came in with a good attitude and enthusiasm. I was ready. Since I prepared, I was no longer nervous; I was excited!" Ms. Tirado won the job offer, and she later learned from her sales manager how she did it. "It was my engagement—I asked her a lot of questions. It was also my knowledge and ambition that landed me the position."

Ms. Tirado found herself arriving at an organization that had certain expectations about how to influence ethically and effectively. One principle she acquired was to listen to the client's needs first before talking about what her organization had to offer. "After I know about their business, their current marketing initiatives, and their struggles, I find solutions that align with Univision." Another principle she has learned is to put prospects at ease by being open about Univision's past successes and limitations. "My job is to make the potential client feel as comfortable as possible. I come with commercials of clients in the category, examples of what worked and what didn't work. My goal is to always be as transparent as possible." A straightforward mission guides Ms. Tirado. "The key is to be honest and stay true to yourself and loyal to your client."

Ms. Tirado is aware of some other practices that make her more impactful. She realizes that she is a strong influencer because of the care she puts into each of her client's marketing plans. "They are never one-size-fits-all. Everyone's goals are different and, as a solutions provider, we must give each client the same attention regardless of the amount they invest." She has also found that keeping clients updated also pays dividends. "During a campaign, I send reports on where advertising aired, the associated ratings, and insights into the target demographic. Providing your client with new information will make them feel like they made the right choice." For someone who is comfortable taking control, it is also notable that Ms. Tirado realizes she needs to continue to be receptive to clients. "I also ask for feedback. We are solution providers, but there is also room for improvement."

Considering the degree to which Ms. Tirado is self-assured and knowledgeable about advertising sales, it is a little shocking to learn that she was not always this way. Even a couple of years prior to graduation, she would never have believed she would work in this area. "When I was in college, sales terrified me. I always said to myself I would never work in sales because I didn't feel like I had the personality." Tirado talked about what changed her perspective on taking on a professional role with influence at its core. "Once I saw there was an opportunity available at Univision, I knew I had to take it. I believed in the brand, the importance of advertising to the Latino market, and how helpful it is to showcase trusted information, services, and products. I realized if you believe in what you are offering it's no longer really sales. It's simply a conversation about how you can help a potential advertiser grow."

Ms. Tirado is committed to her main professional responsibilities, but she has also made a point of applying her influence skills for other worthwhile causes. One project that has given her a feeling of deep accomplishment was working with her alma mater, Penn State Abington—the Penn State campus with the strongest record of serving diverse students but still an institution needing to do more. Ms. Tirado described initiating the campus' first Latino marketing campaign: "Being able to sit down at the table with the marketing communications team of my former school was magical." After several meetings, Tirado helped them develop the "Somos Penn State" campaign that included television spots, event promos, event activation, and digital. The high point of the campaign for Ms. Tirado was speaking to a group of prospective students about her own experience being a child of immigrants and needing to navigate all aspects of the college experience on her own because her parents did not understand how to help. One of the individuals she reassured that day was a young woman who went on to enroll and is making steady progress toward graduation.

Looking toward the future, Ms. Tirado feels positive and trusts that hard work will lead to results. She is fortunate to work under a manager who is knowledgeable, skilled, and supportive. Ms. Tirado looks forward to learning more about handling objections and the importance of telling a story. Tirado also wants to more fully develop her personal brand at the company, "so clients will be even more enticed to work with Univision and me." Ms. Tirado also sees her love for what she does continuing to play a major role. "I will continue to develop growth plans with creativity and passion. Passion really changes things. It's like cooking with love."

Questions:

1. Drawing from the theory section of this chapter, make a case for three influence strategies or tactics that Ms. Tirado used with Univision representatives prior to being provided with an application.

2. Make an argument for the single influence strategy or tactic that best explains Ms. Tirado's efforts in preparing for and completing her interview with Univision.

3. Ms. Tirado emphasized that care is a major part of what makes her successful as an influencer. Do you think one or more of the theories presented in this chapter adequately accounts for care as an influence strategy, or is another theory needed to do so?

4. How can stakeholder influence explain Ms. Tirado's success in securing her position, in carrying out her Univision work, and in making a difference with her pro bono efforts?

APPLYING THE CONCEPT TO YOUR WORK WITH CLIENTS

IDENTIFY THE DOMINANT INFLUENCE FRAME OR STORY

Determining the overall influence strategy used by an organization is a valuable initial step to being helpful in this area. While the influence strategies and tactics used by even a small organization can be numerous and vary considerably, most organizations adopt a primary approach. An organization's top leaders should easily articulate how they are seeking to influence the world. Whether it is easy or difficult to discern, it is often most neatly conceptualized as a single attempted strategic narrative.

EXPLORE THE POLYVOCALITY OF STAKEHOLDER VOICES

Even when an organization seems strongly committed to a coherent influence strategy, a diversity of approaches, and variation in the success of those approaches, should be identifiable. Different stakeholder groups need to be influenced to different degrees, on different matters, and in different ways so that the organization is better able to meet its goals. Stakeholders need to feel like they are heard on different matters and will employ different influence tools to raise their voices. By no means are all stakeholder voices a threat. Some voices might be. Others' voices very likely bring forward perspectives so that the organization can better meet its goals and become more influential with the stakeholder group and beyond.

SPOT OPPORTUNITIES FOR UNUSED
AND UNDERUSED INFLUENCE PROCESSES

Putting aside an organization's overarching goal and its primary means of influence for achieving it, it is a near certainty that an organization has the possibility of using new or revised approaches to influence, especially in the nuances of specific organization-to-stakeholder touch points. Spotting these opportunities can perhaps best occur by stepping back, seeking inspiration in various theoretical models, and creatively brainstorming.

INFLUENCE WITH A LONG VIEW

Large organizations, at least publicly traded ones, can be obsessed with winning an immediate "yes" to bolster quarterly financial results. Small organizations, whether for profit or not for profit, can be hungry for earning an immediate "yes" to generate profits to simply keep the lights on. While monetary and other immediate needs for influence should be acknowledged, it is wise to recognize their omnipresence and not allow them to make the organization myopic. Corporate communication professionals may need to help win the day, but they almost always need to do so in a way that does no appreciable harm to long-term interests, including the ability to influence effectively over the long term.

QUESTIONS:

▪ What is the most essential work my client is taking or needs to undertake in terms of asserting a frame under threat of competing frames?

▪ What is my client's best narrative, and how might we be more effective at sharing it with different stakeholders?

▪ How does my client use persuasion cues with key stakeholders, and how might the influence process be strengthened?

▪ How does a crisis affect the organizational narrative?

▪ How might stakeholders influence organizational narrative during a crisis?

Tools and Processes When Acting for Others

MANAGE THE OVERALL INFLUENCE EFFORT

Whether working in a senior leadership role as an employee of the organization or as a consultant to senior organizational leaders, corporate communication professionals can provide value by coordinating the overall influence effort. This can fulfill several functions, including consistent overall messaging, the ability to scan for and manage potential crises, and an operational hub for day-to-day communications.

SOCIAL MEDIA LISTENING

Arguably, the first principle of influencing effectively is listening to those you likely want to impact. Corporate communication professionals often have the knowledge and skills to systematically follow, analyze, and report on organization-relevant communication by stakeholders or other targets on one or more social media platforms. There can be tremendous value in taking time to listen, and the best listeners are often those who personally identify with those to whom they are listening and, of course, the overall organization. Effective listening is necessary for influence strategy and tactic selection and implementation. It should occur on an ongoing basis and intensify during times of change and ongoing or potential crisis.

TAKING CHARGE OF INFLUENCING A PARTICULAR STAKEHOLDER GROUP

Corporate communication professionals routinely find themselves temporarily in charge of influencing a stakeholder group, often on a particular issue. Internally, this could mean designing and delivering a learning and development program to emerging leaders. Externally, this could mean planning and running a community event. Of course, organizations sometimes place such emphasis on relations with particular stakeholders that they hire stakeholder specialists. Especially with well-defined stakeholder groups and those highly valued by the organization, it can be important that the specialist is a member of the stakeholder group to maximize credibility and influence potential for the organization. An example would be an organization hiring a former elected official as a lobbyist to influence former colleagues on behalf of the organization.

MAKING THE RIGHT IMAGE REPAIR DECISION

Implementing the right decision can become a lot more difficult when the situation is not hypothetical but actual and you are in it with others who you know are suggesting a bad direction. In a crisis, corporate communication professionals can find themselves needing to first influence the very people they are trying to protect. Crises are stressful and cause many, especially those without training and proven models at the ready, to hastily retreat or attack rather than think through the situation systematically and take truly strategic action. Corporate communicators are needed to win the backing of senior leaders and effectively lead messaging efforts when a crisis makes influence particularly hard to exert successfully.

PROFILE OF ORGANIZATIONAL EXPERIENCE:

Amazon

Amazon was started by Jeff Bezos in 1994 and opened for business the following year. The organization was originally called Cadabra, but Bezos quickly renamed it when his lawyer misheard the name over the phone as "cadaver." Initially, Amazon only offered books, and its founder pegged the company's chance of success at 30%. It was not terribly long, though, before sales took off and, in 1997, Amazon went public and was worth almost half a billion dollars (Easter & Dave, 2017; Ramo, 1999).

Bezos was named *Time* magazine's person of the year in 1999, but long before Amazon was a durable profit-making success, he envisioned his company selling pretty much everything (Ramo, 1999). And this ambitious goal has certainly come to pass. In the 21st century's first 20 years, Amazon came to do more than offer a nearly inconceivable number and range of products created by other companies. It became a leader in web services (including cloud computing and ad sales), consumer technologies (including the Kindle e-reader, the Amazon Fire HD, the Amazon Fire TV, and the Amazon Echo), entertainment (including AmazonStudios), and groceries (including AmazonFresh, Whole Foods, and Amazon Go) (Easter & Dave, 2017; Lane, 2018). One of the ways to explain the success of Bezos and Amazon is to consider how influence has been used inside and outside the organization.

A *Forbes* staff writer was able to interview an increasingly inaccessible and circumspect Bezos and learned that one of Bezos's goal has been to preserve the ability of employees throughout the company to be influential by elevating proposals for innovations (Lane, 2018). In observing other companies, Bezos recognized that one of the main explanations for small start-ups being able to overtake large, well-established organizations is that new ideas in big companies must survive the gauntlet of earning managerial approval at multiple levels to win support and get developed. Bezos's work-around for not inadvertently blocking employee-championed ideas at a now-massive Amazon is to permit employees to shop around, if necessary, for just one manager to win support, particularly with ideas for incremental improvements. For truly transformative ideas, Bezos himself attempts to be directly involved and assesses them according to three factors: (1) originality, (2) scale, and (3) return on investment.

The overall internal culture that Bezos fosters at Amazon is controversial at best and toxic at worst. To keep the overall company driving forward, Amazon operates with a kind of social Darwinism (Kantor & Streitfeld, 2015). Employees and managers at various levels sometimes speak of the opportunity to do amazing things and make an amazing difference. Many also speak about how it is commonplace for employees to cry at work because of extreme stress and to find themselves getting forced out if they encounter health and/or family issues requiring leave. And turnover in general is high. One former employee in advertising and marketing cautioned that the organization is potentially having employees seen as "fungible" (Kantor & Streitfeld, 2015). Two of the practices underlying the highly competitive internal environment are the ability of employees to anonymously provide feedback on their colleagues and a wider embrace of data-driven management where the measurement of employees is constant and related blunt changes are common.

One of the ways Amazon has been influential with customers and prospective customers is with the design of their online product pages. Although it can be taken for granted, product page design is really the primary interface between the company and consumers. The typical Amazon product page incorporates many of the major compliance techniques, including reciprocity (e.g., noting free shipping), commitment and consistency (e.g., displaying products others bought along with the current product), social proof (e.g., showing the number of positive ratings), liking (e.g., posting an attractive photo in the case of book authors), authority (e.g., including reviews from established sources), and scarcity (e.g., when appropriate, warning there are only a limited number of the product left in stock).

Amazon used influence in a flashy manner with a wide national audience in how it selected headquarter expansion sites (O'Connell & McCartney, 2018). In 2017, it announced that it was launching a competition to select a second headquarters while keeping its Seattle site. The competition process resulted in bids from over 200 cities. In 2018, it announced that it had chosen two winners, Northern Virginia and New York City. The reality-show-like competition allowed Amazon to win significant tax concessions, learn valuable information for possible future business decisions, and attract free and generally positive visibility. Some initially argued that Bezos and Amazon were entirely victorious (e.g., Matsakis, 2018). Others argued that it was a flawed approach that could backfire in raising expectations for Amazon in the area of CSR (e.g., Ovide, 2018). Amazon's influence approach to the highly visible headquarter expansion initiative seemed to be confirmed as flawed when they withdrew from the New York City expansion in mid-February of 2019 due to the uproar of several progressive politicians and their constituents (Goodman, 2019).

Questions:

1. What is the most convincing narrative frame that Bezos and other Amazon advocates could use to justify a demanding internal culture?

2. To what extent do you think the internal culture at Amazon can reasonably expect to succeed at encouraging internal influence in the form of breakthrough new ideas? Present one idea for making Amazon employees even more influential in terms of advancing Amazon's own goals?

3. Do you agree or disagree that the Amazon product page design primarily addresses the central route rather than the peripheral route in the ELM, and, regardless, do you think it is as effective as it could be? Justify your responses.

4. What single influence theory presented in this chapter best explains the mechanism by which Amazon attempted to reap various gains with its effort to select a location for its new headquarters?

Chapter Conclusion

An early career corporate communication professional cannot go long without facing the fact that the nature of his or her work demands that he or she represents a point of view—and he or she is aiming to impart this point of view on others. Influence, whether direct or indirect, has a fundamentally assertive quality. You may have embraced the field early on because you know you are assertive and want to make a difference in the world. On the other hand, you may have embraced the field for other reasons and know or found out that you are perhaps not so much an assertive point person but rather a team member. Whatever the case, recognize that influence is not some magical quality but a wide set of strategies and tactics that can be learned and honed through practice. Hopefully, this thought energizes you since the motivation to influence is itself an important part of the process. And no matter how good you get at changing the thoughts, feelings, and actions of others, be sure to remain open to being influenced by others. That is a measure of humility and a sign of intelligence and growth.

Key Terms

Compliance
Compliance techniques
Elaboration likelihood model
Framing
Image restoration theory
Influence

Narrative framing or strategic
  storytelling
Persuasion
Polyvocality
Power
Stakeholder
Stakeholder theory

Chapter Discussion Questions

1. Can mastery of one narrow approach to influence be enough to achieve success over time, or does success largely depend on the ability to use several approaches to influence appropriately and effectively? How might this be similar and different for individuals and organizations? Argue with specific examples.

2. What are some examples of inappropriate attempts at influence in the corporate communication field? What are some examples of when you might feel a legitimate obligation to attempt to influence?

3. How would you ideally be mentored so you could become a markedly more influential communicator? Who might you ask to become this mentor?

4. How could one of the compliance techniques summarized by Cialdini could be incorporated into an image repair attempt for an issue you may face in your own career (e.g., temporary unemployment)?

Chapter Activities

1. Partner with a classmate, learn about his or her professional identity and target audience, listen to the person's personal pitch, and then offer at least two ways he or she could make the personal pitch more influential.

2. Working alone or with a partner, generate a list of the top-10 ways a soon-to-be-graduating corporate communication student can exert influence and make it more likely that he or she will secure a desired position upon finishing his or her degree. Be sure to highlight the role of influence in each of your listed items.

3. Pretend no barriers exist and you could represent any single brand in the world. Create a one-page plug for your chosen brand that is innovative, sensitive to the brand and one or more of its stakeholder groups, and incorporates three or more influence strategies or tactics shared in this chapter.

Recommended Readings and Resources

Adam Grant is a professor of management and psychology at the Wharton School of the University of Pennsylvania. He wrote a popular book based in part on his own research that is devoted to the concept of reciprocity as an influence strategy. He described three deal-making styles: givers, matchers, and takers. He found that givers most often benefit the most.

Grant, A. (2014). *Give and take: Why helping others drives our success*. Penguin.

Adam Grant also gave a related TED Talk.

https://www.ted.com/talks/adam_grant_are_you_a_giver_or_a_taker

Nancy Duarte is a leader in the analysis and design of influential presentations. *Resonate* is a thoughtfully designed book that illuminates the structure of some of the best presentations in recent decades while also clearly explaining how you can do it yourself. Her work highlights the importance of effective storytelling and visuals.

Duarte, N. (2010). *Resonate: Present visual stories that transform audiences*. Wiley

Nancy Duarte also gave a related TED Talk.

https://www.ted.com/talks/nancy_duarte_the_secret_structure_of_great_talks

Cliff Atkinson is a popular author who cites research and provides an excellent overall explanation for why traditional use of PowerPoint fails and what should be done about it, especially for key pitches.

Atkinson, C. (2018). *Beyond bullet points* (4th ed.). Microsoft Pearson.

Figure credits

RESEARCH AND ASSESSMENT
The Information to
Chart and Measure Progress

This chapter explains why research and assessment are needed to support various aspects of the strategic communication process. It also introduces different tools for doing so. You will leave the chapter with an understanding of research and assessment appropriateness given the types and stages of different organizational initiatives. You will also begin to apply research and assessment to the development and advancement of your own professional strategies.

Theory and research for this chapter will focus primarily on tactics used in research and assessment for strategic communication, including environmental scanning, social listening, research methods, measurement tools, and the importance of feedback.

The ideas of research and assessment are nothing new to you. Take this example that you recently engaged in: How did you decide where to apply to college? You probably talked to your high school guidance counselor, asked your friends where they were applying and why, and then did some outside research using resources such as *Fiske's Guide*, *Princeton Review*, or other college handbooks. Maybe you gathered some firsthand knowledge by visiting different campuses and asking questions while you were there. *These are all examples of research.* Keeping with the academic theme, what is a type of assessment that you are familiar with as a student? Grades! Grades assess, or evaluate, your performance in a specific class. Although it may sometimes seem like it, grades are not random. They measure your performance against specific criteria or preestablished standards that a professor can then compare your work against. How you perform compared to those criteria determines your grade.

As we have covered throughout this book, strategic communication is about enabling individuals and organizations to reach their goals. For individuals, especially in your current stage of life, this often involves setting personal milestones, such as graduation, attaining a job, and establishing your first independent home, and then enacting communicative actions that help you achieve them. For organizations, this often includes communicating to build an organizational brand, a positive reputation, and stakeholder relationships. While we talked about the importance of goal setting and planning in Chapter 1, in this chapter, we are going to zoom in and look at the processes behind setting goals and making plans. Importantly, we will tie in the concept of assessment. Assessment looks at how we evaluate our communicative actions and look forward. In other words, it helps us answer the questions, *did we achieve our goals,* and *how can we learn from what we have done to achieve more success in the future?*

Orienting to the Concept:
Using Research and Assessment to Ensure Smart Strategy

Research and assessment essentially answer the questions, *where am I going, have I successfully arrived, could I have gotten here in a better way,* and, sometimes, *which way should I go now?* As we covered in Chapter 1, strategy, or a plan of action created to achieve your goals, can be both planned and emergent. Research and assessment can help in both planning your strategy and adjusting along the way as environmental or other factors intervene. Research is the first step strategic communicators take when planning strategy—it helps them to understand what is going on in the environment, what questions to ask, the smartest goals to set, and which path to take. Research lays the groundwork for action, which is the impetus for assessment. Although a conceptually distinct term, assessment is a form of *evaluative research* in that it analyzes data obtained through research to measure the success of a strategy through predetermined *metrics.*

This section of the chapter defines the key terms related to both personal and professional research and assessment.

CENTRAL DEFINITIONS

RESEARCH
Research refers to the collecting and use of data for "the purpose of describing, predicting, and controlling as a means toward better understanding the phenomena under consideration" (Huitt, Hummel, & Kaeck, 2001). As we will discuss throughout this chapter, there are many different methods, or systematic ways, of conducting research, including primary and secondary research.

MEASUREMENT
Measurement is the analysis of data to see if the strategies employed have met the goal set out in the beginning of the campaign or another communication effort. As we will discuss later in this chapter, there are two primary methods of measurement: qualitative and quantitative analysis.

ASSESSMENT
Assessment is the comparison of data to predetermined goals and criteria for the purpose of determining the degree of success and value of the communication strategy or plan.

FEEDBACK AND DATA

FEEDBACK AND DATA

Feedback is information obtained from a target audience or another environmental factor that provides insight into how an individual or organization is perceived by that audience. Feedback is a type of data or information that can be used for analysis and planning.

GOAL

Put simply, a goal is what you are trying to achieve. Goals provide a big-picture view of what you want to accomplish, and they are most effective when paired with **s**pecific, **m**easurable, **a**chievable, **r**elevant, and **t**imely objectives so that they can be measured and assessed.

THEORY AND RESEARCH OVERVIEW

The Research Process in Strategic Corporate Communication

Research is a continuous process of collecting, analyzing, and assessing data to measure where one is in relation to the overall goals and objectives. Research should be the first step in strategic communication. Environmental scanning is the collecting of data from sources relevant to the individual or organization. For example, an organization might use a database such as Nexis Uni—News Sources to search for any mention of its brand name, CEO, or popular products. This provides data or information used for reference, analysis, or planning. Data can then be analyzed to determine a problem or opportunity facing the organization or simply to give a snapshot of what is being said about the organization in the mainstream media at that given time. Social listening is a similar process enacted on social media. Organizations can use tools such as Hootsuite to search for key terms across social media platforms. If scanning and listening are done daily, over time, organizations will have longitudinal data, or data that presents a long-term view of how the organization is being perceived. Organizations can compare this data to their overall goals and objectives and see how they are performing relative to these goals. In addition, they can analyze the data to determine the share of voice (SOV), or how much of the public attention they have, or even just in terms of whether public perception of the company is primarily positive or negative. They then use this analysis to determine the next steps for strategic communication.

Over time, this becomes a continuous cycle of research, action, measurement, and assessment

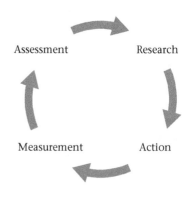

Assessment   Research

Measurement   Action

FIGURE 8.1 Cycle of Research and Assessment

(Figure 8.1) that allows the organization to both plan ahead and course correct in the middle of a campaign.

Research and Assessment Tactics

As you probably gathered from the previous section on the research process, there are many different ways to measure and assess data. This section will break them out into four primary categories: primary and secondary research, and qualitative and quantitative analysis.

PRIMARY RESEARCH

Primary research involves gathering data from firsthand sources, such as through interviews, surveys, or focus groups. Firsthand data allows researchers to gather the first-person perspective or actions of participants. Participants are generally part of a purposive sample, or specially chosen population of people usually involving members of key stakeholder groups. Sometimes, however, the organization may want to know more about general impressions of the organization and will then use a random sample, or participants who have an equal chance of representing the general population.

The following are the most common types of primary research methods used in corporate communication:

1. **Interviews.** An interview is a conversation between two parties (the interviewer and the participant) that is guided by a set of questions prepared by the interviewer in advance of the meeting. Interviews are useful because they can give in-depth information about a chosen topic. Interviews provide a chance for two-way symmetric communication, with plenty of opportunities for feedback and follow-up questions that emerge on the spot as the interview progresses. Some of the drawbacks to interviews are that they are time-consuming, and the data obtained from an interview often cannot be *generalized*, or used to make a general claim, because it only represents the insight of one person.

2. **Surveys.** Surveys are a series of questions administered to participants via pencil and paper or online. They are generally closed-ended, which means participants can only answer from a set number of choices. The most common types of surveys use a Likert scale, which asks participants to indicate how much they agree or disagree with a statement on a scale (most commonly a scale of 1 to 5 or 1 to 7), with the lowest number indicating extreme disagreement/dislike and the highest number indicating extreme agreement/liking. Because of the format, surveys can be administered to multiple people at a time, often numbering in the hundreds or thousands. Higher numbers of participants provide more *statistical power* (ability to detect true differences among participants), *reliability* (consistency), and *generalizability* (the ability to be generalized to the larger population). However, surveys don't offer the detail or insight provided by research methods such as focus groups or interviews.

3. **Focus groups.** Focus groups are essentially group conversations with stake-holders about the organization. Focus groups include between five and 10 participants and a moderator who is usually a representative of the organi-zation. Focus groups can vary in format but often begin with participants sharing their general perceptions of the organization. The moderator can then introduce questions to steer the conversation or introduce sample communication materials to get opinions on the materials. Focus groups can get in-depth insight into how stakeholders feel about the organization or specific campaign materials. Also, because decisions aren't made in a vacuum, it is beneficial to allow conversations to unfold organically, which can provide a truer view of how the participants feel. Conversely, one or two strong voices can "take over," thus skewing the conversation and results. While focus groups allow for more participants than interviews, they enable far fewer people to participate than a survey.

4. **Panel study.** A panel study is a longitudinal research method (i.e., asking the same questions of the same participants over time). Panel studies are useful because they show how participant opinions change over time, typi-cally in response to an intervention, such as a new communication campaign. Most panel studies use surveys to collect the data. Panel studies can be extremely useful because they can show how public perception changes relative to different actions taken by the organization. However, they are difficult to conduct because they rely on having the same people partici-pate over time but getting access and participation from these people over a course of years can be very difficult.

SECONDARY RESEARCH

Secondary research involves using third-party resources, such as organizational documents, news sources, social media posts, existing research studies, government or industry reports, or other similar materials. Secondary research is inexpensive and allows you to cast a wide net for information. Secondary research is also unob-trusive, which makes it generally easier to collect. Accordingly, secondary research is often the first type of research gathered for both planning and evaluation.

The most common types of secondary research methods used in corporate communication are as follows:

1. **Media scanning.** One of the most common ways to gather data through secondary research is media scanning, which is part of environmental scan-ning. Media scanning involves collecting data from media sources relevant to the individual or organization, including major newspapers, trade publi-cations (i.e., publications specific to a particular industry), blogs, and other similar secondary sources. Media scanning is often accomplished by entering key words, including company name, CEO name, popular company products or services, competitor information, and any other relevant key words into a news database (e.g., Nexis Uni—News Sources), search engines, and other industry tools designed to collect data automatically. Ideally, this is done on a

TABLE 8.1 Comparison of Primary and Secondary Research Methods

	Primary	Secondary
Types	Interviews, surveys, focus groups, panel studies	Media scanning, social listening, brand listening, archival and public document searches, big data sources
Benefits	Gets right to the source by directly asking questions to real people	Allows you to collect large amounts of data from a wide time span
	Is customizable—you create the questions that are being asked, so you only collect the information that you need	Can be cheap or free, depending on your source. Can be done on your own, using social media dashboards or by hiring a third-party company to collect and analyze the data
	You have complete quality control	Can provide big-picture information
Drawbacks	Expensive	While you can set some parameters on what you gather, you are not collecting data from the original source, which can lead to more "noise"
	Time-consuming	Must rely on the quality of the source you are collecting from
		You cannot ask specific questions of participants; rather, you must work with what is already published

daily basis so that organizations can ascertain how they are being portrayed in the media, perceived in public opinion, and if there are any crises on the horizon. In addition, by scanning for competitor information and industry key words, organizations can get a more holistic view of where they stand related to specific competitors and their industry in general.

2. **Social listening.** Social listening is an extension of media scanning into the social media arena. It is searching for key words, including hashtags, relevant to your organization, competitors, products/services, and industry across social media platforms. Like media scanning, this can be accomplished by manually searching platforms. However, because of the overwhelming amount of content on social media, most organizations use content management platforms, such as HubSpot, Hootsuite, or Sprout Social. Social listening allows for the same type of analysis as traditional media monitoring, as well as calculating the SOV, or what percentage of the social conversation the organization is receiving relative to other organizations in the search,

and social media sentiment, which considers the overall tenor (positive, negative, neutral) of the media mentions related to the organization. Social listening helps organizations determine where they stand in terms of the overall conversation on social media.

3. **Brand listening.** Brand listening hones in social listening to focus on what is being said on the organization's own platforms. While brand listening is a communication tool that allows organizations to respond to stakeholders in real time, it can also be used in a longitudinal way to gather data about metrics related to specific posts (e.g., how many likes, comments, and shares does each post get), level of stakeholder engagement in the comments, and social media sentiment on the organization's own pages. Brand listening helps organizations determine how they are performing relative to their own goals and standards.

4. **Archival and public document searches.** Archival and public document searches can include white papers, or in-depth reports that present a problem and solution relative to an organization or industry (Kolowich, n.d.), government reports, and organizational archives. While media scanning, social listening, and brand listening can provide organizations with information about where they stand in terms of coverage, SOV, and sentiment and engagement on traditional and social media, archival and public documents can be useful for researching for specific information relative to industry regulations, past organizational campaigns, and industry ideas or opinions.

Measurement and Assessment Tactics

Once data has been gathered using the research methods described earlier, it is time to analyze in order to assess what it means in relation to the organization. The two types of analysis are qualitative, which answers questions of *how* and *what*, and quantitative, which answers questions of *why*, and seeks to establish *association, relationship, or cause and effect* (Creswell, 1998), as well as *how many* and *how often*. While we are talking about analysis in terms of qualitative and quantitative, it is worth noting that methodologies (described in the previous section) can also be considered qualitative or quantitative, as the way that data is gathered lends itself to certain types of analysis. For example, surveys are often considered a quantitative method of gathering data because they are analyzed using quantitative analysis, such as statistical analysis.

Arguably, triangulation, which involves using multiple methods and both qualitative and quantitative analysis, offers the best results because it provides a multidimensional way to view results.

QUALITATIVE ANALYSIS

Content analysis. Qualitative content analysis involves coding a text for specific themes and then making statements about the nature of the text based on those themes. Coding refers to "the analytic process through which data are fractured, conceptualized, and integrated to form theory" (Strauss & Corbin, 1998, p. 3). Basically, coding is assigning our interpretive meaning over the literal meaning of words

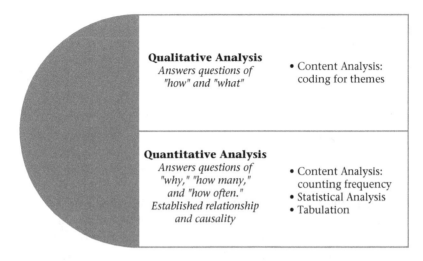

Qualitative Analysis
*Answers questions of
"how" and "what"*

• Content Analysis:
  coding for themes

Quantitative Analysis
*Answers questions of
"why," "how many,"
and "how often."
Established relationship
and causality*

• Content Analysis:
  counting frequency
• Statistical Analysis
• Tabulation

FIGURE 8.2 Comparison of Quantiative and Qualitative Research Methods

and thoughts in a given text. In qualitative analysis for corporate communication, a text can be a corpus of newspaper coverage about the organization, social media content on one's own or others' social media pages, focus group transcripts, and more. Fracturing the data involves breaking it down and categorizing the text in terms of concepts, properties, or dimensions (Strauss & Corbin, 1998). Once the data is sorted in this way, you can conceptualize, order, and relate the coded data in a way that provides insight into the question at hand. This can be done without predetermined parameters, in which case the researcher would assign conceptually related pieces of the text labels that describe each phenomenon that is emerging from data. Alternately, researchers may have a specific question that they are trying to answer, in which case they would enter the analysis with a predetermined set of codes and code the text according to the already established codebook. For example, if you wanted to know how your organization was performing on social media, you could perform content analysis in which you read through one month's worth of stakeholder feedback on your company's Facebook page and group responses in categories that "make sense." You may come up with codes such as "complaints," "compliments," "questions," "product comments," and "conversational." You would then study the text associated with each category, as well as what each category means, to make an overall statement about the state of your social media engagement on Facebook. From there, you could make recommendations for change if necessary. Conversely, may want to answer a more specific question, such as, "What are the different types of inquiries obtained through our company's Facebook page," and then code the data with a preexisting coding scheme, including product/service, customer service, background, sustainability/CSR. In this case, you would not be looking for *how many* times each type of inquiry takes place but rather the meaning behind the different types of inquiries, which could give you insight into what stakeholders are interested in and why.

Each type of coding has benefits and drawbacks. Coding without a predetermined coding scheme allows for a more holistic understanding of the text but can become overwhelming and is more subject to the interpretation of the person conducting the analysis. Using a predetermined coding scheme allows for quicker and more succinct analysis of the data but with the drawback of potentially missing some of the information that the data set provides.

QUANTITATIVE ANALYSIS

Content analysis. Yes, you are reading correctly. Content analysis can be conducted quantitatively as well. Quantitative content analysis involves coding not to determine meaning but to determine quantity. You would follow the same steps as those detailed in the previous section about qualitative content analysis, but then instead of looking for meaning, you would count how many times each code occurred to determine the prevalence (which implies importance) of each theme. In keeping with the previous example of coding inquiries on your organization's Facebook page, this would tell you not what the inquiries mean but simply how often each type of inquiry occurred in a one-month time frame. This could highlight which areas of your company stakeholders are most interested in or which areas of communication you need to clarify.

Statistical analysis. Statistical analysis is used to analyze survey data and make statements about the beliefs and preferences of respondents in terms of percentages. Data can be compared among groups and within groups, measure how closely related two variables are, determine if one variable predicts another, and more. For example, a stakeholder survey could ask questions about stakeholders' general social media use (e.g., how heavy their social media use is in terms of time spent daily, number of platforms visited daily, number of friends on each platform), social media use relative to the organization (e.g., do they follow the organization, how often do they like, comment, or share content), and outcomes, such as identification with and loyalty to the organizational brand. Using a statistical program like SPSS, statistical analysis could show *if* there is a relationship among these variables, *how strong* the relationship is, and if this relationship is stronger relative to demographic data, such as gender, race, and age.

Tabulation. Tabulation involves the simple counting and sorting of quantitative data. An example would be counting and sorting the number of likes, comments, and shares of posts on your organization's Facebook page, the number of unique visitors to each of your social media platforms, how many people used a specific promo code, and more.

APPLYING THE CONCEPT TO YOUR OWN SITUATION

USING RESEARCH TO ASCERTAIN YOUR CURRENT POSITION

The general cycle of research-action-measurement-evaluation that we use for organizations can also be applied to us as individuals. As you prepare to enter the workplace, you want to perform preliminary research to figure out where you stand in relation to your goals, your peers, and field expectations.

While we will talk about the importance of goals and SMART objectives in the next section, you likely have an intuitive sense of who you are, how you want to be perceived, and how you plan to accomplish this. Your goals serve as a marker for what you want to achieve. So, before you even set an overall goal and corresponding objectives, you have to conduct research to figure out where you already stand. So, for example, if you know you have a general goal to work in the communication field, you would want to conduct research to find out what types of jobs are available in communication and what types of qualifications they require. You could accomplish this by using secondary data, such as the job site Indeed. You could then compare your existing skills and experiences to the listed job criteria and, based on what you find, set an objective to obtain an internship in the next semester.

You not only want to see where you stand in relation to yourself but also in relation to your peers. What experiences and qualifications do others who are entering the communication field straight out of college have? You can research other communication programs online and take note of the experiences that students at other institutions are having in their programs, join campus clubs related to your major or similar majors to see what other students in your school are doing, or join a professional organization, such as the Public Relations Student Society of America (http://prssa.prsa.org/) or the communication honors society Lambda Pi Eta (https://www.natcom.org/student-organizations/lambda-pi-eta) to network with your peers.

Other ways you might research to ascertain where you stand are Googling yourself, conducting a personal social media audit (which we will discuss in the "Tools and Processes for Self-Action" section), and soliciting feedback via an informational interview. The data that you receive from these activities can tell you what types of information are publicly available about you and how industry professionals perceive you. How you analyze this data, or the conclusions that you draw from them, can help you determine your next steps.

THE IMPORTANCE OF GOALS AND SMART OBJECTIVES

As we discussed in Chapter 1 and alluded to in the previous section, goals and objectives serve as an overall statement of where you want to be and the steps you need to take to get there. Commonly, you will set one goal for yourself that serves as your "big idea" and then two to three concrete and measurable objectives that will get you there. SMART objectives are as follows:

S – Specific
M – Measurable
A – Achievable
R – Relevant
T – Timely

Essentially, you want to know exactly what you are measuring and what your time frame for measurement is. If your objectives aren't measurable, you will never be able to determine if you've met them or not, and you will likely not move toward your goal in a substantive way. Likewise, if you don't put an end point on your objective, it will lose its power.

A relevant goal for you right now might be the following: *To obtain a career in a strategic communication field upon graduation.*

Three objectives to help you reach your goal might be as follows:

1. Narrow down my field of interest to three subareas of strategic communication by the end of the first semester of senior year.

2. Research job qualifications for each area and make sure I have a minimum of the three most relevant skills and experiences for each subfield by the end of the first semester of senior year.

3. Apply for 15 jobs in the month before graduation.

Broken down in this way, accomplishing your goal seems much simpler and more achievable than simply saying, "I want to get a job when I graduate." Engaging in a SMART goal setting process creates a clear path that you can follow to get to where you want to be.

MEASURING PERSONAL PROGRESS

Just as performing an evaluation at the end of a campaign can determine the success of that campaign, taking stock while you are working toward your goal and once you've reached your goal can show you what you've achieved, what worked, and what you can learn from the journey to do even better in the future. While it is unlikely that you will use surveys or focus groups, you can use self-reflection, personal metrics, and outside feedback to determine your progress.

Journal and take notes. Journaling has proven benefits for helping us battle depression, gain perspective on our lives, and learning more about ourselves in general. But did you know that journaling can have benefits when it comes to your career as well? Just as with traditional journals, there are several ways that you can approach work through journaling. For example, you can keep a more task-based journal focusing on goal setting, a daily idea or task log, and note taking/brainstorming. Or, you could take a more reflective approach that involves lessons learned, personal and professional wins, advice, venting, or vision-board-style goal setting.

Tabulate. A more quantitative method of measuring personal progress, tabulation, simply involves counting metrics that you find important. This will be highly dependent on your own situation but could involve counting how many goals you have reached, projects you have finished, new contacts you have made, or how much money you have brought in (if you are account based). Just as with all measurements, you have to decide what is important to *you* and then measure it.

Solicit feedback. Getting feedback from peers, supervisors, and clients can be an extremely effective way to measure your personal progress. You can get both on-the-spot feedback or feedback related directly to what you are doing, as well as more reflective feedback, such as how you have progressed over the long term. When choosing someone to give you feedback, it is important to ask someone with whom you have done substantial work, as well as someone who will be honest but tactful and has your best interests in mind. We will also talk about how to solicit feedback from potential employers or industry leaders in the "Tools and Processes for Self-Action" section of this chapter.

Again, you have to know what, specifically, you want to assess. While you may want a "big-picture" overview of how you are doing, it is important that you pinpoint specific areas that you are most interested in and then create your questions accordingly. That is, make sure you are asking questions that will get you the information you want. While soliciting feedback can be a stressful and even awkward experience, if you choose the right people with the right mind-set, it can be a great learning experience.

QUESTIONS:

- What has been the explicit or implicit basis for my career positioning so far?

- How might research and assessment be most helpful as I seek to progress in my career in the near future?

- What research and assessment tactics are likely to be most useful for advancing my career strategy and my career itself?

Tools and Processes for Self-Action

SOCIAL MEDIA AUDIT

Do you plan what you post on social media, or do you fly by the seat of your pants? Do you try to keep it professional, or is it an open place for self-expression? Regardless of how you answered these questions, you are at a time in your life when a social media audit is necessary. A social media audit is a systematic inquiry into your online presence. The following template, adapted from Freberg, 2019, can help you to ascertain your current position and make changes relative to your personal and professional goals, ultimately resulting in a stronger personal brand:

1. You might be tired of hearing it, but all measurement starts with knowing what type of information you are trying to find. Start with your goals. Do you have goals for social media? If not, now is the time to make some. You will then measure everything you find out in your audit against these goals. Some goals might include professional reflecting of your brand (revisit Chapter 2 if you need a refresher), posting a certain number of times, connecting with a certain number of people, garnering a specific amount of engagement, or connecting with leaders in the local communication field. As a side note, if you aren't considering the career implications of social media as you create your goals, you should be. A professional and credible social media presence can make you a stronger job candidate, as well as give you practice in tailoring your messaging for specific stakeholders. Because everyone uses platforms differently, you may have very different goals for Snapchat than you do for Twitter. Feel free to make some platform-specific objectives, but each of them should either support, or at least not interfere with, your overall goal and/or brand that you want to reflect.

2. Analyze each of your platforms in terms of the following:

- Any photos or images on your page

- Your social media handle or name

- How many posts you have created over the time frame of your choosing

- Average engagement (likes, shares, comments) for each of your posts. You can look at raw numbers or how much engagement you are getting proportionate to how many followers you have

- The sentiment of your posts. Are you generally upbeat? Negative?

- The sentiment of the comments you receive

- Google yourself. Does any of your social media content come up when you search the Internet? Is it favorable or not?

- Evaluate the types of posts that garner the most engagement and portray you in a way that reflects your personal brand

3. The next step is to compare these metrics to your goals. Are you meeting your social media goals, or is there a gap between your social media goals and your social media reality?

4. Create action steps based on your findings.

SOLICITING FEEDBACK FROM PROFESSIONAL LEADERS

An informational interview is an informal interview with someone in your field of interest. Informational interviews are not interviews for a specific position but rather provide you with an opportunity to ask questions about careers in the field. Informational interviews give you the opportunity to practice your interview skills and serve as a research tool through which you can gain valuable information about the field, as well as feedback on your experience and presentation skills. Because corporate communication is a diverse field with many subareas, you shouldn't limit yourself to one interview. Set up interviews in a variety of areas that you are interested in.

How do you nail an informational interview?

1. **Do your research.** Research the field. Research the relevant subareas (e.g., external communication, social media). Or if you have already identified specific organizations in which you want to work, research those organizations.

2. **Find a contact and reach out.** There are several ways to secure an informational interview. Many of them come back to your personal and academic networks. Check with your family. Do you have a family member or a friend of a family member in the field you want to enter? Check with your professors and campus Career Centers. Most professors have at least some contacts within the field they are teaching and are usually more than

happy to connect you with them. Check with your peers. You never know who has a parent/aunt/uncle/family friend in a relevant position. Campus Career Fairs are also a great place to connect with potential interviewers. Feeling brave? Check LinkedIn for alumni or even try to connect with someone who holds a relevant position in an organization that you are interested in. Many professionals are happy to give back.

3. **Prepare.** Decide what you want to know and formulate questions that will get you those answers. Develop open-ended questions rather than "yes/no" questions. Use the research that you did in step one to help you with your questions. Most informational interviews last approximately 30 minutes; make sure you develop and sequence your questions to get the most important information in that amount of time.

4. **During your interview.** Be professional in terms of dress, speech, and demeanor. According to job search site Monster, dress and act for the position you want to obtain (Martin, n.d.). Be courteous and interested. Ask your questions but also follow the lead of the person you are interviewing.

PROFILE OF INDIVIDUAL EXPERIENCE:

Kwan Morrow

Kwan Morrow is the founder of KM Digital Relations, a strategic communication firm that focuses on social media strategy. Mr. Morrow said that data analysis is the "bread and butter" of his service and how he proves his value to clients. He not only uses research and analysis for clients but also to chart and track his own professional career. Mr. Morrow entered the field 10 years ago when social media use for organizations was in its beginning stages. Because he was charting new territory, he had to rely on research and assessment to create his own course through the social media landscape. Mr. Morrow said, "Starting out, I constantly researched how companies were using social media, the latest strategies, and how it could fit into a company's overall marketing. When I began to interview for positions, the companies were pleasantly surprised with my familiarity with it and it made it much easier for me to find the perfect job."

FIGURE 8.3 **Kwan Morrow**

Once he started working, research and analysis continued to be an important part of his success. Because social media was still new, he didn't have a boss with years of experience to guide him. To close the gap, he researched non-stop, both at work and after hours, as a way to prove his value and sell the importance of social media, as he said, "Literally creating my career ladder as I climbed it." As he continued to progress in his career and worked toward opening his own agency, Mr. Morrow kept a continual eye on how much companies were spending on social media, using that as a barometer of the importance companies were placing on the medium, as well as the opportunity for him to grow his career. Mr. Morrow also noted the growth in social media marketing positions, which further justified his decision to pursue a career in the field.

Professionally, research and assessment are a large part of his work with clients. He describes the research-action-measurement-evaluation cycle as follows:

> Research is key to setting a strong foundation for any strategy, projects, or initiatives we do for clients. That research can include their industry and competitive landscape, their previous results from similar campaigns, and the challenges and pain points their target audience are facing.

> Based on that research we set tough, but realistic goals for their initiatives. Everything we do after that point is aligned with achieving those goals. It drives the strategy and tactics and keeps the campaign focused.

> Measurement is a key part of success. We measure what went right and why, but also what didn't work so well so that we can learn and apply that to future campaigns. The most important type of data in this stage depends on what they were trying to achieve and the goals they set. At its core, probably the most important piece of data is how many new leads or sales were driving for clients. Other campaigns may be focused on driving more awareness, for example, for a new product launch. In these cases, we want to know how many people are seeing the associated content and clicking through to the website to learn more about it. But of course, being social media, we're also interested in the data that tells us how much people are engaging with our social content—likes, retweets, clicks, comments, shares, favorites, etc.

In terms of conducting research and analysis for either personal or professional reasons, Mr. Morrow said, "We live in a data-driven world. But that data doesn't always have to come from sophisticated algorithms and machine learning. Speaking from a social media perspective, oftentimes the best research is accomplished by getting as close to the front lines as possible and observing what's working and what's not. When assessing the results, go into it with an open mind. If you start your research looking for specific outcomes, you're more likely to be so focused on finding evidence to support those outcomes that it's easy to miss the truly valuable data just below the surface."

The advice that Mr. Morrow has for anyone entering the field of corporate communication is as follows:

▪ Take in as much feedback as possible from as many sources as possible. This will help you spot trends and connect the dots, which is where the real insights come from.

▪ Take negative feedback seriously but not personally. It's often the most valuable type of feedback. Decide how relevant it is, learn from it, and keep moving forward.

Questions:

1. Mr. Morrow said that the most important type of data used for evaluation depends on the goals set at the beginning of the project. How can you relate this to charting your own career path?

2. How can you apply Mr. Morrow's insights about research and analysis to preparing for, and growing in, your own career? Create three action steps you can derive from this insight.

3. How can you balance the need for specific goals to guide your research and analysis with Mr. Morrow's advice to keep an open mind and not start your research looking for specific outcomes?

APPLYING THE CONCEPT TO YOUR WORK WITH CLIENTS

USING RESEARCH TO ASCERTAIN THE CURRENT ORGANIZATIONAL POSITION

To set meaningful goals, you have to know where you are starting from. What exactly does this mean? It means engaging in preliminary research to see where you stand relative to yourself, competitors, and the industry at large. Earlier in the chapter, we discussed the various methods involved in media monitoring, or scanning the media to find out what is being said about your organization, who is saying it, what it means, and how it relates to what is being said about your competitors. The most effective methods of research to ascertain your organizational position are as follows:

▪ Environmental scanning

▪ Social listening

- Surveys

- Focus groups

By using these methods, you can measure the following:

- SOV

- Sentiment

- Customer satisfaction

While these methods are useful in ascertaining organizational position before starting a campaign, all of these methods should be employed on a routine basis to measure the efficacy of the organization's external communication, market share, brewing crises, and relationship to competitors.

SMART GOALS AND OBJECTIVES FOR THE ORGANIZATION

Just as SMART goals and objectives can direct our individual actions, they are also important anytime an organization takes action. Because goals are often temporally bound, meaning that we aim to reach them in a certain amount of time, new goals come into play once an organization has achieved previous goals and wants to further that action or go in a new direction, when a new product or service is launching, or during a time of organizational change. SMART goals often accompany campaigns, or long-term, targeted communication endeavors. However, they can also be relevant to other organizational actions, such as finance/revenue, social media metrics/ engagement, market share, customer service, employee satisfaction, and more.

While goals and objectives can be influenced by internal and external organizational context, they should always stem from the organization's mission and values. Ultimately, all organizational communication and action should be a reflection of *what the organization stands for and believes*. In that way, achieving objectives leads to reaching goals, which leads to fulfilling the organization's mission and reinforcing its values. The bonus of approaching SMART planning as a fulfillment of the organizational mission is that it can lead to better internal/external alignment of the organization. That is, if all of the organization's actions and communications line up with its stated goals, then the organization will be acting authentically across organizational boundaries. What people on the inside see is what people on the outside see. When there is alignment between organizational identity ("what the organization thinks it is") and what stakeholders see and experience, identity reputation alignment occurs (Coombs & Holladay, 2010, p. 175). As you will see in the Zappos case study later in this chapter, this can lead to a stronger, more positive reputation.

QUESTIONS:

- How, if at all, has your client already used research and assessment to guide strategic communication efforts?

- How is strategic communication research and assessment most needed by your client at this time?

- What research and assessment tactics are most applicable to the needs of your client, and how should they be adapted for maximum success?

Tools and Processes When Acting for Others

ASSESSING (SOCIAL) SOV

SOV is one of the ways you can analyze the data you get through media monitoring. It is an awareness or exposure metric that shows how much of the market your brand has permeated relative to your competitors. In short, it is a measure of how your exposure compares to that of others in your market/field. In terms of traditional media, such as advertising, SOV can be calculated by dividing your brand's advertising by total market advertising (e.g., brand advertising/total market advertising = SOV). In some ways, calculating SOV is like qualitative content analysis in that you are counting the number of times something occurs. With SOV, you are adding the layer of calculating how many times this happens relative to how many times it happens to others, out of the whole pool of data.

In social media terms, social share of voice (SSOV) is a measure of how often people mention your brand either directly or indirectly (Sehl, 2019). SSOV is calculated in much the same way as traditional SOV: add your total mentions plus the number of competitor mentions to get the total number of industry mentions. Then divide your brand mentions by the total number of total industry mentions and multiply by 100 for a percentage ([your brand mentions/total industry mentions] * 100 = SSOV) (Schleyner, 2018). This is often not done manually but rather through social media dashboards, such as Hootsuite or HubSpot. It may also be helpful to calculate SOV for your two or three closest competitors for a more detailed view of where you stand.

Why is it important? In the case of SSOV, more is most often considered better, as it can be seen as a proxy for popularity and influence (Sprout Social). As with traditional SOV, it is also a measure of exposure to your brand. In addition, SSOV can offer several strategic benefits, including the following (Sehl, 2019):

- **A look at the "big picture" of your specific market.** What brands are people talking about, what are they saying, and where do you fit into the mix?

- **The efficacy of your campaigns and messaging.** If people are talking about you, then you know that you are reaching them. If you add sentiment analysis (analyzing the sentiment or tenor of the data in terms of positive, negative, and neutral), you will also know if people are saying good or bad things about your brand.

■ **Learning more about your stakeholders.** Once you know who is talking about you, then you can segment the data demographically, geographically, and by tenor. This will tell you who you are and aren't reaching and to what effect.

USING "BIG DATA"

Approximately 90% of the data in the world was created in the last 2 years (Peterson, 2018). That is a staggering statement. Advances in technology over the last 20 years, especially Internet-based technology, has led to a proliferation of available information that businesses of all types can use to inform decision making, improve performance, and even predict behaviors (Weiner & Kocchar, 2016a, 2016b). Such information, when gathered for the purpose of analysis, is referred to as big data. Put simply, big data is "high-volume, high-velocity and/or high-variety information assets that demand cost-effective, innovative forms of information processing that enable enhanced insight, decision making, and process automation" (Gartner, n.d.). Such data includes the information generated as we navigate the Internet, use GPS-equipped smartphones, are active on social media, use call centers, create marketing leads, generate lifestyle and economic data, create large volumes of e-mail or other electronic repositories, and more (Peterson, 2018; Weiner & Kocchar, 2016a;). In industry terms, big data refers not only to the data itself but also to the process of analyzing large volumes of data for patterns.

Big data is marked by four properties: volume, velocity, variety, and value (Weiner & Kocchar, 2016a, 2016b). *Volume* refers to the large amount of data and its finely detailed nature; *velocity* is the speed at which the data can be gathered and analyzed; *variety* refers to the types of data; *value* is the unprecedented level of insight and predictive power that big data brings to the process of research, analysis, and evaluation. Big data can be used to perform many of the research methods discussed previously, including content analysis and sentiment analysis. This may seem strange given the role human interpretation plays in qualitative content analysis. However, text reading tools, such as SAS Sentiment Analysis, can group data by key words associated with sentiment, giving a fairly accurate account of the overall tenor of a text. NodeXL, another analysis tool for big data sets, can be used to map out the relationships among social network users using social network analysis. However, human analysis remains an important part of the process. In the case of automated sentiment analysis, human researchers still have to go through to check the coded data (often only a percentage of the data that constitutes a representative sample) and make sure that the codes are applied correctly. For example, automated coders often cannot read sarcasm and may code something as "positive" even when the true meaning is negative. While NodeXL can map relationships, it is up to the human researcher to decide if the most central person in the network is acting as an influencer, and if so, if that is positive or negative. In short, it is up to humans who understand the *context* of the data to decide what the data actually means.

THE BENEFITS OF BIG DATA FOR STRATEGIC COMMUNICATION

Big data is increasingly becoming a valuable tool in strategic communication, and it is important for you to understand it as you move into the field of corporate communication. As we have discussed throughout this chapter, research and assessment are a continual part of the communication process: they precede goal setting and action, should take place during action to make sure you are on the right track, and follow extended periods of action, such as campaigns to determine efficacy. Big data allows for more informed decision making and planning.

Big data enhances analysis in many areas, including sentiment analysis, stakeholder analysis, social listening, media monitoring, and more, all of which can assist in assessing the reach, influence, and action-based outcomes of organizational initiatives. This information can be used to create more targeted objectives, strategies, and tactics, enhancing overall communication and relationships (Weiner & Kocchar, 2016a).

While big data holds a lot of promise for enhancing the strategic communicating function, like any tool, it must be used correctly and with intention. Weiner and Kocchar (2016a) recommend asking the following questions before integrating big data into the organization's communication strategy:

- What is the goal of data-driven communications?

- How will the data and findings help achieve objectives?

- What is the source of the data?

- In what ways will the data applications interact/interrelate with others?

- What can be done to ensure data alignment?

- Regarding talent, does the team have big data skills for critical thinking and statistical analysis? Who will lead the initiative? Who will conduct the analysis?

- Are tools available to capture relevant content to produce accurate data?

- What can be done to create an environment that encourages discovery and learning through data (rather than "data as a scorecard")?

- How much investment will be required? Do the intended findings and subsequent applications merit the investment?

PROFILE OF ORGANIZATIONAL EXPERIENCE:

Zappos

Zappos, an online retailer of shoes and clothing, is a company known for its excellent customer service and the promise to "deliver happiness." Zappos is a great example of the importance of data and how, in order to have meaning, research and data must be intrinsically connected to other areas of the organization, including leadership and culture. Good research isn't just about collecting numbers. You have to know where you are starting and what your end goal is for you to know what your metrics *mean*.

CEO Tony Hsieh wanted Zappos to be someplace people would want to work, even if they weren't getting paid, and in turn share this feeling of happiness with customers (Tjan, 2010). When he first took the helm of the company, Hsieh primarily hired friends who shared his ethos. Before Zappos was financially stable, Hsieh and others in the company took little to no pay to keep the company going (Hsieh, 2010). Although money was an integral part of his plans for the business, Hsieh's bottom line was connectedness, fun, and creating something bigger. Hsieh said, "A lot of companies fall into the trap of just focusing on making money, and then they never become a great company" (Hsieh, 2010, p. 121).

In 2003, Zappos set the goal of $1 billion in gross merchandise sales by 2010. To do this, Hsieh realized that despite the company's immediate need to get through cash-flow issues, Zappos needed to think long term. He decided that their big vision was to build Zappos's brand and culture around the best customer service. From then on, the mission to have the best customer service drove all future actions and goals, including becoming the number one e-commerce company (Hsieh, 2010).

Great customer service at Zappos was built on delivering WOW service and having a strong, positive company culture. Delivering great customer service became an overflow of employees' commitment to the organizational culture. WOW service "goes beyond fulfilling basic customer expectations and does so in a creative, unexpected way" (Solomon, 2018, para. 1). One of the main ways that Zappos does that is through opening up as many direct channels of communication with customers as possible, including the often-forgotten phone. Hsieh (2010) said, "On most websites, the contact information is usually buried at least five links deep and even when you find it, it's a form or e-mail address that you can only contact once." We take the opposite approach. We put our phone number (1-800-927-7671) at the top of every single page of our website, because we actually want to talk to our customers. And we staff our call center 24/7" (p. 143). Members of the call center, called the Customer Loyalty Team (CLT), are encouraged to build emotional connections with callers by going the extra mile. This can mean anything from bonding over the fact that they have the same name, to finding out-of-stock shoes with a different vendor, to surprising customers with upgraded shipping.

Given Zappos's bottom-line goals and objectives, their measurement differs from the typical call center key performance indicators (KPIs) of "time to resolution" and "call times." In typical industry terms, the shorter those two metrics are, the better. But Zappos uses metrics to measure the customer service experience, including the following:

- **Total call time.** Zappos focuses on the percentage of time a CLT member spends on the phone out of his or her day. Not only are CLT members expected to spend as long as it takes to build a connection on each phone call, but they are also expected to spend 80% of their time interacting with customers (Verill, n.d.).

- **WOW moments.** Zappos employs a 100-item Happiness Experience Form that measures factors such as if the CLT member attempted to make a personal emotional connection, build rapport, and address unstated needs (Verill, n.d.).

- **Active chats.** Zappos employees are expected to treat online chats the same way they treat phone interactions: by building a personal connection and providing a WOW experience. Chat efficacy is measured similarly to phone calls, with the added metric of "abandonment time" or times when there is an open chat, even though the customer is no longer on the chat (Verill, n.d.).

- **Customer satisfaction.** Zappos uses a Net Promoter Score from customer satisfaction surveys (Verill, n.d.).

In addition to these KPIs, Zappos also monitors and rewards attendance and punctuality, measures the strength of internal employee networks by having employees rate familiarity with colleagues, and engages in one-on-one "culture reviews" with employees to give and get feedback on areas such as core values, performance, leadership, and growth potential (Verill, n.d.; Cheng, 2013).

Zappos hit its goal of $1 billion in gross merchandise sales in 2008, two years ahead of schedule. Hsieh credits achieving this success to focusing resources on Zappos's "BCP" (brand, culture, pipeline). By identifying what was most important, building the business around it, and using the right metrics to measure success, Zappos was able to accurately gauge progress toward goals and achieve success.

Questions:

1. Although this case study implies that Zappos is taking a successful route to research and measurement, do you agree? What might the company be missing? What suggestions might you have for improvement?

2. Take a look at one of Zappos's social media platforms. Do both Zappos's and customers' comments indicate that Zappos is successful in its goal of delivering the best customer service? Why or why not? Do you have any suggestions for Zappos based on what you see?

3. What connection do you see between Zappos's measurement of internal and external factors? Why is this important?

Chapter Conclusion

This chapter focused on the importance of charting a path for strategic communication that includes preliminary research, goal setting and action, and evaluation. Knowing where you are and where you want to go are the first steps to setting the right course. Knowing which questions to ask and how to answer them through data collection and analysis are how you know if you're on the right course and, ultimately, if you reached the correct destination. This process has value for both organizations and individuals. While formal research and assessment can sometimes seem like an intimidating process, hopefully, this chapter showed you that when you ask the right questions and collect the right data, you can get powerful answers.

Key Words

Assessment

Big data

Brand listening

Campaigns

Coding

Content analysis—qualitative

Content analysis—quantitative

Criteria

Data

Environmental scanning

Feedback

Focus groups

Generalizability

Goal

Hootsuite

Informational interview

Interviews

Longitudinal data

Measurement

Media scanning

Methods

Preliminary research

Primary research

Purposive sample

Qualitative

Quantitative

Random sample

Research

Reliability

Secondary research

Share of voice

SMART goals

Social listening

Social media audit

Social media sentiment

Social share of voice

Statistical analysis

Surveys

Statistical power

Tabulation

Triangulation

Chapter Discussion Questions

1. Why is triangulation important? Which methods do you think complement each other and why?

2. Taken together, what are all of the methods and metrics we discussed in this chapter an indicator of? Why is this important to the organization?

3. Read the Forbes article titled "How Big Data Became 'Big Bad Data.'" What are your thoughts on the benefits and drawbacks of big data? Do your

actions regarding sharing/protecting your data line up with your stance on the subject?

4. Much of the data that we discuss in this chapter comes from individual people on public platforms, such as social media pages. Do you think collecting and analyzing this data is an invasion of privacy? Do you see any ethical dilemmas associated with using social media data in research and analysis?

Chapter Activities

1. Conduct a brief study about your college/university. Choose a topic related to your school (e.g., quality of the dining hall/cafeteria). Create a brief survey (approximately 15–20 questions) and five focus group questions that ask your target audience about their impressions of this topic. Administer your survey and conduct a focus group. Analyze your results. How did your results differ between the two types of methods? What did your survey data tell you that your focus group data didn't, and vice versa? Did you find one more useful than the other? How does this emphasize the benefits of triangulation?

2. Conduct a social media audit of your personal accounts as described in this chapter. Use both qualitative and quantitative analysis. What did this audit tell you about your social media presence? Were you surprised? Create one goal, two objectives, and three strategies for your future social media postings based on these results.

3. Go through the steps of selecting someone with whom you could conduct an informational interview. Conduct research and prepare your questions. If you feel ready, reach out and schedule the interview! If you choose to do the interview now, record what you got out of it and what you might change for next time.

Recommended Reading and Resources

"Do You Know the Difference Between a Goal and an Objective?"

https://www.fastcompany.com/776233/do-you-know-difference-between-goal-and-objective

"Understanding Goals, Strategies, Objectives and Tactics in the Age of Social"

https://www.forbes.com/sites/mikalbelicove/2013/09/27/understanding-goals-strategies-objectives-and-tactics-in-the-age-of-social/#87650e74c796Hootsuite.com

Hootsuite is a social media content management platform that allows businesses to research, plan, and post social media content. The company's website is full of interesting and useful articles about concepts discussed in this chapter.

"Why You Should Keep a Work Journal" https://www.inc.com/jessica-stillman/why-you-should-keep-a-work-journal.html

"How to Get the Feedback You Need"

https://www.inc.com/jessica-stillman/why-you-should-keep-a-work-journal.html

"Informational Interviewing"

https://www.monster.com/career-advice/article/informational-interviewing

"3 Steps to a Perfect Informational Interview"

https://www.themuse.com/advice/3-steps-to-a-perfect-informational-interview

LEADING AND MANAGING
Taking Care of the Overall Strategic Communication Enterprise

This chapter addresses the ongoing processes of leading and managing strategic communication for you and any organization you may represent. It references different conceptions of leadership and management created to apply to organizations that we extend to individuals. The topic of leadership is addressed in some traditional respects yet is considerably broadened in terms of how it has come to be known from a communication standpoint. The long-standing topic of management is likewise considered in general terms and as something uniquely communication oriented. The area of project management is explored for its overall growth and value to many working as corporate communication professionals. The topics of diversity, equity, inclusion, and intercultural communication are also introduced. It is important for corporate communication professionals to regularly self-reflect on these matters and keep them front and center in the work they do for others. The issue of the corporate communication professional sometimes leading in the foreground and at other times leading in the background is an important theme throughout this chapter.

Orienting to the Concept:
Strategic Communicators as Leaders

Not too long ago, communication professionals were predominantly seen as tacticians. Only in the past 20 years have most large organizations added corporate communication leadership roles, such as vice president of corporate communication or strategic communication. Prior to that time, the communication function was relegated to the marketing or human resource departments. There may have only been a communication coordinator or director. Top leaders, typically without high regard for the value of communication expertise, made decisions and instructed rank-and-file communicators to simply get the word out.

The situation has changed. Most organizations realize that, for better or for worse, communication is vital to their prospects. Accordingly, they want to unlock the power of corporate communication and are willing to give high formal status to those professionals who lead the effort. This has been driven in part by the recognition that we live in a fast-paced information society in which scandals can take down even the best brands, even those not viewed by the general public as communication centered.

The complexity and high stakes of communication in large organizations are also evident in other corporate communication areas, and this affects leadership possibilities in our field. Corporate communication professionals are not just powerful leaders employed at the most senior levels of large organizations; for instance, many corporate communication professionals working as consultants are notable leaders too. This is just one example. There is room to rise in almost all corners of the field. This is an exciting time to be venturing out because it is a time of potential.

The topic of leadership in corporate communication involves grasping how leadership is a fundamentally communication-based activity, how various types of leadership knowledge and practice can help strategic communicators in doing work for others, and how corporate communication professionals can thrive and advance in their careers.

Management as it relates to corporate communication can sometimes be minimized since it does not have a visionary quality. However, many management insights and applications exist that can enhance the work that strategic communicators do, particularly in terms of getting the complex work done.

Last but not least, knowledge and skill in the areas of diversity, equity, and inclusion are foundational components for working effectively in our field, especially for leaders and managers.

CENTRAL DEFINITIONS

LEADERSHIP

While a mainstream view of leadership may continue to emphasize a leader's influence on others to achieve a common goal (Northouse, 1997), a view more sensitive to diversity and a communication orientation is leadership as a complex influence process involving one or more leaders, followers, and other stakeholders (modified from Rost, 1991).

MANAGEMENT

Management is the administration of an organization and involves the processes of forecasting, planning, organizing, directing, coordinating, and controlling (Fayol, 1917).

PROJECT MANAGEMENT

A project is "a temporary endeavor undertaken to create a unique product, service or result" (pmi.org, 2019). Project management involves using the processes of initiating, planning, executing, monitoring and controlling, and closing to complete a project (pmi.org, 2019).

STRATEGY

While strategy has several aspects or definitions, a central feature is that it provides a high-level plan (Mintzberg, 1998) or guiding policy (Rumelt, 2011) for achieving goals.

TACTIC

A tactic is an action selected to advance a strategy.

THEORY AND RESEARCH OVERVIEW

Transformational Leadership as Highly Communicative

Transformational leadership has been an established theory of leadership for many decades (Northouse, 1997). It is notable here because it has been researched in terms of its communication characteristics (e.g., Men, 2014a, 2014b), and it may be a leadership style that is of heightened importance in an era where worker engagement and an ethical approach are valued.

Transformational leadership is an inspirational form of leadership closely connected to charismatic leadership and contrasting with transactional leadership, the latter a deal-making approach concerned with narrow self-interest (Yukl, 2006). Two primary figures in the development of transformational leadership are Burns and Bass (Yukl, 2006). Burns (1978) sees transformative leaders as mediating differences among different constituencies and motivating others to achieve outcomes beyond short-term self-interests. Bass (1995) emphasizes that a transformative leader is not only someone with emotional appeal (i.e., charisma) but also a person who succeeds at actively engaging others to become involved in reaching shared goals. Notably, while Burns limits the definition of a transformational leader to someone who works in the long-term best interests of those they lead, Bass acknowledges a transformational leader may betray followers' long-term interests (Yukl, 2006). Further, Burns views a transformational approach as distinct from a transactional approach, but Bass accepts that the same leader can use both transformational and transactional means (Yukl, 2006).

Research on internal organizational communication demonstrated that transformational leaders often use face-to-face channels and tend to have followers who are satisfied and communicative (Men, 2014a). Related research has shown strong links among transformational leadership, positive symmetrical communication, and positive employee–organization relationships (Men, 2014b). Other research determined that charismatic and other human-oriented leadership is highly communicative as opposed to task-oriented leadership, which is far less so (De Vries, Bakker-pieper, & Oostenveld, 2010). In addition, this research found that leaders' supportiveness, assuredness, and preciseness are vitally important when communicating with subordinates (De Vries et al., 2010).

CHARACTERISTICS OF TRANSFORMATIONAL LEADERS

- Mediate differences
- Motivate others
- Build relationships
- Human centered
- Focus beyond short-term self-interests
- Emotional appeal
- Engage others
- Focus on shared goals
- Highly communicative
- Often prefer face-to-face channels

Leadership as Fundamentally Communicative and Involving Leadership Narratives

Much of the theorizing on leadership assumes a leader's point of view (Northouse, 1997) and a psychological perspective (Mayfield & Mayfield, 2016). In contrast, communication scholars in recent decades have tended to take a discursive approach that considers leadership as a fluid, meaning-making process heavily involving followers as well as leaders. Gail Fairhurst is a dominant voice in articulating leadership as a communication phenomenon. In a landmark article, she and a coauthor outlined the following value commitments for such an approach to leadership (Fairhurst & Connaughton, 2014, p. 8):

1. Leadership communication is transmissional and meaning-centered.

2. Leadership (communication) is relational, neither leader-centric nor follower-centric.

3. Influential acts of organizing are the medium and outcome of leadership communication.

4. Leadership communication is inherently power-based, a site of contestation about the nature of leadership.

5. Leadership (communication) is a diverse, global phenomenon.

6. Leadership communication is alive with the potential for reflexivity, moral accountability, and change.

The work of Carroll and Levy (2010) very much fits the model put forth by Fairhurst and Connaughton (2014) and provides focus and practicality with the notion of leadership as a communicatively constructed identity. These authors point out that a leader is both a subject and an object. They explain how successful leadership often involves relatively expansive subject-initiated identity work. In general terms, the leader's ability to communicatively create alternative narratives is central to leadership. Although leaders and developing leaders will never be completely free of constraints, the power to author and coauthor desirable narratives is at the heart of what it means to have the capacity for leadership growth.

The Need to Diversify Leadership, Including the Concept Itself

Chin and Trimble (2015) provide an excellent overview of how nondominant groups continue to be underrepresented in leadership roles and how certain popular conceptions of leadership have played a role in blocking access. Despite the considerable racial and ethnic diversity in the United States at the present time and the statistical likelihood that there will be no dominant group in the United States in 2050, only a small percentage of Fortune 500 CEOs and directors are visible minorities. Likewise, women are glaringly underrepresented in these positions too.

Chin and Trimble (2015) point out that this unfair situation in the work world has, in some ways, been shaped by notions of leadership that have tended to universalize characteristics that are based on norms for White heterosexual men in Western settings, especially in the United States. Demographic realities alone dictate that our ideas and practices of leadership must better reflect the diversity within the United States and around the world. Important actions include increasing diversity, ensuring inclusion, and welcoming different understandings of effective leadership based on different cultures and contexts.

Diversity Leadership as the Management of Ongoing Tensions

Corporate communication professionals not only have an opportunity to self-develop in terms of diversity-related competencies; they also have an opportunity to directly and indirectly lead others in terms of diversity, equity, and inclusion. Mease (2016) has shown that as corporate communication professionals (for Mease, diversity consultants specifically) go about this work, they are frequently forced to manage two tensions flowing out of an overall responsibility to further both social justice and organizational goals. One tension is between emphasizing broad or narrow constructions of diversity. This tension can manifest in many organizations' more general definitions of diversity versus most activists' definitions that focus on historically oppressed people. A second tension is between focusing on change at the organization level or individual level. Communication professionals tend to value efforts targeting large-scale change over individual-level change; however, commitment of resources is frequently a factor in advancing organizational change. Mease (2016) offers that these tensions are not meant to be resolved but rather embraced, as their management is itself the fundamental diversity work that is necessary organizationally.

Hot-Button Diversity Issues Leaders Must Engage

The diversity landscape in the United States has changed in fundamental ways in recent years that effect all professionals and especially leaders. Three drivers of change have been the Black Lives Matter (BLM) movement, the #MeToo movement, and the growing recognition of the need for protections for members of the LGBTQ community. The BLM movement launched with the acquittal of George Zimmerman in the shooting death of unarmed African American teen Trayvon Martin in 2013 (Bates, 2018). The #MeToo movement surged with the litany of sexual abuse allegations against Hollywood producer Harvey Weinstein and many other prominent men beginning in 2017 (Schmidt, 2017). The LGBTQ movement does not have such a singular inflection point in recent years; however, public polling (McCarthy, 2018) provides one source of evidence for greatly increased acceptance of those with nonheterosexual identities and lifestyle choices.

All three movements have brought attention to structural inequality and much individual-level prejudice and worse, resulting in victimization of historically disenfranchised groups and unfair privilege for historically dominant groups. The upshot of working and leading in this environment is that it is now mainstream to foreground diversity, equity, and inclusion issues in organizations. For members of historically disadvantaged groups, it is increasingly normal to directly claim these identities and confront injustices in the professional world. For members of historically dominant groups, it is time to acknowledge privilege and be an advocate for those who have faced and, in many cases, continue to face injustices, especially by supporting individuals with nondominant identities as they speak with their own voices and advance as leaders.

The Importance of Intercultural Competence for Leaders

All corporate communication professionals need to be adept at intercultural communication, but this is especially the case for those who lead. Intercultural interactions certainly occur when a person travels to another country. They can also occur when working in our home country with those from other places. Deardorff's (2006) process model of intercultural competence provides a way to assess and develop intercultural abilities. The model highlights attitudes, knowledge, skills, and outcomes. Respect, openness, and curiosity are key attitudes. Cultural self-knowledge, wider cultural understanding, and sociolinguistic awareness are notable knowledge components. The skills of listening, observing, interpreting, analyzing, evaluating, and relating are vital for knowledge development and realizing desired outcomes. Adaptability, flexibility, ethnorelativity, and empathy are valued internal outcomes. Communicating appropriately and effectively with others amounts to the primary valued external outcome.

Leading in Different Ways and Developing as a Leader

Leadership does not necessarily mean holding a formal leadership title. Therefore, many, if not most, have the potential to act as a leader. Effective informal leadership is not only a way of making a positive difference for the organization. It can also be a way for someone to establish or enhance his or her credibility and transition to a formal leadership role. Even those holding a formal leadership position may still find themselves using informal leadership in some of their professional interactions. Informal leadership has been shown to involve political will and political skill within a social network (Shaughnessy, Treadway, Breland, & Perrewé, 2017). The skill to lead informally and the wider set of abilities related to navigating a social network largely amount to communication abilities that can be honed.

Johansson, Miller, and Hamrin (2014) have proposed the concept of the communicative leader. The behaviors and principles associated with this concept provide a template for assessing leaders and developing leaders, including in terms of self-development. While all leaders communicate, a communicative leader is someone "who engages employees in dialogue, actively shares and seeks feedback, practices participative decision making, and is perceived as open and involved." The four core communication behaviors of these leaders are as follows: (1) structuring (including planning, allocating, and goal setting), (2) facilitating (including coaching, training, and providing feedback for success), (3) relating (including being friendly and generally supportive), and (4) representing (including gathering information and influencing beyond the unit). The eight principles of communicative leadership are as follows: (1) foster employee self-management, (2) help structure reports' work, (3) set clear expectations, (4) respect employees and set the tone for a positive climate, 5) solve problems and make decisions appropriately and effectively, (6) connect employees' efforts to larger goals, 7) effectively frame messages and events, and (8) support the sensemaking of others.

Managing Strategic Communication Campaigns

Much corporate communication work, especially relatively larger initiatives, takes the form of campaigns. While leadership certainly plays a part, much of the campaign process, especially the handling of the overall endeavor—from planning to pitching to executing to finalizing assessment—is best understood as managerial in nature.

Experts in the campaign process stress the need for research and an overall management process involving the alignment of goals (i.e., the direction of movement), objectives (i.e., measurable demonstrations of movement), strategies (i.e., approaches for achieving objectives), and tactics (i.e., actions for fulfilling strategies) (Austin & Pinkleton, 2006). These authors note that a campaign plan, program proposal, or research report can all be structured in terms of the following sections, with minimal variations: (a) executive summary, (b) situational analysis and research needs, (c) research goals, (d) objectives, (e) research hypotheses, (f) research strategies, (g) results, (h) analysis, (i) proposed communication plan, (j) conclusion, (k) references, and (l) appendices. The core sections of a plan, proposal, or report basically correspond to the flow of how the activities are operationally managed and otherwise carried out.

PROJECT MANAGEMENT PROCESSES

Although project management has its origins in the construction, engineering, and military fields (Cleland & Ieland, 2006), its contemporary form applies to almost all fields. The temporary and unique nature of project management makes it highly relevant to much of what corporate communication professionals seek to accomplish. Not only can the project management concept be applied to a whole corporate communication campaign, but it can also be applied to narrower aspects of a campaign as well as other corporate communication work that is not understood as campaign related.

Over the last 50-years, the field of project management has become very well defined and organized, especially through the Project Management Institute (PMI), the leading not-for-profit professional association for project management (pmi. org, 2019). Strategic communicators at any level in their careers can learn about and apply project management methods on their own or formally study and earn certifications through PMI.

FIGURE 9.1 Characteristics of Transformational Leaders

Here is an elaboration of the five project management processes presented earlier in this chapter under the "Central Definitions" section: (1) initiating—establishing that there is a need and likely return on investment; (2) planning—organizing project resources and communications and creating a task time line; (3) executing—taking direct project-related action, including assigning tasks; (4) monitoring and controlling—getting feedback and making necessary adjustments; and (5) closing—making sure the project goals are achieved and shared with relevant parties and completing any final communications, including documentation to support the success of future projects (PMI, 2017).

APPLYING THE CONCEPT TO YOUR OWN SITUATION

LEADERSHIP IS LIKELY AN IMPORTANT ASPECT OF YOUR INDIVIDUAL BRAND

Maybe you have no experience as a formal leader. Maybe you have no ambition to become a formal leader. Nonetheless, the topic of leadership remains directly relevant, if for no other reason than you will position yourself in relation to leaders beyond yourself, and this will affect not only your individual brand but also how you develop. As a corporate communication professional, you are more likely to enjoy working under and for transformative leaders and leaders who grasp that good leadership qualities are predominantly communication phenomena.

Also, it is important to recognize the potential of informal leadership opportunities for advancing your individual brand. Sometimes you will be offered these opportunities. More often, you will have opportunities to create these opportunities.

At least consider the immediate and longer term benefits of saying "yes" to these defined and less-defined offers. Demonstrating informal leadership is a way for you to test your talents and interests. And fulfilling informal leadership opportunities can demonstrate your initiative to those around you.

Regardless of your own leadership status now or your current aspirations for fulfilling a formal leadership role in the future, it is probably a smart move to keep the possibility open. Potential, emerging, and established leaders often have higher status and more influence and control.

COMMIT YOURSELF TO BEING AN INCLUSIVE LEADER

If you have experience as a member of a nondominant community (especially in terms of race and/or ethnicity, gender, sexual orientation, and socioeconomic status), there is a good chance that you know what it is like to face unfair treatment, and you probably find that you can easily empathize with others in such circumstances. If you have experienced relative privilege, it may be more difficult to recognize how membership in one or more historically dominant group can function as an unfair advantage. Therefore, it may be a challenge to reflect on the advantages you probably gained from your dominant identity/ies and empathize with those who have encountered and possibly continue to encounter substantial system-level and interpersonal barriers.

Leadership is closely associated with power. Take time to deeply assess what gave you access to whatever power and position you may hold. Commit yourself to not only advancing your own power but also fostering the empowerment of diverse others. Do more than welcoming others into the leadership circle. Adjust for the fact that different individuals face different levels of access to entry. Also, find ways to help diverse individuals thrive as leaders, as much as possible, on their own terms. These commitments and demonstrable abilities will likely receive even higher value in the coming years as this nation and the world become more diverse. Raising up others may, paradoxically, be the surest way of raising up yourself.

ANTICIPATE NEEDING TO DEVELOP AS A LEADER

There is a lot to leadership. A successful leader is more likely to be someone who commits themselves to their ongoing development than someone who pretends, however confidently, to have mastered leadership. The single relatively straightforward concept of the communicative leader (Johansson et al., 2014) offers plenty of challenges with its four core communication behaviors (i.e., structuring, facilitating, relating, and representing), each entailing knowledge and skills that demand revisiting even once they are initially grasped. Of course, even visiting and revisiting one model and its corresponding set of competencies is not enough given the complex challenges of leadership. And an exploration of leadership insights that have begun to stand the test of time should not come at the expense of consideration of cutting-edge thinking and practices. In any case, before and while you lead for clients, you will need to lead your own brand.

APPRECIATE THE NEED TO DEVELOP
AS A MANAGER AS WELL AS A LEADER

Although presently not nearly as attention grabbing as the concept and practice of leadership, the concept and practice of management are vital to corporate communication and, likewise, need to be learned anew throughout a professional communicator's career. Leadership may be simplified as more of an "organized vision thing." Management may be simplified as more of a "mobilizing to accomplish the vision thing." Here the breadth and depth and ongoing development of project management by the PMI shows how strategic communicators can be continually aided and challenged in their growth. Before and while you manage client work, you will need to manage your own brand.

QUESTIONS:

- Who is the leader I might most want to model myself after?

- What is my personal experience of diversity, equity, inclusion, and inter-cultural issues, and how can I responsibly represent myself and broadly support others in these areas?

- What does it mean to be an effective leader and (separately) an effective manager of my own career?

- How do I most need to develop as a leader and manager of my own career, including likely enlisting the help of others?

Tools and Processes for Self-Action

TAKING AN INVENTORY OF YOUR INFORMAL AND
FORMAL LEADERSHIP AND MANAGEMENT RECORD

Taking a chronological or topical approach, generate a list of your key experiences and demonstrated competencies as a leader or manager. It is perfectly fine if you include activities outside your core professional area, including activities from early in your life. Also, identify three pivotal moments that shaped your views on leading and managing. These may be the same as some of your key experiences when you were a leader or manager yourself, or they be times when you learned from the negative or positive example of others acting in these capacities.

CREATING YOUR LEADERSHIP AND MANAGEMENT DEVELOPMENT PLAN

If you are like most people, you probably see lots of different ways you could get better at leading and managing within the broad context of advancing your own career. This realization can be overwhelming. To make your development plan more motivating than deflating, identify just three ways to make yourself better as a leader and manager in the coming year. For each of the three goals you have listed, indicate two or three key steps you need to take. If possible, add a time line for completing your steps and achieving your goals.

GENERATE NARRATIVES THAT ESTABLISH OR ADVANCE YOU AS A LEADER
Narratives or stories that position you as a leader help you focus and boost your confidence. They can also be helpful as you present yourself to others. These narratives do not necessarily need to be a part of your standard self-introduction. They can just be stories that you organically drop into conversations and other free-flowing communications. These stories can directly or indirectly highlight your leadership and management experience or potential. They can capture instances when you got things exactly right, or they can be times when you learned important lessons.

PROFILE OF INDIVIDUAL EXPERIENCE:

John Burk

John E. Burk received his PhD in speech communication from Southern Illinois University in 1996. He is a human resources manager at Intel Corporation focused on aligning talent, teams, leaders, and organizations to execute business strategies within high growth organizations. He leads organizational design, development, and change management initiatives for the businesses he supports. Previously, John served in senior executive roles in government and as an educational technology consultant in secondary and higher education, in addition to being a faculty member at Arizona State University. He is a frequent presenter at conferences and has several publications in journals and handbooks.

FIGURE 9.2 John Burk

While John is an expert on leadership communication, he also remains a student. He has continued to be inspired and impacted by three leadership giants: former U.S. secretary of state Colin Powell, former U.S. president Jimmy Carter, and former Pakistan prime minister Benazir Bhutto. John explained, "Colin Powell is my model for my leadership approach and style: Listen first, get the best from your team, and let your team decide the way to execute. Jimmy Carter is my model for servant leadership: Lead by doing, and be authentic, humble, kind, and gracious. Benazir Bhutto is my model for understanding the risks of leadership and doing what is right: Commit to a cause greater than yourself, literally greater than your own life."

John has many thoughts about what has helped him to continue to develop in his career, but four stand out for him. His 30-years of military experience was milestone-based, and he learned and applied different leadership communication principles in moving from frontline leader to middle manager to senior leader to strategic leader. In advancing from frontline project manager positions to supporting the strategic execution of senior leaders in business and industry, John has seen the importance of using leadership communication training to build trust and create a climate of transparency. His time as a graduate student and his ongoing experience as a scholarly practitioner allows him to reflect deeply and share his ideas with others. He has written articles and book chapters on leadership communication, group/team communication, and organizational communication. John is also particularly proud of challenging the White and male norms in leadership communication. One way he did so was by getting his students at Arizona State University to write a paper on the leadership style and leadership successes of a woman and/or a person of color. John described why a more inclusive conception of leadership is so vital: "We must expand our view of leadership since we live in a diverse society. Take time to recognize the Parkland High School survivors' leadership in advocacy. Take time to recognize the global leadership for cultural and societal change in the work of Nadia Murad and Malala Yousafzai."

John's single leadership high point so far is when he was the senior leader/brigade commander for a 2,200-person organization consisting of five subdivisions and 23 frontline organizations. Employees were concurrently deployed overseas and in Arizona, the latter involving domestic emergency response operations. John summed up their achievements: "I led a core team of incredibly capable leaders that delivered extraordinary results." John noted that shining a spotlight on others' accomplishments was effective and satisfying for all concerned. "I ensured the disparate organizations came together for reward and recognition events that instilled pride in their individual and organizational accomplishments."

Things have not always proceeded smoothly for John. It was especially difficult when he once worked under a new leader who seemed to have a style entirely unlike his own. John commented on how he chose to handle the situation. "I focused on what I could achieve within my scope of work. I knew I needed to move on at the right time. The situation was unsustainable for both of us. I moved on when I completed the assigned work and a new opportunity arose."

Based on a great deal of study and experience, John is well positioned to provide guidance to others interested in leadership advancement. He encourages leaders to recognize their limitations and act accordingly: "Be willing to seek and acknowledge feedback. And develop a team around you. No one is a perfect leader. Perfection is not the goal. Authentic leadership is the goal and the key to success." For the aspiring leader who may be frustrated with his or her own progress, John offered, "Focus on getting small wins that demonstrate leadership. Seek stretch assignments. Step up when asked or fill a gap on your own initiative." When asked to reflect on the frequency with which business leaders have disappointed in recent decades, John expressed concern for the lack of ethical leadership, noting the likes of Bernie Madoff and the notoriety of toxic leaders, those bullying and demanding followership, like Steve Jobs and Elon Musk. He also urges us to highlight ethical leaders such as Bill and Melinda Gates and Howard Schultz.

In terms of managing the demands of leadership across an entire career, John emphasized the need to maintain a wide perspective. "On a daily basis, assess what is truly important to accomplish and let the rest go. Be self-reflective. Observe and learn from other leaders. Study leadership profiles and practices. Take time to recharge." He also stressed authenticity and commitment to continuous improvement. "Be yourself. It is okay to be vulnerable. There is no best style or approach. Listen and learn. Leadership, like life, is a journey not a destination."

Questions:

1. What, if any, of John's accomplishments would you characterize as informal leadership as opposed to formal leadership?

2. For one of John's formal leadership roles, indicate how he might have had to balance the diversity tensions described by Mease (2016).

3. How has John shown a commitment to diversity, equity, and inclusion? For one of the positions he has held, indicate two additional such efforts he could have taken (i.e., efforts not detailed in the case).

4. What is one thing about John's leadership journey that you admire and would want to accomplish yourself? What is one thing about your leadership journey that you intend to be different than his?

APPLYING THE CONCEPT TO YOUR WORK WITH CLIENTS

GETTING CLEAR ABOUT ACTIVELY LEADING
VERSUS SUPPORTING YOUR CLIENT'S LEADERSHIP

Whether the client you are serving is an employer paying you a full-time salary or an organization contracting with you (or the organization you work under) on a limited basis, it is important to clarify the nature of leadership on the projects in which you are involved. Sometimes corporate communication professionals are sought out to develop a leadership vision that they may or may not then be tasked with making operational. Sometimes corporate communication professionals concentrate on managing or comanaging the implementation of others' leadership visions. Regardless of who is taking charge of the backroom leadership and management issues, it needs to be clarified who is the face of leadership and management. Make sure you always know your roles and responsibilities. Ask if you are unsure.

PROMOTING A MEANING-MAKING VIEW OF COMMUNICATION RATHER THAN SIMPLY A TRANSMISSION-BASED VIEW

Intelligent and accomplished people schooled in disciplines other than communication, including some very senior leaders you may be representing, may think of the concept of communication as simply the transmission of information. At the extreme end, this can be a concrete view assuming there is an objective reality that exists and must be shared with others in as literal a manner as possible. According to this outlook, communication is just a tool to inform and connect individuals about fixed realities.

Most corporate communication professionals hold a constitutive view of communication. This is a much broader, complex, and dynamic view of communication. Here communication is seen as essential to all meaning-making. Everything is up for grabs. The nature of messages, situations, and other seemingly stable constructs like identity are all malleable.

Supporting clients, especially clients who are formal leaders, in grasping a constitutive view can be foundational to them grasping the value of you, your strategic advice, and your strategic capabilities. A constitutive view underlies the concept of a transformational leader and other highly applicable scholarly insights into leadership. Also, it makes the nuances of broader issues like diversity, equity, and inclusion far easier to appreciate and act upon appropriately and effectively.

MANAGEMENT AS THE SKILL SET FOR MAINTAINING THE COURSE

Leadership, in terms of who holds a top title and who establishes the strategic direction, can get the glory, but those championing corporate communication management should not be overlooked. Clients frequently need help working out the details of planning, acting, dealing with contingencies and unforeseen developments, and backend assessment. Creating task time lines, assigning work to team members, and ensuring that team members are provided feedback and are held accountable are largely managerial responsibilities you may find yourself handling. The discipline, perseverance, and stamina of management may very well be needed to make the big ideas of leadership come to life.

QUESTIONS:

- How can you best establish credibility as a leader in the eyes of the client(s) you most want to represent?

- What client leadership matters can you responsibly lead and manage on your own versus those that may require you to partner with others?

- Are there particular client leadership matters you would not be willing to represent as a corporate communication professional? Explain.

- To what degree are you comfortable working in professional roles where client-leaders may get much of the acclaim for your ideas and hard work?

Tools and Processes When Acting for Others

INITIAL CONSULTATIONS AND COACHING TO ENSURE THE FOUNDATION OF LEADER CREDIBILITY

Sometimes you will work directly for a leader to advance the agenda tightly associated with that leader. Other times you will work under a leader but have your work framed as generally supporting a group or division or the overall organization. Regardless of the arrangement, it is wise for you and the leader or leaders with whom you are associated to address some foundational issues. The purpose is to do your best to make sure they have basic credibility and are not presently doing anything that could jeopardize it. This can be accomplished with one or more initial interviews, possibly combined with some executive coaching. This approach is more appropriate and easier to carry out if you are looked upon as an established professional. These duties may fall to someone else if you are a junior member of a partnership or team.

Brainstorm basic questions ahead of time to learn about the leader's and organization's histories and context. Inquire about what has gone well and what has not. Learn about and support the leader's own reflecting process in terms of his or her patterns of success and difficulty. Pay special attention to the person's leadership and management philosophies and practices. Listen for indirect clues and talk directly about the leader's approach to diversity, equity, inclusion, and intercultural issues. Be prepared to directly address problematic issues by describing not only what is at stake for others but also what is at stake for the leader. Support the development of the leader with clear positive alternative behaviors, including appropriate and effective ways of talking to and about different individuals and groups. Practice communication skill development with the leader, if necessary.

USING CONTRACTS AND OTHER WRITTEN PLANS

In a fast-moving world, it can be easy to forget to invest the time in creating written contracts and other written plans or dismiss their importance entirely. The problem with a carefree and unsubstantiated approach to these aspects of work-life is increased exposure to uncertainty and other forms of risk for all concerned. It is a good basic business practice to have a written contract in place between you and your employer whether the company is paying you a salary, paying you on a part-time basis, or paying you as a contractor. Likewise, it is a good basic business practice to develop a written plan for the scope of any project you have a role in designing or implementing. Normally, a contract is a private matter between you and the point person for the organization paying you. The plans for the corporate communication projects in which you are involved are typically shared among many individuals (e.g., those co-leading and comanaging the initiative). The principle remains the same, though. Written documents provide a framework for clarifying the goals, responsibilities, and relationships of the involved parties. Invest time in them. Get help, if necessary, to understand them, including by working with an attorney. Written documents are a normal part of corporate communication work, especially if you are a leader interfacing with other leaders.

SUPPORTING ORGANIZATIONAL LEADERSHIP WITH INTERNAL CAMPAIGNS OR OTHER PROJECTS

While internal corporate communication should be generally understood as multidirectional, there is no question that initiatives are often launched by top leaders with the intention of being positively engaged by those employed lower down in the organization. These internal communication efforts need to be designed with sensitivity to the fact that they may leak to external audiences; however, they are chiefly created to reflect senior leaders' intentions and resonate with other insiders who are tasked with some level of implementation. Corporate communication professionals serving these top leaders can help in framing and executing these campaigns that frequently begin with information cascades and emphasize the general strength of immediate supervisor–subordinate relationships.

SUPPORTING ORGANIZATIONAL LEADERSHIP WITH EXTERNAL OR COMPREHENSIVE CAMPAIGNS OR OTHER PROJECTS

Efforts to support top organizational leadership in designing and executing small or large external initiatives need exceptional awareness of how communications can be seen differently by various stakeholders and unintended audiences. Large external campaigns regularly address multiple stakeholder groups and use multiple platforms. Corporate communication professionals can be involved in framing, planning, and executing the campaign. Keep in mind that any campaign or project carried out by a corporate communication professional on behalf of an organizational leader has implications for how that leader's reputation is perceived.

PROFILE OF ORGANIZATIONAL EXPERIENCE:

Costco

Costco is a membership-based warehouse store that emphasizes quality and value. The warehouse store concept began in 1976 with the launch of Price Club in California by Sol Price. The first Costco opened in 1983 in Washington State under the leadership of Jim Sinegal and Jeff Brotman. In 1993, Price Club and Costco merged. Upon merging, the company became known as PriceCostco. However, in 1997, the company simply became known as Costco. From 1983 to 2011, Jim Sinegal was CEO of Costco. He was succeeded in this role by Craig Jelinek (Costco, n.d.).

Costco's business model involves making the bulk of its profits from yearly membership dues, stocking a relatively small range of products, purchasing in vast quantities, and then passing on the savings to its members (Lutz, 2014; Meyersohn, 2018). It ranks globally as the second largest retailer in terms of sales (Meyersohn, 2018). Costco has done remarkably well against its main competitors, such as Sam's Club/Walmart, Target, and Amazon (Lutz, 2014; Meyersohn, 2018). For instance, Costco's annual financial growth rates outstripped Sam's Club's rates to the point that the Sam's Club CEO was forced out (Wahba, 2017). And with Costco's member resubscription rate holding steady at 90% and its bargain pricing intact, the company is doing fine in its competition with Amazon (La Monica, 2015; Meyersohn, 2018).

In an era where many companies have a revolving door of CEOs, it is notable that Costco has only had two individuals in the CEO role since 1983. This may speak to the lack of scandals both for these individuals and for the company. Current CEO Jelinek was known for keeping a low profile, even on the eve of becoming CEO (Allison, 2011). David Schick, one of the few Wall Street analysts who met him at the time of his promotion to CEO, described Jelinek as "uniquely patient" and focused on "a very long-term view" for Costco (Allison, 2011).

Costco also stands out for the way it treats its employees. It pays them considerably more than its closest competitor, Sam's Club. It provides good healthcare coverage for its employees. It is committed to hiring from within. The financial generosity of the company toward its employees has caused nagging from Wall Street since the beginning. Yet, ironically, this unwavering loyalty by CEOs Sinegal and Jelinek has turned out to provide investors with decades of incredible financial returns, even versus Sam's Club/Walmart, which has held down and at times cutback spending on employees (B. Stone, 2013; Vocoli, 2015).

Although Costco supposedly has no PR staff (B. Stone, 2013), it has certainly demonstrated masterful messaging. Paying a living wage and providing quality healthcare benefits are material expenditures that function as and trigger positive messaging. The company's financial outlays create a high-level of engagement by Costco employees in terms of providing excellent customer service and decreasing employee turnover. Specifically, Costco generates much more profit per employee than Walmart and spends less on hiring new employees (CSImarket, n.d.; Vocoli, 2015). This culture of valuing employees is also seen in encouraging employee suggestions, allowing managers to show initiative, and hiring from within. For example, employee suggestions resulted in the introduction of skylights and solar panels in Costco warehouses around the world, and these changes brought considerable savings in energy costs (Vocoli, 2015). Costco's long-standing and authentic valuing of employees has been instrumental in creating loyalty not only from employees but also members (i.e., customers) and has also held the attention of investors, at least with the financial growth it has facilitated. Costco demonstrates a social enterprise strategy that involves the generation of positive media attention and has current members and prospective members feeling good about spending at the company (Anderson, 2018; Short, 2013; Z. Stone, 2013).

Questions:

1. Costco derives much of its positive brand image from employee-initiated communication about their satisfaction with the organization. What are two or three leadership actions that have facilitated such success?

2. To what extent have CEOs Sinegal and Jelinek exemplified a transformational or communicative approach to leadership? Choose one of these approaches and explain your point of view.

3. Diversity, equity, inclusion, and intercultural themes are not foregrounded in the Costco narrative. Is it necessary for Costco or any organization to directly address these themes to be dealing with them responsibly and effectively?

4. Many would read the Costco case and conclude that the company has done everything right. Propose a communication-centered enhancement to the company's overall strategy (beyond what you may have suggested in an earlier answer) and explain why this would be beneficial for various Costco stakeholders.

Chapter Conclusion

Leadership and management are topics that seem to many as already known and yet, once you do a deep dive, you can quickly realize their theoretical and practical complexity. The nature of leadership has changed in notable ways in recent decades, especially as a communication view has been applied in academia, and the everyday world has become more fluid. Leadership can be about an individual leader with an agenda to advance, but it can also be about a person with a certain formal or informal position relating with others in ways that make the flows of influence tough to distinguish. Management of strategies may seem less high profile than developing the strategies, yet the complexity of implementation makes management of paramount importance. The rise of project management reflects this value. Finally, diversity, equity, inclusion, and intercultural issues can seem peripheral, but they are central matters in how we self-present, position ourselves as leaders, and support clients as leaders.

Key Terms

Black Lives Matter	Equity
Communicative leader	Inclusion
Diversity	Leadership

Leadership narratives

Lesbian, gay, bisexual, transgender, queer

Management

MeToo or #MeToo

Process model of intercultural competence

Project management

Project management processes

Transactional leadership

Transformational leadership

Chapter Discussion Questions

1. Should a corporate communication professional always strive to position him or herself as an informal leader (if not a formal leader)? Explain.

2. Diversity, equity, and inclusion issues are sometimes difficult to address in organizations. What are some ways that corporate communication professionals can get client organizations to engage these topics appropriately and effectively and lead in these general areas?

3. What should early career corporate communication professionals do or not do to hold open the possibility of becoming widely admired industry leaders in the coming decades?

4. In relation to Mease's (2016) work, what is an organization that has successfully balanced social justice and general organizational goals in terms of its handling of diversity and closely aligned topics?

Chapter Activities

1. Identify a leader and propose two narratives that the person should newly or more actively communicate to enhance his or her own credibility, as well as the credibility of the person's organization. Provide an example of what message should be shared and with whom.

2. For one of your answers to question one, apply the five project management processes to operationalize your idea.

3. To help expand the very concept of leadership, speak with someone who self-identifies with a nondominant group and learn how his or her understanding of "good leadership" may have been shaped by the person's nonmainstream experience.

Recommended Readings and Resources

Erica Weintraub Austin and Bruce E. Pinkleton are long-established experts on corporate communication management. Although their book emphasizes PR, it is a top resource for scholars and practitioners concerned with all types of corporate communication campaigns and projects.

Austin, E. W., & Pinkleton, B. E. (2015). *Strategic public relations management: Planning and managing effective communication programs* (3rd ed.). Routledge.

The concept of leadership may have eclipsed the concept of management in popular discourse, but the concept of project management has taken off. PMI is the premier hub for its development. PMI publishes the *Project Management Body of Knowledge*, offers credentialing programs, and organizes local chapters around the world. Project management competencies are a valuable add-on for many corporate communication professionals. A project management certificate can make you more marketable, and completion of a certificate is sometimes recognized as progress toward a graduate degree, such as a master's in business administration.

https://www.pmi.org/

There are many acclaimed books on leadership. Some of these do not have a strong theoretical orientation. Others have a theoretical orientation that is not necessarily communication oriented. Google a list of these books; read one that looks interesting and explore what its author's recommendations mean from a communication point of view. For instance, the following book by Brené Brown encourages leaders to embrace their own vulnerability. This is a psychological orientation. What might it mean to communicate your own vulnerability in an appropriate and effective way for you and those you lead or manage?

Brown, B. (2018). *Dare to lead*. Random House.

CHANGE

Staying on Top of an Important and Fast-Moving Field

T his chapter emphasizes the importance of looking ahead and continued learning. We will return to the core concept of strategic communication within the field
of corporate communication, offering a long view of the field that emphasizes which
elements have stayed consistent and how the field has evolved. We will examine
the importance of flexibility, forward-thinking, and adaptability as personal traits
that can lead to professional success within the field. You should finish this chapter
with a sense of the evolving field you are entering and the importance of strategy
as an overall guiding force for personal and organizational success.

This chapter will explore the idea of change as applied to both the field of strategic corporate communication and you, as an individual, setting out for a career
within the field. We will begin with a focus on change and the accompanying concept
of adaptation. We will then cover a brief review of the corporate communication
field, considering the major changes it has undergone in recent years, as well as
what has stayed consistent. Changes will be examined on both the macrolevel
(contextual changes) and microlevel (tactical changes). Then we will cover personal
traits and professional practices important to adapting to and anticipating change
and the importance of embracing change to build on skills and practices already
learned. We will conclude with an emphasis on the concept of strategy as the central
element around which personal and organizational success is built.

Orienting to the Concept: Change as the Only Constant

Think back 10 years. What did you look like? What was your favorite thing to do?
What were your goals?

What about now?

Now, think about your surroundings 10 years ago. What was the world like? What
was missing that we have now (Instagram?!). What did we have then that we no
longer have?

The importance, and inevitability, of change has been underscored by philoso-
phers throughout history. Ancient Greek philosopher Heraclitus of Ephesus asserted
that "life is flux," or that everything changes, and change is the only constant in
life (Mark, 2010). Lao Tzu, an ancient Chinese philosopher, said, "Life is a series of

natural and spontaneous changes" (Meah, n.d.). We have all experienced change; sometimes it is abrupt and alters our entire course, and other times it is gradual and hardly noticeable until we look back in time.

Not surprisingly, communication plays a large role in both bringing about and reacting to change. It is through communication that ideas are molded and shared. It is through communication that change is proposed, resisted, accepted, or adopted. It is through communication that we seek to reduce the uncertainty brought about by changing circumstances and ultimately decide which direction to take.

Accordingly, both bringing about and adapting to change plays a large role in strategic corporate communication. For example, in Chapters 4 and 7, we talked about the role of persuasion in strategic communication and how corporate communication professionals can use persuasive messaging to affect the perceptions and actions of stakeholders. In Chapter 9, we talked about how good leadership can be a transformational experience, changing the way one looks at or orients to different situations. Just as strategic corporate communication can be an agent of change, it has also undergone several changes since the advent of the field. We will cover both types of change in this chapter.

CENTRAL DEFINITIONS

CHANGE

At its simplest, change refers to the act of becoming something different. Lewin (1947) refers to change as unfreezing, moving, and refreezing. However, change is not finite and is not always planned. Change results from a combination of internal forces and external forces. Because people and organizations are inextricably intertwined with their environment, change is rarely, if ever, one or the other. For example, we may think we want to change our jobs because of internal drive, but that drive is likely fueled by the media we consume, social contacts we have, or the current social and economic environment. Similarly, organizations adopt new technologies, ways of communicating, or systems of management because it will improve their operations, but those ideas are influenced by stakeholder demands and what other members of the field are doing.

ADAPTABILITY

Adaptability refers to the capacity one has to adjust to a new context or situation. Closely related, adaptation refers to the process of change by which one (animal, human, or social unit) becomes better suited to one's environment.

PROFESSIONS AND FIELDS

A profession is an occupation that includes a systematic knowledge base and formal training (Saks, 2016, p. 172), for example, doctors and lawyers. A field is a collection of organizations that are bound by a set of professional parameters, including "key suppliers, resource and product consumers, regulatory agencies, and other organizations that produce similar services or products" (Dimaggio & Powell, 1983, p. 148). A field represents "an intermediate level between organization and society and is instrumental to processes by which socially constructed expectations and practices become disseminated and reproduced" (Greenwood, Suddaby, & Hinings, 2002, p. 58). While the terms profession and field have unique definitions, they both represent a sociological approach to grouping workers and organizations according to shared parameters, cementing them as a social unit. Related to change, the interrelatedness of organizations bound as professions within a field means that changes and norms are socially constructed as each organization influences, and is influenced, by the rest of the field.

THEORY AND RESEARCH OVERVIEW

As we have discussed throughout this book, we use communication to assign meaning, create identity, and share values. We do this on behalf of ourselves, as well as organizations. Communication is a continual process, because as we communicate meaning into existence, it affects our environment, as well as others within that environment. As a result, as our environment evolves, we communicate to find meaning within new contexts and relationships, which in turn (again) changes our environment.

Because humans make up organizations, organizations make up professional fields (such as corporate communication), and these fields exist within a larger society, looking at how entire fields of practice change draws on multiple levels, including intrapersonal, organizational, and institutional level. That is, understanding how and why we change as individuals and how this plays out on organizational levels can also shed light on how entire fields of practice change. In this section, we will unpack theories regarding different levels of change to provide a holistic view of the concept.

Intrapersonal Change
Change on the individual level can be thought of as intra (or internal) personal change. How and why do we, as individuals, decide to make a change? There are many social science theories that consider this question, such as social cognitive theory, the theory of planned behavior, and the transtheoretical model (TTM; Table 10.1). Each theory posits different variables and relationships among the variables that influence how, when, and why we change. However, there are some

TABLE 10.1 Types of Change

	THEORY	DESCRIPTION
Intrapersonal Change	**Social Cognitive Theory**	There is a reciprocal relationship among who we are, our behavior, and our environment. Our decision to adopt a behavior is influenced by our behavioral capability (i.e., are we able to perform the behavior), what we see modeled by others, reinforcement for the behavior (positive or negative), anticipated outcomes, and our self-efficacy or ability to successfully perform a behavior.
	Theory of Planned Behavior	A combination of our attitude, subjective norms (what we think those who are important to us feel about the behavior), and perceived behavioral control (how much control we think we have over the outcome) lead to behavioral intentions, which lead to behavior.
	TTM	Change occurs in stages, including precontemplation, contemplation, preparation, action, maintenance, and termination.
Group/Organizational Change	**3-Step Model**	Change occurs in a three-step process: unfreezing, moving, and refreezing. This occurs when we leave a state of equilibrium.
Macrolevel Change	**Community Ecology Theory**	Populations of organizations evolve within a community and change as a result of variation, selection, and retention processes. There is a reciprocal connection between micro and macrolevel change.
	Institutional Theory	A five-stage process for change, including *de-institutionalization, pre-institutionalization, theorization, diffusion, and re-institutionalization.*

commonalities among the theories that point to the most important elements of how and why we change (Fishbein et al., 2001):

- **Intentions.** Behavioral theorists state that intention, or having the purpose or goal of doing something, precedes the actual behavior. So, you must intend (or purpose) to change before you will actually change.

- **Environmental constraints.** Environmental constraints are external limitations placed on your ability to take action—for example, a lack of money or legal barriers. The fewer the environmental constraints to overcome to change, the more likely we are to adopt change.

- **Anticipated outcomes.** To adopt change, we must believe that the new behavior or state of being will bring more positive rewards than our current behavior or state.

- **Norms.** Norms can refer to any normalized social standard on the societal or interpersonal level, including how one's most relevant social contacts feel about the change or behavior in question or how socially desirable the change is. Norms can also include perceived social pressure related to adopting or changing behavior (Azjen, 1991, p. 188). According to the theory of planned behavior, we are often more likely to change if we perceive a lot of pressure to do so, or if we perceive that others with significant social value to us agree with the change.

- **Self-standards.** If the change is consistent with our desired self-perception and it does not violate personal standards, we are more likely to adopt the change (Fishbein et al., 2001, p. 5).

- **Perceived self-efficacy.** We are more likely to adopt change that we feel we can successfully engage in. This can be influenced by our perception of skill, resources, knowledge, and more.

- **Emotion.** We are more likely to adopt a behavior when we have a positive emotional reaction to it (Fishbein et al., 2001).

While these factors can affect whether we will adopt change, the TTM model (Prochaska & DiClemente, 1983) proposes that we go through six stages in the process of changing, each of which can be influenced in different ways:

1. **Precontemplation.** We do not perceive a reason to change.

2. **Contemplation.** We have begun to identify a change we want to make but have not yet committed to making it.

3. **Preparation.** We start making small changes in anticipation of making a larger, more impactful change.

4. **Action.** We have adopted the change and have the intention of continuing to behave in a way that is consistent with supporting the change.

5. **Maintenance.** Once we have adopted the change and engage in plans and actions to continue this course of action, we are in the maintenance phase. In this stage, our conviction toward the change, which has become our new status quo, is solidified.

6. **Termination.** There is no desire or intention to return to our old state.

The TTM was originally proposed as a model for behavior change relative to smoking cessation, so it does not necessarily take into account the fact that once we reach a new state, we are unlikely to stay there forever. While we may maintain a new state relative to a health behavior, such as not smoking, in situations that pertain to our social and professional lives, we are likely to continue to evolve as our needs and situations change.

Notice that even these intrapersonal theories of change include external influences, such as subjective norms and environmental constraints. As we mentioned earlier, change does not happen in isolation, but rather, is influenced by our networks and our environment. The next sections will examine change related to organizations and the field of corporate communication.

Group and Organizational Change

Individuals and group interaction affect change at the group and organizational levels. A simple, but intuitive model of group change is the 3-step model (Lewin, 1947), which positions change as a process of *unfreezing*, *moving*, and *refreezing*. According to the 3-step model, we live in a state of *equilibrium*, which is balanced by driving and restraining forces. An example of equilibrium is when supply and demand are equal, thus creating a state in which opposing forces are balanced. When one of the forces slips out of place, equilibrium is destabilized. When this equilibrium is destabilized, beliefs and behavior are unfrozen. Moving involves taking into account "all the forces at work" and evaluating all possible options. Ideally, this involves moving from a less desirable to more desirable set of behaviors (Burnes, 2004). Finally, refreezing involves "stabilizing" the social unit within the new, quasi-stationary equilibrium achieved through moving. While the 3-step model was developed to explain group change, it is the simplicity of its processes that allow it to be adapted to several levels of change. Indeed, its similarity to the macrolevel theories of change discussed in the next section underscores the multilevel interdependency of change.

Macrolevel Change

Macrolevel change, or change to an entire field, is often more of an evolution that an abrupt change. While this evolution is often precipitated by a "jolt," such as a regulatory, technological, or social event (Greenwood et al., 2002), the adoption of change is often slow moving and involves the integration of new knowledge and parties, trial and error, and negotiation of meaning and identity. As defined earlier, a field is a set of organizations that share a set of parameters that include general goals, partners, rules, norms, and skills. Fields can be considered loosely coupled networks that consist of various populations, each of which may also have membership in other fields or communities. Within a field, there can be various populations, including organizations that produce similar services or products, regulatory agencies, consumers/stakeholders, and suppliers (DiMaggio & Powell, 1991). Over time, shared practices and beliefs emerge from the repeated interaction among similar organizations (Greenwood et al., 2002). In addition, pressures from markets, stakeholders, regulatory agencies, and others demand the adoption, maintenance, or dissolution of specific behaviors. Collectively, these influences are called *isomorphic forces*, in that over time, in response to coercive (regulatory forces), to reduce uncertainty, or gain and maintain legitimacy, organizations within a field begin to adopt the same behaviors, which leads to institutionalized norms

(Dimaggio & Powell, 1991). When organizational behavior is *institutionalized*, it means that the behavior has become an accepted standard across the field and is the commonly accepted way to behave and "get things done." Therefore, for an entire field, such as corporate communication, to change, new ideas and practices must be introduced and filtered through the existing norms and values of the field before they can become adopted or rejected as a new way of doing things.

Macrolevel theories of change often position change as a result of recognizing the need for change, trying out new ideas and methods, choosing the most desirable method, and adopting the change. The choices made during the change process, indeed often driving the need for change, are attributed to the larger environment within which the organizations exist. For example, community ecology theory posits that populations of organizations evolve within a shared space known as a community. Similar to the idea of a field, a community consists of different populations or various types of organizations that have some effect on each other or a shared interdependency. These communities are part of a larger environment with which they share both reactive and proactive action. Elements of the larger field can include the economy, globalization, and other social or technological forces. Organizations within the field change as a result of variation, selection, and retention processes. *Variation* is the recognition of alternative possibilities for action, either from the environment or generated within the community (Bryant & Monge, 2008). Selection involves choosing one or more of the variations, and retention involves the institution of the selected variation(s) (Bryant & Monge, 2008).

Institutional theory, or the theory of how organizations respond to the pressure to legitimize organizational practices, which leads to both organizational- and field-specific standards, suggests a five-stage process for change, including *de-institutionalization*, or the breaking down of previous norms and behaviors; *pre-institutionalization*, or trial and error involving individual members of the field; *theorization*, which includes specification of the problem/opportunity and a compelling solution, and justification of new possibilities for the field; *diffusion*, or spreading of the new ideas; and *re-institutionalization*, when "cognitive legitimacy" is achieved, the change becomes a taken for granted norm (Greenwood et al., 2002; Tolbert & Zucker, 1996). Another internal or external jolt can set the process off all over again.

There are several social and communicative factors that underscore change processes.

Precursor to change. Referred to as the "jolt," institutional theory in which anything that destabilizes equilibrium presents a problem that cannot be resolved in current conditions, or it provides an opportunity for moving to better conditions and can serve as a triggering event for change.

Group dynamics. Within the field, member institutions can be both cooperators and competitors. That is, although individual organizations may compete for clients and other stakeholders, they have a vested interest in the overall success of the field. This can require cooperation to ward off shared environmental threats and pool resources to keep the field moving forward. Simultaneously, there is pressure on individual organizations to innovate and stand out from the others. As a field evolves, new members will enter, and others will leave as both a precursor and result of change. Related, the boundaries of a given field or community exist in a state of flux and evolve as members adopt or drop norms, values, standards, and behaviors (Greenwood et al., 2002).

Communication processes. Messaging, dialogue, argumentation, debate, information sharing, presentation, justification, legitimizing, and collaboration are all communication processes that contribute to change at the field level. These happen at the organizational level, as organizations individually work to integrate, or reject, new ways of doing things. For example, as Internet-based communication began to rise as a possible way to communicate with stakeholders, organizations had to decide if having an organizational website was worth the time and resources it would take to create and maintain it. They had to convince individuals in the organization of its efficacy and alter the standard practice of using media relations and advertising as the primary vehicles of communicating with stakeholders to create new types of messaging for the Internet. This happened through management communication, peer communication, upward feedback, and trial and error. Over time, as organizational members and external stakeholders saw the benefits of web-based communication, more resources were diverted to support the practice, and organizational websites became an institutionalized practice.

These communication processes also occur at the field level, as members from various organizations meet in social settings and professional settings or come together to oppose new legislation. Key places that this happens are trade publications (news magazines and blogs related to a specific industry) and professional associations. We will discuss the importance of professional and community associations in the "Tools for Self-Action" section later in this chapter.

Corporate Communication as a Changing Field

Strategic communication has been an ever-evolving concept, changing as business and social environments have evolved. In Chapter 1, we described strategic communication as being planned, targeted, and goal oriented. As a field, corporate communication employs strategic communication to coordinate internal and external communication processes with the goal of creating positive stakeholder relationships and furthering organizational goals (Elving, 2012). In the beginning, the field was less relationship oriented and more organization centric, with an emphasis on management over relationship. That is, early strategic communication efforts primarily focused on managing employees, external stakeholders, and organizational reputation for the benefit of the organization. As we discussed in Chapter 1, corporate communication shares roots with management and organizational communication, marketing, and PR. Early communication tactics included one-way asymmetric communication, such as press agentry and publicity stunts, which sought to gain attention for the organization at all costs. Internally, this included a focus on top-down communication between management and employees, often with few mechanisms for feedback. As the field evolved, media relations became an important vehicle through which organizations could gain legitimate publicity. Internally, communication evolved from primarily one way and top-down to represent more upward and lateral communication. Since the late 1990s, organizational websites have provided an always-open gateway between the stakeholder and the organization, allowing for direct communication between the two parties. With this advance began an era of increasingly direct communication without the need for a gatekeeper. And the rest is history. Or, more accurately, the future of the field.

While organizational success and the bottom line are still key foci of corporate communication, recent changes in both technology and the organizational mind-set have shifted the field to a focus on relationship and dialogue, giving the stakeholders more of a voice and making them more "partner" than "target."

Where We Are Now

While this entire text has been dedicated to providing you with the skills and mind-set to be successful in the field as it is now, this section will break down the major changes we've seen over the past decade into six major categories, each of which reflects important strategic and tactical trends in corporate communication.

DIGITAL

The continued rise of the Internet and its accompanied adoption in corporate communication is the biggest shift the field has seen and arguably acts as the impetus for all other changes. Public brand websites make it possible to for organizations to have a 24/7, global presence, essentially acting as hubs for organizations' external communications and gateways to the brand. Internally, organizations can use intranet sites (websites available only to employees) to share and store information, build organizational culture, and connect employees who are not co-located. External websites not only represent a macrolevel conceptual change but have also changed the way that strategic communication is practiced on the tactical level. In addition to traditional media, such as newspapers, trade publications, and television/radio news, news blogs such as the *Huffington Post* and *News Insider* now represent viable news outlets that organizations work with to gain coverage.

Whereas media releases coupled with advertising were formerly the primary vehicles for external communication, organizational websites and social media have changed the way organizations and stakeholders communicate with each other. There is no longer a necessary mediator, or third party, between the organization and stakeholders. While brands still create media releases, they go to both the media and directly to stakeholders via the digital newsroom on corporate sites. While organizations still greatly benefit from free, widespread media coverage that results from good media relations, this is no longer the only, or even primary, way of communicating with stakeholders.

Social media has also become a mainstay of external communication. Statistics show that 90% of brands use social media to increase brand awareness, maintaining between four and 10 social profiles (Hootsuite, 2018). To this end, the Internet and rise of social media has "democratized" information in that stakeholders can "talk to" organizations via social media, as well as to each other. Stakeholders can choose to work with an organization if they have a complaint or publicly circumvent the organization by posting on its own social media, the organization's social media, or in some other public forum. Accordingly, stakeholder communication can now be both "one-on-one" and "one-to-many" within the same "conversation." For example, a brand can make a post on social media for all stakeholders and then engage with individual stakeholders in the comments. The individual communication, although direct between the stakeholder and brand, is public for all to see. As we discussed in Chapter 3, this forces a certain level of transparency on the part of the organization because stakeholders can praise or criticize, even publicly protest, an organization right on its very own Facebook page.

RELATIONAL AND STAKEHOLDER CENTERED

Just as the rise in digital communication in strategic communication has led to more transparency, it has also led to a more relational orientation to the organizational/stakeholder relationship. Organizations can use the direct access they have to stakeholders to engage them through two-way communication, more customized and timely content, and relational activities, such as polls and contests. As we discussed in Chapter 4, the field has experienced a shift toward embracing a dialogic approach to communication by which the needs of the organization and stakeholders are mutually highlighted. Stakeholder communication is not solely seen as a means to achieving a better bottom line but rather as a way to increase trust and understanding. In addition, we've seen a shift to highlighting CSR and sustainability in business practices as recognition of the effect of business practices on social and environmental areas of society.

STAKEHOLDER-GENERATED CONTENT

Accompanying the rise in digital stakeholder-centered comments is the rise of *stakeholder-driven* communication, such as influencer marketing, customer advocacy, and employee advocacy. A social media influencer is an area expert who has gained credibility and a large following on social media. As the name implies, influencers can influence the buying decisions of their followers. Brands often engage with social media influencers for influencer marketing in which the organic endorsement of the influencer acts like a celebrity endorsement, but rather than being a traditional celebrity, they are "celebrities" in a given industry or other social arena and therefore have influence with followers who are also interested in that same area (Influencer Marketing Hub, n.d.). Customer advocacy is the principle of word of mouth applied to social media. This can happen without direct prompting from the organization, especially when the organization does a good job with social content and stakeholder interaction. Brands can also increase customer advocacy with strategies, such as providing incentives or giving back to the community (Alton, 2018). Employee advocacy is when employees take to social media to extol the virtues of their employers. Many organizations are now setting up employee advocacy programs through which organizations provide employees with the incentive and tools necessary to share their organizational experiences and impression of the brand via their own social media (Patel, 2017). While this could be risky for both the employee and the organization, the correct organizational environment, outlook on employee advocacy, and social media policy can make this a powerful word-of-mouth tool for organizations and a rewarding experience for employees.

MOBILE

Research shows that as of 2019, 57% of organic search engine visits originated from a mobile device and that three out of four mobile searches lead to follow-up action on the part of the stakeholder (The state of mobile search–statistics and trends, 2019). It is approximated that approximately $118 billion was spent on retail purchasing through mobile devices in 2018 (Morrissey, 2018). While mobile use is not new, the field has to continually adjust practices to optimize the opportunities that mobile provides. A recent survey showed that customers feel that there is a trade-off between mobile-friendly pages and content, with content lacking when pages are optimized for mobile use. Participants also indicated that being able to access content "anyway I want" was the most important aspect of a mobile brand experience (Falkow, 2014). One major way that brands are engaging stakeholders is through mobile apps. Mobile apps are increasingly being used as a way to enhance brand experiences for stakeholders and increase stakeholder loyalty through strategies such as discounts, promotions, coupons, and the ability to make purchases and order food so that it is ready and waiting.

DATA DRIVEN

Although it can be difficult to determine return on investment for social media, there is a proliferation of analytics software available that allows communication professionals to determine who their information is reaching, what affect it is having, and how this can impact current and future stakeholder behavior. As we discussed in Chapter 8, strategic corporate communication is driven by research and analysis, and big data has helped to not only identify what works and doesn't work but also to predict behavior. Social media sites can serve as large data repositories about stakeholder behavior, and third-party analytical software can provide additional insight to both performance and behavior. The collection, analysis, and utilization of data carries with it ethical implications for both privacy and how practitioners use data.

INTEGRATING ARTIFICIAL INTELLIGENCE

Artificial intelligence can be used to perform several functions in communication fields, including writing data-driven stories, creating media lists, assisting in crisis management, transcribing audio and video, predicting media trends, and monitoring social media (Marx, 2017). For example, social media management dashboards such as Hootsuite already play a big role in planning, scheduling, and analyzing social media content. According to Melissa Hoffman, editor/content director of PR News, one of the major challenges going forward will be learning how to enhance, not threaten, the communications role through the use of artificial intelligence (Marx, 2018).

WHERE WE ARE GOING

While it is impossible to predict how strategic communication will evolve, it seems likely that it will follow the path of digital progress. This means a more stakeholder-centric mind-set and stakeholder-driven content. As digital and mobile media continues to create a more customized experience for stakeholders, organizations will continue to adjust to creating content for audiences that are finely segmented. In addition, figuring out the ethical and social implications of an increased reliance on technology and finding balance between the role of technology and the role of the human practitioner may be major challenges for the field moving forward.

Areas of the field that are unlikely to change are the founding values of strategy, goal setting, and ethics. Specific strategies and tactics will continue to evolve. However, the importance of understanding stakeholders, creating a strategic plan driven by SMART goals, and staying true to the organization's mission and values in all communication will supersede the tactical changes in the field. The relational orientation of the field, which rests on mutuality between the organization and stakeholders is a concept that may get stronger but will not go away. Likewise, as the field evolves, ethics should remain a guiding light. As we enter into uncharted communication territory involving artificial intelligence, big data, and other changes, maintaining a focus on integrity, transparency, and honesty is perhaps the most important direction the field can take.

APPLYING THE CONCEPT TO YOUR OWN SITUATION

THE IMPORTANCE OF LEARNING

As a college student, you may think that your time for "learning" is almost over. You will soon graduate, get a job, and start "doing." However, learning never stops. To be successful, we have to embrace learning at all stages of our lives. This means seeking out new information, points of view, skills, and partners who will help us put what we are learning into action. Indeed, learning and doing are not two ends of a spectrum; learning *is* doing, and without learning, we can't get anything done.

Learning has been defined in many ways, with an emphasis on acquiring knowledge or skill. However, learning is both a social and communicative process that "leads to change, which occurs as a result of experience, and increases the potential of improved performance and future learning" (Ambrose, Bridges, DiPietro, Lovett, & Norman, 2010, p. 3). Thus the ability to learn and integrate new information, experiences, and skills into our lives can act as a critical agent of positive change. Many modern educational approaches, such as John Dewey's experiential learning, illustrate that the idea of learning works best when we are active participants in the experience. According to Dewey (1938), all learning is socially constructed and influenced by the social environment in which the learner is interacting.

However, learning also comes from within. For example, *figuring out how we learn best*, also known as metacognition, and then putting those practices into place, can greatly impact our ability to learn. Self-directed learning, which has been linked to student success, employs metacognition in a four-step process, including assessing learning readiness, setting learning goals, employing metacognition, and evaluating efforts (Ambrose et al., 2010, p. 30).

Arguably, before we employ any learning practices, we have to *believe* we can learn and change. Our mind-set, or attitudes and beliefs about ourselves and the world around us, affects everything from the actions we take to our response to situations we are in. Related to learning, Dweck (2006) defines mind-set as the view we adopt for ourselves. Identifying your mind-set can improve your ability to learn and affect positive change in your life.

MIND-SET

Do you believe that intelligence is fixed and you either have it or you don't, or do you believe that you can always change how intelligent you are? Do you believe that having to work hard at something means you are not smart, or does working hard to figure something out make you feel more accomplished? The statements in the first half of each sentence represent a fixed mind-set, while the statements in the second half of each sentence reflect a growth mind-set. People with fixed mind-sets believe that "we are who we are" and that our intelligence, morality, and personalities aren't able to be substantially changed (Murphy & Dewck, 2016). Conversely, people with growth mind-sets believe that we can change and that through learning and experience, we can significantly change our basic human traits (Murphy & Dweck 2016). According to Carol Dweck (2006), a pioneer in research on mind-set, "The fixed mindset makes you concerned with how you'll be judged; the growth mindset makes you concerned with improving" (p. 13).

So how is mind-set related to change? Mind-set affects not only how we view ourselves but also the types of goals we set, our view of effort, and the chances we are willing to take. For example, people with a fixed mind-set tend to play it safe and stick with activities that they know they are good at. They feel smarter when they are performing well and not making mistakes (Dweck, 2006). This means that they are unlikely to embrace change that feels risky or may lead to failure. With a fixed mind-set, failure can define you. Change can take us outside of our comfort zones and put us in situations where success may look like failure because we aren't getting things right immediately.

However, not getting things right immediately but continuing to try *is* the definition of success for someone with a growth mind-set. Such a person would believe that trial and error is how we get better, how we improve our intelligence, and how we succeed. For someone with a growth mind-set, working hard and achieving something new is a success. Therefore, someone with a growth mind-set is much more likely to embrace change because it requires taking risks and learning something outside of their established set of skills or experiences.

Changing our mind-set from fixed to growth can help us learn how to embrace change and, in turn, grow and better ourselves. Dweck (2006) outlines several ways that we can shift our mind-set:

1. **Think differently about your mind.** In her research, Dweck (2006) found that teaching people that the brain is a muscle that grows stronger the more we use it allowed students to become more open to extending more effort, learning new study skills and, eventually, shifting to a growth mind-set. Students who were taught about how the brain works and a growth mind-set performed better at the end of the semester than did a group of students who were given the same study skills but without education about how the brain works.

2. **Learn about the brain.** Dweck (2006) also found that educating students about how the brain works can also make a difference. For example, she found that when students were taught about transferring knowledge from working memory to long-term memory, they were better able to articulate why they did or did not retain certain knowledge. This understanding empowered them to take failure not as an indictment on their ability but rather as a need to adapt their learning style or try something new.

3. **Not personalizing failure.** Learning how to step outside of failure and see it as an experience rather than a personality flaw can help someone shift from a fixed to a growth mind-set. In addition, realizing that rejection is not always *about you* but perhaps about the situation or where other parties in a situation are coming from can also help us to depersonalize and learn to accept failure.

4. **Taking the extra step.** Mentally reframing failure from a negative to a positive isn't always enough. A true mind-set shift involves acting on the opportunity to improve. This could include soliciting feedback, helping someone else who outperformed you or seeking help the next time you are in a similar situation.

5. **Recognizing the positives.** Acknowledging the positive effects of embracing change can make a big difference in your view of, and willingness to, change (Young Entrepreneur Council, 2015).

6. **Embracing vulnerability.** Perhaps the flip side of not personalizing failure is the ability to acknowledge that sometimes it is okay to mess up. It happens to everyone and opening up to help and feedback does not make us weak (Young Entrepreneur Council, 2015).

7. **Eliminate the "sunk cost" mind-set.** Don't be afraid of expending time and effort to learn even if the payout isn't obvious or immediate. Likewise, don't be afraid to walk away from something you have put a lot of resources into if changing course is the better choice (Young Entrepreneur Council, 2015).

QUESTIONS:

- How can I continue to improve myself?

- How can I stay relevant in my field?

- What can I do to lead, or adapt to, change?

Tools and Processes for Self-Action

CULTIVATING ADAPTABILITY

Adaptability is how open and willing you are to changing. Adaptability is important because, as we established earlier in the chapter, our environment is constantly in flux. In both personal and professional situations, the ability to adjust expectations and actions makes us flexible and able to create solutions and new opportunities when our external conditions inevitably change. While, by nature, some people are more comfortable with change than others and, therefore, more adaptable, adaptability can also be learned. Much like mind-set, adaptability can be cultivated by shifting the way we think and undertaking actions that provide new pathways. Boss (2014, 2015) outline several ways to cultivate adaptability:

- **Be open to uncertainty.** Simply accepting the fact that uncertainty is a part of life and reframing it as an opportunity rather than a disadvantage is a first step toward becoming more adaptable.

- **Shifting motivation and focus.** This can involve reframing the situation and looking at the benefits that will come from adapting and recognizing when to maintain focus on existing goals while involving a critical thought process to move through a challenging situation (Bailey, 2014).

- **Develop courses of action.** Think ahead and create scenarios about what could happen if you choose a specific course of action. Then create contingencies for those scenarios. This provides you with a series of "go-to" plans that make you more prepared, more comfortable, and, ultimately, more adaptable.

- **Don't blame or dwell.** Both blaming others and dwelling on possible or actual "failure" will only hold you back. Accept what has happened, learn from it, and move on.

- **Experiment.** Try new things. Focus on learning. As we discussed earlier in the chapter, learning never stops.

- **Know what you stand for.** Knowing your values provides an anchor as you embrace change. You can be willing to try new things and change, but you won't lose yourself in the process or go down a path that you are entirely uncomfortable with if you let your values guide you.

PROFESSIONAL DEVELOPMENT AND TRAINING

This section will discuss training and professional development from a holistic point of view, emphasizing not only formal classes and organizational opportunities but also participation, networking, and an attitude of openness.

MENTORSHIP

Mentoring is the process of providing guidance for someone who has less experience. The role of a mentor is to provide the information, support, and access that a less experienced counterpart needs to acclimate to a new environment and succeed. Most often, mentoring takes place within a formal institution, such as a workplace or school. Mentoring can be informal, such as when two people pair up without specific direction provided by the institution, or formal, when the institution has in place a specific program and set of guidelines for pairing senior and junior members for the purpose of guidance and learning.

Mentors provide two types of support. Career related and psychosocial (Kram, 1985). Career related support includes everything from coaching, sponsorship, gaining exposure and visibility within the organization, protection, and job- or task-related assignments designed to help the mentee grow (Allen, Ebby, Poteet, Lentz, & Lima, 2004). Returning to the idea of networks, good mentors provide access to their networks, providing mentees with the benefits of indirect ties, or new contacts that they make through their mentor. These are contacts they likely wouldn't have been able to access on their own and provide a source of both structural and cognitive social capital. Because of the network-based structures of many organizations in the contemporary work climate, these ties often span organizational boundaries, providing mentees with a set of diverse, multilevel ties (Higgins & Kram, 2001). Psychosocial support focuses on helping mentees create identity and a sense of competence and effectiveness within their professional role, which can include actions such as role modeling, acceptance, confirmation, and friendship (Allen et al., 2004, p. 128). Mentoring results in two primary types of outcomes for mentees: objective career outcomes (e.g., promotion, compensation) and subjective outcomes (career and job satisfaction, career commitment) (Allen et al., 2004).

So, how can you get involved in mentoring? As you enter the workplace, find out if your organization has a formal mentoring program. If it does, you will likely get paired up soon after entering the organization. If your workplace doesn't have a mentoring program, seek someone out. You can approach your boss and ask if they will mentor you, or if they could recommend someone in your department who could serve as a member. Or, if you begin to develop a good relationship with someone who has experience, and whose work you admire, you could approach them directly and ask them to be your mentor. Attending meetings of professional associations in your field is another great way to meet a mentor (see "Tools and Processes When Acting for Others" later in this chapter for more information about professional associations). Once you are working with a mentor, be a good mentee. Listen to what your mentor is saying and keep a growth mind-set. Be respectful of your mentor's time and expertise. Be mindful of representing both yourself and your mentor well, especially in situations related to the contacts or access he or she had shared with you. And when it is time, pay it forward by becoming a mentor.

PROFILE OF INDIVIDUAL EXPERIENCE:

Matthew Johnson

Matthew Johnson, enterprise supply chain communications leader— pharmaceuticals for Johnson & Johnson, has experienced firsthand how the field of strategic communication has evolved over the last 20 years. Throughout his career at Johnson & Johnson, Mr. Johnson has worked as director, Corporate Communica-

FIGURE 10.1 **Matthew Johnson**

tion at Johnson & Johnson Corporate, external affairs leader at Ethicon Global Franchise, and in his most recent role in which he leads a team responsible for internal and external communications across the Johnson & Johnson pharmaceutical ("Janssen") supply-chain organization. The depth and breadth of his experience over the last two decades has given him a long view of the field, how it has changed, and the importance of evolving. While he feels that the core principles of strategic corporate communication have remained the same, the environment in which these principles are enacted and, subsequently, *how* they are enacted has changed greatly.

Mr. Johnson cited the expansion of globalization, the Internet, and social media as fundamental agents of change for how we communicate and our expectations as information consumers. He said, "When I professionally entered the field in the late 1990s, two-way online mechanisms were still very new and mobile devices with Wi-Fi capabilities weren't widely accessible, even in developed countries. The mass dissemination of information on a global scale was still highly controlled, streamlined and regulated. Today, with the democratization of information and the seemingly unlimited, unfiltered communication mediums across the world, communication professionals are increasingly critical in helping individuals and organizations adapt to these dynamics, anticipate needs and meet the changing expectations of audiences."

These changes have meant transforming both the mind-set and media through which organizations communicate both externally and internally. Globalization, concurrent with the rise of the Internet, has changed what it means to be both local and global, in that "everything local is now potentially global." Concurrent to these changes has been the rise of social media, which has dramatically altered the way we connect, share, and consume information. According to

Mr. Johnson, strategic communication professionals have faced the challenge of figuring out how to effectively cut through the "noise" in this oversaturated global news market to deliver accurate and compelling messaging to our key stakeholders.

To adapt to the changes and challenges faced by communication professionals, Mr. Johnson has employed a combination of embracing new trends and staying true to enduring ideals. Professionally, he has served as a strategic counselor and worked with senior leaders to lead change from the smallest of changes to the largest of organizational transformations. He credited his success in this area to the following:

- A steadfast commitment to transparency and accountability. Without that, you do not have trust and without trust, you cannot lead forward.

- A clear purpose or "north star," such as the Johnson & Johnson Credo, is critical. This will guide every decision you help to influence, especially during the toughest of times.

- Alignment with the Arthur Page principles (https://page.org/site/the-page-principles). These have served me well and helped me apply my core values when consulting on challenging issues.

- Bringing an objective outside-in perspective to work. It is very easy to become siloed or to have a narrow view when you are entrenched in a tough situation. My ability to lift up and provide diverse perspectives rooted in data is a capability that has been valued in my career.

- Keeping a finger on the pulse of stakeholders to anticipate their needs and represent their views in tough situations.

In terms of adapting to changes on both a personal and professional level, Mr. Johnson suggested a variety of strategies that help him gain insights, test ideas, and stay connected.

- Become a media and news consumer.

- Stay on top of emerging trends in both the field and the industry.

- Embrace and practice what you learn. It's not enough to study emerging trends; you have to be willing to put them to use.

- Don't be afraid to make mistakes. Failing fast is a catalyst for growth.

- Maintain a globally diverse network of professional contemporaries.

- Find mentors who challenge you, and when it is time, pay it forward and become a mentor. Your legacy is not your own.

- Remain open and embrace change.

Here's Mr. Johnson's key piece of advice for embracing change with integrity: "It is important to remain open to new ideas and different ways of thinking—even when they conflict with our established paradigms—but never at the expense of our value system."

Questions:

1. Which of Mr. Johnson's strategies for adapting to change do you think is most useful for you? Why? Name two action steps for employing this strategy in your life.

2. Mr. Johnson mentioned the difference between the mass dissemination of information being highly controlled, streamlined, and regulated and the current democratization of information and multiple, unfiltered communication mediums. Based on what you have learned throughout this book, what are some of the key ways strategic communication professionals have adapted to this change?

3. What do you think it means that "everything local is now potentially global?" How do you think this has changed the field of strategic corporate communication?

APPLYING THE CONCEPT TO YOUR WORK WITH CLIENTS

UNDERSTANDING THE ENVIRONMENT

As we discussed earlier in the chapter, change comes from both internal and external forces. While it may be tempting for organizations to jump on the latest trends happening within the field, it is important for strategic communicators to focus on what is happening both inside and outside of the organization. Systems theory examines the reciprocal relationship between an organization and its environment. Individual organizations are nested within several larger systems, such as professional fields, industries, supply chains, and geographic locations. Each of these larger systems, called suprasystems in systems theory, provides inputs to an organization in the form of rules, norms, legislation, raw materials, labor, and more. The more open an organization's boundaries, the more inputs it can take in. Within the organization, processes such as mission, rules, norms, and workflows take these inputs and create outputs, which go back out into the environment. These outputs affect the suprasystem, which in turn affects inputs, and the cycle starts again.

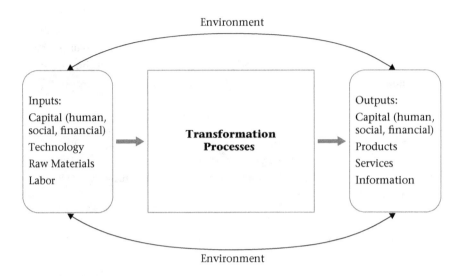

FIGURE 10.2 **Systems Theory**

Organizations with more open boundaries will take in more inputs, whereas organizations with closed boundaries are likely to only take in what is necessary, which can lead to working with outdated information or resources, thus possibly stifling innovation and change. While open boundaries tend to provide more benefits and greater opportunities for success and innovation, too many inputs can be confusing or overwhelming if the organization does not have processes in place for dealing with the inputs that are entering the system. Thus strategically managing organizational boundaries can be a key element in bringing about productive change without overloading the system. One way to accomplish this is through establishing boundary spanners. A boundary spanner is an individual who links the internal and external organizational environment. Acting as a boundary spanner can be valuable for you, as an individual, as well as for your organization. A typical example of a boundary spanner is a salesperson whose role is to translate the value of organizational product/services to clients while at the same time bringing the needs and wants of clients back into the internal system as feedback toward how the organization can improve its products, services, and processes. As a boundary spanner, one can integrate what is going on in the environment with what is happening within the organization, ultimately benefiting both. In addition, as the boundary spanner has a unique set of connections relative to others in both the internal and external environments, this person often reaps the benefits of being a broker of important information.

However, boundary spanning isn't limited to working with stakeholders who are customers. Rather, boundary spanners can be part of interorganizational collaborations (e.g., research and development, collaboration to solve a shared problem) or collaborations with strategic partners to further organizational goals (e.g., the media relations function, through which strategic communicators work with members of the media to gain coverage for the organization). In each of these cases, the information that is shared by crossing boundaries enables the organization to better understand its environment, as well as engage in change processes that can benefit both the organizational and supra-systems.

In the "Tools and Processes When Acting for Others" section of this chapter, we will look in more detail at two ways that you can act as a boundary spanner for your organization: benchmarking and joining professional and community organizations.

CREATING A CULTURE OF CHANGE

Organizational culture is a combination of the values, assumptions, and beliefs that undergird an organization, and the resulting communicative and behavioral actions that make up daily organizational life (Deetz, Tracy, & Simpson, 2000). An organization's culture is often what sets it apart from other organizations. For example, think about what it means to be a member of your college or university as opposed to someone from a school that is comparable in size and other factors but that has a different mission or values. The differences that you can identify likely relate to organizational culture. Organizational culture is not only linked to organizational identity but also serves as a form of management. Because organizational culture is created and shared through communication, rules, rituals, and other symbolic behavior (e.g., workplace dress, what is punished versus what is rewarded, mission statements), it can also serve as a management function as employees figure out what it means to be a "productive" member of the organization. According to Deetz et al. (2000), "a positive corporate culture creates employee potentials and the context in which they can be realized" (p. 4).

Returning to the idea of mind-set, research shows that *organizations* can also adopt either a fixed or growth mind-set (Harvard Business Review, 2014). Organizations with a growth mind-set encourage employees to take risks, even when the risk can affect the whole organization. This can involve rewarding employees for more than just successes but also for "useful lessons learned" (Dweck, 2016, para. 6). Such organizations support collaboration and provide opportunities for learning and growth to all employees. They also tend to promote from within, taking the time to cultivate employee skills, as well as value potential, capacity, and a love of learning" (Harvard Business Review, 2014, para. 8). This fosters a more innovative culture that is open to risk, which in turn cultivates a workforce that is open to change and challenge. The payoff for organizations with a growth mind-set is greater employee empowerment and commitment.

QUESTIONS:

- ▪ How can I guide my client through the next five years? 10 years?

- ▪ How can I help my client stay relevant in its industry?

- ▪ How can I help my client lead the industry?

- ▪ How can we build organizational systems that are flexible and adapt to change?

Tools and Processes When Acting for Others

BENCHMARKING

The process of benchmarking involves looking at direct counterparts to determine best practices among competitors or other organizations in one's field. The goal of benchmarking is to determine performance gaps in an organization, see how other organizations perform in these areas and use this information to implement improvements. Benchmarking can be done independently as an organization chooses a set of metrics against which it compares itself to relevant competitors or can include collaboration among several organizations in which competitors become cooperators in working together to improve both the individual and field-based practices. Benchmarking can also move outside the scope of a given industry to see how other industries invoke comparable solutions or processes.

Benchmarking is a proactive precursor to planned change in that it seeks and addresses weaknesses and performance gaps within an organization and finds solutions before the problems become acute. It can be implemented before a problem is apparent or at the early stages of problem development. For example, in the early 1980s, Xerox was facing heavy competition from Japanese and other competitors. After completing the benchmarking process, they implemented changes to reduce manufacturing costs and improve a quality control program called "Leadership Through Quality" (ICMR.org). By opening their system, looking to the best practices of others, and being willing to implement change, Xerox was able to survive the competition and continues to be a strong player to this day.

PROFESSIONAL AND COMMUNITY-BASED ASSOCIATIONS

In Chapter 3, we discussed the importance of networking. Not only is it great for when you are starting your career, but it will benefit both you and your organization throughout your career. Networking is important related to change because, like benchmarking, it allows you to meet people who are in the same profession and share ideas and best practices. It also helps you to build social capital with others in the field, which has many benefits, including building trust on both individual and organizational levels and creating relationships through which you can share information and assistance. One of the best ways to network on behalf of your organization is to join professional associations. As the name implies, professional associations are focused on a specific profession or industry. Professional associations generally operate on a membership basis and provide members with access to directories that include other members, informational resources, and networking events. Professional associations often make a statement about the field, such as providing a code of ethics or professional behavior that set best practices for the field. In addition to setting field standards, professional associations can act as "agents of change" as they allow for conversation and debate around ideas and practices. Over time, professional identities are reconstituted through these discussions, as new practices become legitimized and adopted. There are usually one or two key organizations that represent the entire field and several smaller regional associations that provide more targeted information and networking opportunities.

Key organizations in the United States for strategic communication include the following:

Public Relations Society of America (PRSA) www.prsa.org. The PRSA was founded in 1947 and is the largest professional organization serving the communications community in the United States with over 30,000 members. The mission of the PRSA is to "make communications professionals smarter, better prepared, and more connected through all stages of their career" (PRSA, n.d.). The PRSA maintains a member directory and job bank, and it holds one national conference each year. There are regional chapters, as well as the Public Relations Student Society of America. The PRSA Foundation is a 501(C) (3) charitable organization committed to promoting diversity to serve the public good and to "address the needs of a diverse world" (PRSA, 2018). The PRSA code of ethics is commonly cited as the field's guiding set of ethical principles.

International Association of Business Communicators (IABC) www. iabc.com. Founded in 1970, the IABC hosts regional and international conferences, has upwards of 80 regional chapters throughout the world, and has its own 501 (C) (3) foundation, the IABC Foundation, with the mission to "generate resources to fund and support strategic initiatives in line with IABC's purpose and to demonstrate the power of professional communication as a force for good in business and society" (IABC, n.d.). Consistent with the goals and missions of most professional associations, IABC maintains a member directory and a repository of articles and resources for business communication, and the association has its own set of guiding principles for the field titled The Global Standard.

While PRSA and IABC are probably the two largest associations for communication professionals in the United States, there are numerous others that operate on both national and international levels, including https://page.org/site/the-page-principles, the Association for Women in Communications (www.womcom.org), the Global Alliance for Public Relations and Communications Management (https://www.globalalliancepr.org), the International Public Relations Association (www.ipra.org), and the American Marketing Association (www.ama.org). Each of these organizations provides membership resources, including networking and events, to individuals in strategic communication.

In addition to professional associations, organizations such as the local chamber of commerce can provide a great place for networking across sectors relative to a specific geographic location. Most cities and towns have a chamber of commerce that consists of representatives from local businesses and civic leaders, with the intention of working toward the goal of creating a strong and vital community that promotes opportunities for businesses and community members alike. Given the importance of the environment in which an organization operates to the success of the organization, chambers of commerce provide an excellent opportunity for organizations to participate in creating the kind of environment in which they, and those around them, can succeed.

PROFILE OF ORGANIZATIONAL EXPERIENCE:

3M

The company now known as 3M was founded in 1902 in Two Harbors, Minnesota. Originally named Minnesota Mining and Manufacturing Company, the 3M was created to mine for corundum, a mineral used to make grinding paper and sanding wheels. Today, 3M operations span 12 industries, ranging from automotive to health care and communications. 3M has seven brands that make many of the product staples we take for granted in day-to-day life, including Scotch® Brand Tapes, Post-it® Super Sticky Notes, and Scotch-Brite® cleaning products. Needless to say, the company did not get from mining for minerals to creating dental crowns without a combination of embracing change and staying true to core principles.

This process of change was sparked by a series of failures early in the company's history, which forced it to alter its course and innovate (McGlade, 2017). When mining for corundum, the company founders found no customers for the mineral, which was used to create grinding wheels, so they decided to create their own grinding wheels. When this did not work, they changed to making sandpaper, only to find out that they were actually mining a different mineral, anorthosite, which they could not use for manufacturing. Minnesota Mining and Manufacturing then started to import garnet to make their sandpaper. Not only did the product not work, but poor planning in the creation of the factory led the floors to collapse under the weight of the raw materials (3M, n.d.; McGlade, 2017). During this time, salaries were cut and then discontinued (3M, 2002). However, perseverance, two large investors, and new company leadership led to the company's first successful product, 3M™Three-M-ite cloth, which came to market in 1914.

Rooted in this series of initial failures, 3M developed an organizational culture of innovation. Early on, they took chances on employees who were open-minded, optimistic, and sometimes known as "wild eyed" inventors (3M, 2003). One of these early inventors, Richard Drew, worked on finding a solution for tapes that left residue when being peeled away. After 2 years, he was to stop and work on other projects, but he persisted on his own time, eventually creating what is now known as Scotch™ tape. They build on this spirit by providing employees the opportunities and support necessary to learn and succeed and making this part of their culture (Govindarajan & Srinivas, 2013). For example, the company designates the roles of "scout," entrepreneur," and "innovator" to employees (Scholz, 2017). Scouts gather research and identify "problems worth solving" (Scholz, 2017). 3M also conducts research both inside and outside of the organization through internal collaboration among employees in a series of formal and informal forums, and field visits with customers. In addition, they invite customers into their innovation centers. Entrepreneurs work together to "remove the unknown" and innovators work on bringing the product to market. The three designations are cross-functional, disbanding and recombining depending on where they are in a project. In addition, they work on multiple projects at a time to keep innovation fluid and moving forward.

Not only has 3M stayed relevant through innovation and adaptation, but they have also played a part in many "firsts" that led to major cultural shifts. For example, 3M™ Sound Recording Tape allowed for the ability to play back sound recordings, Scotch® Magnetic Tape was used to record television programs for the first time, and Tartan™ Turf was the first synthetic grass surface, which is now known ubiquitously as turf. This success was driven through a focus on building on the past and looking toward the future. In the words of former CEO W. James McNerny Jr., "In extending our market reach, 3M's formula for success has remained the same: first, identify customer needs, and second, use 3M technology to pioneer innovative solutions to meet these needs" (3M, 2002, p. 1).

Questions:

1. How do you see the interplay of group, organizational, and macrolevel change in the evolution of 3M?

2. How did 3M cultivate an organizational culture of growth mind-set?

3. What elements of systems theory do you see at play in 3M's story?

Chapter Conclusion

Change is all around us and is part of our daily lives. From making resolutions on January 1 to changing some element of our behavior, to changing our major, to changing our mind-set; change is something we do both purposively and passively. Corporate communication is not immune to change; as a field, corporate communication has undergone technological, tactical, and relational changes. Being able to adapt, embrace, and even lead change is critical to being successful. Understanding how and why you engage in change on both personal and social levels can help you make better, more conscious choices about the direction you want to take personally and professionally.

Key Terms

3-step model of change
Adaptability
Artificial intelligence
Change
Community ecology theory
Customer advocacy
Employee advocacy
Field

Group and organizational change
Influencer marketing
Institutional theory
Intrapersonal change
Macrolevel change
Mentorship
Mind-set
Mobile apps

Profession

Professional associations

Professional development

Social cognitive theory

Social media influencer

Systems theory

Theory of planned behavior

Theory of self-regulation and
   self-control

Transtheoretical model

Chapter Discussion Questions

1. What do you consider to be a good definition of learning? Based on what was discussed in this chapter, name three ways that you will continue to learn postgraduation.

2. How does understanding organizations as part of a larger system affect your conceptualization of change? How do you recognize these same forces in your own life?

3. Can you think of an example of equilibrium in your life? Has it ever been destabilized, and if so, what was the effect? If not, what are the actions you have taken to maintain equilibrium?

4. Do you have any predictions about the corporate communication field that you would add to the list from this chapter? What are they and why? How do you see yourself fitting into the future field?

Chapter Activities

1. Spend some time reflecting on your mind-set. Do you find that you have a fixed mind-set or a growth mind-set? While Dweck (2006) points out that all of us have both mind-sets, one or the other is typically predominant. If you find that you have a fixed mind-set, take steps to move toward a growth mind-set. First, list three assumptions you have about your success and failure. Now, using what you learned in this chapter, list one to two strategies you will use to combat these assumptions. Then reflect on a situation in the past where you experienced what you perceived as a failure. What were your thought processes? Now write about how you could reframe your reaction to the situation. Finally, list three action steps you will take the next time you are in a similar situation. If you believe you already have a growth mind-set, still take the time to reflect on a situation in which the outcome was not what you expected or hoped. What was your thought process? Create three action steps you will take next time you are in a similar situation. Is there a way to enhance your growth mind-set?

2. Visit the website for PRSA (www.prsa.org), IABC (www.iabc.com), and at least one of the other organizations noted in the "Professional and Communi-ty-Based Associations" section of this chapter. Browse the websites, paying special attention to the "About," "Mission," "Ethics," and "Resources" sections of each site. Take notes on the similarities and differences of each. Now,

compare what you have written about each and try to make some general statements about the field of strategic communication. What are some of the current trends, expectations, skill sets, ethical outlooks, and resources that are dominant in the field right now? What is useful (and/or not useful) about being a member of these associations? How does this affect you as a future professional communicator?

3. Using the information from this chapter, identify someone who might serve as a good mentor for you as you progress through your degree, or if you are about to graduate, as you begin to enter the communication field. Contact them for a preliminary conversation, using some of the strategies described in this chapter.

Recommended Readings and Resources

"12 Powerful PR Trends That Will Shape Your Strategy for 2019"

https://b2bprblog.marxcommunications.com/b2bpr/pr-trends-pr-strategy
This article provides a current look at trends in PR, with advice for how to put the information into action.

"Social Media Advocacy: How to Build a PR Program Advocate"

https://blog.hootsuite.com/social-media-advocacy-brand-advocate/
This article provides clear and detailed information about creating a social media advocacy program.

"How to Find a Great Mentor—First, Don't Ever Ask A Stranger"

https://www.forbes.com/sites/kathycaprino/2014/09/21/
how-to-find-a-great-mentor-first-dont-ever-ask-a-stranger/#2038a26bdfa1

"Looking for a Mentor? The 7 Best Places to Start"

https://www.entrepreneur.com/article/294093

This article provides tips for finding a mentor at various stages of your career.

GLOSSARY

3-step model of change A theory that positions change as a process of *unfreezing, moving,* and *refreezing.*

Adaptability The capacity one has to adjust to a new context or situation.

Applied ethics An ethical approach concerned with ethical behaviors in the day-to-day world versus the theoretical study of ethics.

Artificial intelligence (AI) The use of computer systems to accomplish tasks usually done by humans.

Assessment The comparison of data to predetermined goals and criteria for the purpose of determining the degree of success and value of the communication strategy or plan.

Attribution theory Theory concerned with explanations for the cause of an event along with corresponding emotions of either anger or sympathy among onlookers.

Beliefs Confidence in the existence of something not rigorously provable.

Big Data High volume and variety information derived from a number of sources, including information generated as people engage/are monitored in electronic activities (e.g., navigating the Internet). Big data must be analyzed using advanced programming that can handle such large loads of information and provides enhanced insight, decision making, and process automation. Big Data refers not only to the data itself but also to the process of analyzing large volume data for patterns.

Brand What an overall entity is essentially known and recognized as. Subsumes the concepts of identity, image, and reputation.

Brand listening Brand listening homes in social listening to focus on what is being said on the organization's own platforms.

Campaign(s) Ongoing and coordinated communication endeavors that communicate different elements of the strategic plan and other related organizational actions to various stakeholder groups.

Change The act of becoming something different.

Channel The vehicles through which we create and share messages.

Coding Assigning interpretive meaning over the literal meaning of words and thoughts in a given text.

Communication audit A comprehensive analysis by which organizations evaluate their current communication efforts with internal and external audiences.

Communication campaign Ongoing and coordinated communication endeavors that communicate different elements of the strategic plan and other related organizational actions to various stakeholder groups.

Communication competencies Core elements and skills related to effective communication.

Communication self-assessment A personal analysis in which a person analyzes his or her own communication competencies.

Communicative leader A type of leader who engages in dialogue, feedback, and participative decision making with employees. Communicative leaders are often perceived as open and involved.

Community ecology theory A theory of change that studies how populations of organizations evolve within a shared space known as a community through the process of variation, selection, and retention.

Compliance Whether a targeted person will positively respond to a request.

Compliance techniques Strategies that increase the likelihood of compliance from another person.

Consequentialist ethics or **consequentialism** A type of ethics concerned with outcomes and maximizing the net good.

Constitutive communication A view that situates communication as a process of meaning development about social phenomena ranging from self and social structure. Accordingly, from a constitutive point of view, it is through communication that we create shared realities by (re)negotiating meaning through every interaction.

Context Context is the setting for anything or anyone that is considered the focus. Alternatively, context is what is outside a frame, and the process is complicated by the fact frames exist within other frames.

Content analysis (qualitative) A research method in which bodies of text are coded for meaning by the researcher.

Content analysis (quantitative) A research method in which key words in bodies of text are tabulated by the researcher.

Coordinated management of meaning (CMM) Theory based on the idea that we create our social worlds in communication with one another, and we, in turn, are shaped by them. CMM posits that even a seemingly straightforward conversation between two people can become complex as the conversational partners differently prioritize the contexts of culture, episode, identity, and relationship that surround any speech act.

Corporate citizenship See *corporate social responsibility.*

Corporate communication A field that employs strategic communication to coordinate internal and external communication processes with the goal of creating positive stakeholder relationships and furthering organizational goals.

Corporate social responsibility (CSR) An organization's efforts to positively contribute to social issues.

Corporate social responsibility (CSR) campaign A campaign that has the key goal of advancing organizational commitment with a specific initiative.

Crisis A time of instability for an organization, typically preceded by a triggering event or something that alters the normal state of the organization and/or its environment.

Criteria A standard by which something is judged.

Customer advocacy The principle of word of mouth applied to social media.

Culture A relatively unique blend of communication behaviors shared by a group of people.

Data Information that can be used for analysis and planning.

Deontological ethics Principles for taking action that are not tied to the consequences of action. It is ethics focused on means versus ends, including valuing the treatment of humans.

Dialogic communication A communication approach that individuals share their own perspectives and remain open to appreciating the perspectives of others.

Dialogic ethics An ethical approach that suggests a past focus on ethical judgment be replaced with a focus on ethical learning while acknowledging an important limit in the inability for dialogue to be forced. A major goal of dialogic ethics is to create shared ground.

Dialogic theory of communication A communication perspective that emphasizes the importance of a mutual orientation to all communication enacted by the organization.

Diversity The inclusion of people of various races, ethnicity, gender, sexual orientation, socioeconomic status, age, physical abilities, and ideologies.

Dramaturgy Part of Goffman's identity theory, dramaturgy serves as the overall theatrical metaphor to explain how we think about ourselves and relate to others.

Ego network One's own network or the network from an individual actor's point of view.

Elaboration likelihood model A theory of persuasion that posits that people follow one of two routes to persuasion based on factors such as motivation and ability to process the message. Recommends different messaging strategies based on the stakeholders' level of interest in and relevance to the subject of the message.

Embedded The way actors are tied within their social network.

Employee advocacy When employees use social media to support their employers.

Environment The social setting of particular human activities and, therefore, can function as a synonym for context.

Environmental scanning The collecting of data from sources relevant to the individual or organization.

Equity A sense of fairness and equality.

Ethics A major area of philosophy that is concerned with the thinking behind what is right and wrong. Ethics can also refer to any instance of deciding right and wrong and to refer to one school of thought on the subject of right and wrong.

Feedback Information obtained from a target audience or other environmental factor that provides insight into how an individual or organization is perceived by that audience.

Feminist ethics Accounts for the role of both morality of compassion and care as well as rights-based moral reasoning.

Field An officially recognized category of similar types of organizations.

Focus groups A research method in which people are gathered in a group and asked questions about a specific topic by an organizational representative for the purpose of assessing the group's opinions and attitudes regarding the topic.

Framing A metaphor for defining meaning in a situation. Within the loosely bounded social spaces of everyday life, there is more data than can possibly be processed and fully unified in terms of attempting to have what might be called total meaning.

Goal Long-term, overarching purpose. What you want to achieve.

Group and organizational change Change that takes place among groups of people and/or throughout the organization.

ICT succession theory A communication theory that states that using complementary media in sequence can increase the likelihood that communicators will reach their intended audiences.

Identity An individual's or organization's self-concept; how we want to be seen, particularly by those we judge to be important to us.

Image How an entity is perceived from an external perspective, especially by important stakeholders, at a certain point in time.

Image repair theory (also known as image restoration theory) A crisis messaging strategy for dealing with matters that involve responsibility and offensiveness. A detailed typology of messages and the selection and construction of a given message should take into account the following criteria: what needs the most attention; what will the most important stakeholder group accept as true; what evidence and resources does the entity have at its disposal; what is the optimal medium for communication with priority stakeholders?

Impression management Part of Goffman's identity theory that states an entity communicates with an audience by using verbal and nonverbal means to present a socially ideal version of the role they are adopting.

Influence The ability to affect others' thoughts and/or behaviors. Influence also refers to the process or processes of changing the thoughts and/or behaviors of others.

Inclusion Providing equal access and opportunity to all people in a given population.

Influencer marketing A type of marketing where the organic endorsement of the influencer acts like a celebrity endorsement.

Informational interview An informal interview with someone in your field of interest. Informational interviews are not interviews for a specific position but rather provide you an opportunity to ask questions about careers in the field.

Institutional theory A theory of how organizations respond to the pressure to legitimize organizational practices, which leads to both organizational and field-specific standards via a five-stage process, including *de-institutionalization, pre-institutionalization, theorization, diffusion*, and *re-institutionalization*.

Intercultural communication Communication among and between people of different cultures.

Intercultural communication competence Intercultural communication that emphasizes the importance of relationship, the importance of identity, and the importance of context.

Interorganizational network The networks organizations build within their various communities. Through interorganizational networks, organizations can leverage communication to gain access to resources, create powerful coalitions, or enact social initiatives.

Interview A conversation between two parties (the interviewer and the participant) that is guided by a set of questions prepared by the interviewer in advance of the meeting. Interviews are useful because they can give in-depth information about a chosen topic as well as the opportunity for two-way symmetrical communication.

Intrapersonal change Change on the individual level.

Leadership A complex influence process involving one or more leaders, followers, and other stakeholders.

Leadership narratives Communication strategies used to co-construct leader identity among leaders and followers.

Longitudinal data Data that presents a long-term view of the phenomena under consideration.

Macrolevel change Change on a societal level. Related to corporate communication change to an entire field.

Macrostructure Easily identifiable, large-scale social structures, such as organizations and nations. It also refers to somewhat less defined, large-scale social systems.

Management The administration of an organization and involves the processes of forecasting, planning, organizing, directing, coordinating, and controlling.

Mass media Media communicates one-to-many and includes television, news, radio, and billboards. Mass media was traditionally the only way organizations could reach stakeholders outside of interpersonal interaction in physical locations.

Microstructure Microstructure refers to the avenues and constraints that are created in small-scale social interactions, such as single conversational turns spoken in relation to previous conversational turns.

Measurement The analysis of data to see if the strategies employed have met the goal set out at the beginning of the campaign or other communication effort.

Media Media is something that acts as a mediary between or among parties. Within corporate communication, "media" takes on two primary meanings: mediated electronic channels through which messages are communicated, and *the media*, which refers collectively to news and information outlets such as newspapers and television and Internet news sources, including bloggers.

Media relations The practice of developing relationships with members of the media and creating materials, such as press releases and media kits, to influence organizational coverage in the media.

Media richness theory Considers the effect media choice has on our comprehension of, and reaction to, messages related to the degree to which each type of media helps us reduce uncertainty. Characterizes media as rich or lean related to the number of communicative cues a given type of media allows.

Media scanning Part of environmental scanning. Involves collecting data from media sources relevant to the individual or organization, including major newspapers, trade publications (i.e., publications specific to a particular industry), blogs, and other similar secondary sources.

Message The basic outputs (and inputs) of strategic communication. How actors create and share meaning about ourselves. In the field of corporate communication, they are the basis for brand building and relationship building and essential to the flow of everyday organizational life.

Message map A tool for distilling an organization's core message and then coordinating other messages around that main message.

Methods Ways and systems of gathering and analyzing data.

Mind-set Our attitudes and beliefs about ourselves and the world around us, particularly related to our own abilities and successes or failures.

Mobile media Media that is unique in that it allows the user to make mediated communication portable.

Morality An informal system for guiding behavior; rational members of a community share it.

Narrative framing Using the structure of stories to influence.

Networking The communicative process of leveraging your network contacts and strategically seeking out new contacts to add to your network.

Objective Measurable, finite purposes that move toward the completion of goals.

One-way communication Communication pushed out to stakeholders from the organization, with no mechanism for feedback or elaboration.

Online/Social media Media tied to the Internet that enables both one-to-many and one-to-one communication.

Organizational identity An organization's self-concept. How it wants to be perceived by stakeholders.

Persuasion The deliberate use of spoken or written language to get others to adopt a position and/or behavior.

PESO model A conceptual model that characterizes the various ways that organizations can communicate with stakeholders as paid, earned, shared, and owned.

Polyvocality Relating to the range of stakeholder voices present in corporate communication.

Portfolio Professionally assembled samples of an individual's work that serve as a representation of their overall skill set. Portfolios are taken on job interviews as a way to present a candidate's skills and talents related to the job.

Postmodern ethics A body of ethical approaches that assume that an understanding of context is required for exploring matters of right and wrong, that the individual is inextricably connected to others, and that the very language of ethics only has meaning as it is socially situated.

Process model of intercultural communication competence A way to assess and develop intercultural abilities. The model highlights attitudes, knowledge, skills, and outcomes. Respect, openness, and curiosity are key attitudes. Cultural self-knowledge, wider cultural understanding, and sociolinguistic awareness are notable knowledge components.

Profession An occupation that includes a systematic knowledge base and formal training.

Professional associations Organizations centered on a specific profession or industry that act as a repository for professional standards and skills, as well as serve as good venues for networking.

Professional development Training or other actions undertaken to advance one's career.

Professional ethics Also known as applied ethics, professional ethics are ethical behaviors in the day-to-day world versus the theoretical study of ethics.

Project management Project management involves using the processes of initiating, planning, executing, monitoring and controlling, and closing to complete a project.

Power The ability to achieve a particular outcome without needing to rely on influence. To have power in a situation means to have full control.

Preliminary research Research done at the beginning of the research and analysis process to ascertain where the organization stands relative to its own goals, competitors, and the industry at large.

Primary research Research that involves gathering data from firsthand sources, such as through interviews, surveys, or focus groups.

Punctuated equilibrium theory (PET) A theory of change and maintenance that regards organization identity as shifting between periods of slower, incremental change and faster, disruptive change.

Purposive sample Specially chosen population of people for study, usually involving members of key stakeholder groups.

Qualitative research Research measurement and assessment tactics that answer questions of *how* and *what*. Generally paired with research methods such as interviews, focus groups, and secondary research.

Quantitative Research measurement and assessment tactics that answer questions

of *how many* and *how often*. Generally paired with research methods such as surveys.

Random sample Study participants who have an equal chance of representing the general population.

Rational ethics An approach to ethics derived from attempts to use logic to determine qualities or principals that can be applied to all kinds of situations. Rational approaches are universal, meaning they are intended to apply to all people in all circumstances.

Reputation The evaluation an internal and external stakeholder makes about how well an organization is meeting its expectations based on its past behaviors.

Research The collecting and using data for the purpose of better understanding specific situations or making predictions.

Secondary research Research using third-party resources, such as organizational documents, news sources, social media posts, existing research studies, government or industry reports, and other similar materials.

Share of voice (SOV) How much of the public attention an organization has as measured by media or social media mentions.

Situational crisis communication theory A crisis communication theory that is concerned with explanations for the cause of an event along with corresponding emotions of either anger or sympathy among stakeholders.

Situational theory of publics Explains how the perception of problems and the likelihood of related action are dependent on the contexts in which a stakeholder group is embedded.

SMART goals and objectives Objectives that are specific, measurable, achievable, relevant, and timely.

Social capital The intangible collection of resources ingrained in our social structure.

Social cognitive theory Social science theory that states we learn and change behaviors by observing others.

Social constructionist perspective The perspective that humans develop through social interaction with others.

Social listening The collecting of social media data from sources relevant to the individual or organization.

Social marketing See *corporate social responsibility (CSR)*.

Social media audit An analysis conducted by an individual or organization that compares individual/organizational goals against the content, comments, and analytics on their social media platforms. When a gap between goals and reality are identified, a plan for change is developed.

Social media influencer An area expert who has gained credibility and a large following on social media.

Social media sentiment The tenor (positive/negative/neutral) of social media communication about a specific organization or initiative.

Social networks The social structures through which we come together and are connected to others.

Social share of voice (SSOV) Percentage of the social conversation the organization is receiving relative to other organizations during social listening.

Stakeholder Groups and individuals that affect or are affected by an organization.

Stakeholder communication Communication between and among an organization and its stakeholders.

Stakeholder mapping model (SMM) A theoretical model that adapts the stakeholder salience model to online communication by adding the dimensions of connectivity and content.

Stakeholder networks A whole network view of an organization's stakeholder groups (e.g., consumers, shareholders, employees) and how the structure of these relationships affect organizational outcomes.

Stakeholder salience model (SSM) A model that classifies stakeholders according to power, legitimacy, and urgency. Based on the grouping of these attributes, stakeholders are determined to be more or less salient to the organization at specific points in time.

Stakeholder theory A social theory based on the idea of creating value between the stakeholder and the organization and acknowledging the roles of humanity, relationship, and ethics.

Strategic communication Strategic communication is planned and targeted communication aimed at achieving positive outcomes for specific goals.

Strategy The plan for how you will reach your objective.

Statistical analysis A type of quantitative analysis that uses special software to look for trends, similarities, and differences between or within populations under study.

Structuration theory A social theory that attributes equal weight to structure and actors in creating and perpetuating social systems.

Surveys Research methodology that contains a series of questions administered to participants via pencil and paper or online. They are generally closed-ended, which means participants can only answer from a set number of choices.

SWOT analysis Organizational analysis that assesses strengths, weaknesses, opportunities, and threats relative to the organization to determine whether to take further action.

Synergy A sense of cohesiveness and unity among messages.

System A complex organism composed of many parts that interact with the environment around it.

Systems theory A biological and then later social science theory that emphasizes the notion of a part or process embedded in a larger whole that is translatable to a contextual understanding.

Tabulation The simple counting and sorting of quantitative data.

Tactic Tasks related to implementing the strategy.

Teleologic ethics See *consequentialist ethics* or *consequentialism*.

Theory Guiding frameworks that describe and predict what types of communication will be most effective in different circumstances.

Theory of planned behavior Theory of intrapersonal change that states a combination of our attitude, subjective norms (what we think those who are important to us feel about the behavior), and perceived behavioral control (how much control we think we have over the outcome) lead to behavioral intentions, which lead to behavior.

Transactional leadership A deal-making approach leadership concerned with the narrow self-interest of the leader.

Transactional model of communication A model of communication that added the idea of feedback to the earlier transmission model of communication.

Transformational leadership An inspirational form of leadership closely connected to charismatic leadership through which employers engage with, and inspire, followers.

Transmission model of communication An early, linear model whereby a sender created a message, which was encoded, sent through a channel, and received and decoded by a receiver.

Transtheoretical model (TTM) A theory of intrapersonal change that states change occurs in stages, including precontemplation, contemplation, preparation, action, maintenance, and termination.

Triangulation Combining quantitative and qualitative methodologies to create a clearer picture of a phenomenon being researched.

Two-way asymmetrical communication Communication originating from an organization that allows for stakeholder feedback, but not in a way that prioritizes stakeholder concern or equality.

Two-way symmetrical communication Communication originating from an organization that allows for stakeholder feedback that is used to generate mutual understanding and responsiveness.

Utilitarianism See *consequentialist ethics* or *consequentialism*.

Values Qualities desired as means or ends and/or qualities apparent in the communications or other actions of individuals or organizations.

Virtue ethics An ethical approach that emphasizes character traits, such as honesty or benevolence, as a key aspect of ethical behavior.

Whole networks Networks from the point of view that examines all of the connections within a specific boundary condition (e.g., a town or an organization).

REFERENCES

3M. (n.d.). *Timeline of 3M history.* https://www.3m.com/3M/en_US/company-us/about-3m/history/timeline/

3M. (2002). *3M proud past, bright future: A century of innovation 2002 annual report.* Annual Reports. http://www.annualreports.com/HostedData/AnnualReportArchive/3/NYSE_MMM_2002.pdf

3M. (2003). *A century of innovation: The 3M story.* http://multimedia.3m.com/mws/media/171240O/3m-century-of-innovation-book.pdf

9to5mac.com. (n.d.). Jony Ive: Chief design officer. https://9to5mac.com/guides/jony-ive/

Abratt, R., & Mingione, M. (2017). Corporate identity, strategy and change. *Journal of Brand Management, 24*(2), 129–139. http://dx.doi.org.ezaccess.libraries.psu.edu/10.1057/s41262-017-0026-8

Alexander, L., & Moore, M. (2016). Deontological ethics. In E. N. Zalta (Ed.), *The Stanford encyclopedia of philosophy* (Winter 2016 ed.). https://plato.stanford.edu/archives/win2016/entries/ethics-deontological/

Allen, T. D., Eby, L. T., Poteet, M. L., Lentz, E., & Lima, L. (2004). Career benefits associated with mentoring for protégés: A meta-analysis. *Journal of Applied Psychology, 89*(1), 127–136.

Allison, M. (2011, June 28). Costco president Craig Jelinek keeps a low profile. *Seattle Times.* https://www.seattletimes.com/business/in-person-costco-president-craig-jelinek-keeps-a-low-profile/

Alton, L. (2018, March 1). How to encourage customer advocacy on social media. *Adweek.* https://www.adweek.com/digital/how-to-encourage-customer-advocacy-on-social-media/

Ambrose, S. A., Bridges, M. W., DiPietro, M., Lovett, M. C., & Norman, M. K. (2010). *How learning works: Seven research-based principles for smart teaching.* John Wiley & Sons.

Anderson, G. (2018, June 6). Costco workers get a raise and the retailer gets more good press. *Retail Wire.* https://www.retailwire.com/discussion/costco-workers-get-a-raise-and-the-retailer-gets-more-good-press/

Argenti, P. A. (2016). *Corporate communication* (7th ed.). McGraw Hill Education.

Arnett, R. C., Arneson, P., & Bell, L. M. (2007). Communication ethics: The dialogic turn. In P. Arneson (Ed.), *Exploring communication ethics: Interviews with influential scholars in the field* (pp. 143–184). Peter Lang.

Arnett, R. C., Fritz, J. H., & Bell, L. M. (2009). *Communication ethics literacy: Diaglogue and difference.* SAGE.

Ashforth, B. E. 2001. *Role transitions in organizational life: An identity-based perspective.* Lawrence Erlbaum.

Ashwill, M. A. & Du'o'ng, T. H. O. (2009). Developing globally competent citizens: The contrasting cases of the United States and Vietnam. In D. K. Deardorff (Ed.), *The SAGE handbook of intercultural competence* (pp. 141–157). SAGE.

Atamian, L. (2017). Why is Walmart a sustainability leader? *Huffington Post.* https://www.huffingtonpost.com/entry/why-is-walmart-a-sustainability-leader_us_5a329da5e4b00caf3d59eae8

Austin, E. W., & Pinkleton, B. E. (2006). *Strategic public relations management: Planning and managing effective communication programs* (2nd ed.) Lawrence Erlbaum.

Azjen, I. (1991), The theory of planned behavior. *Organizational Behavior and Human Decision Processes, 50*, 179–211.

Bacon, J. (2018, April 14). Philadelphia mayor 'heartbroken' after black men arrested at Starbucks. *USA Today*. https://www.usatoday.com/story/news/nation/2018/04/14/philadelphia-police-chief-officers-did-nothing-wrong-starbucks-arrest/518123002/

Baig, E. C. (2017, October 6). Apple's Jony Ive on creating the iPhone: Loathing made us do it. https://www.usatoday.com/story/tech/columnist/baig/2017/10/06/apples-jony-ive-creating-iphone-loathing-made-us-do/740010001/

Bailey, S.T., (2014, March 27). 4 tips for being more flexible and adaptable. *BizJournals*. https://www.bizjournals.com/bizjournals/how-to/growth-strategies/2014/03/4-tips-for-being-more-flexible-and-adaptable.html

Ballinger, J. (1992, August). The new free-trade heel. *Harper's, 285* (1707), 46–47.

Balmer, J. M. T., & Burghausen, M. (2015) 'Explicating Corporate Heritage, Corporate Heritage Brands and Organisational Heritage', Journal of Brand Management 22(5), 364–84.

Bandura, A. (1989). Human agency in social cognitive therapy. *American Psychologist*, 44(9), 1175–1184.

Bary, E. (2018, August 4). Apple officially becomes first US company with $1 trillion market cap. *MarketWatch*. https://www.marketwatch.com/story/apple-crosses-threshold-needed-for-1-trillion-market-cap-2018-08-02

Bates, K. G. (2018). A look back at Trayvon Martin's death, and the movement it inspired. NPR. https://www.npr.org/sections/codeswitch/2018/07/31/631897758/a-look-back-at-trayvon-martins-death-and-the-movement-it-inspired

Bennett, S. (2014). 88% of companies are using social media for marketing. *Adweek*. https://www.adweek.com/digital/social-media-companies/

Benoit, W. L. (1995). *Accounts, excuses, and apologies: A theory of image restoration strategies*. State University of New York Press.

Benoit, W. L. (1997). Image repair discourse and crisis communication. *Public Relations Review*, 23(2), 177–186.

Benoit, W. L. (2015). Image repair theory in the context of strategic communication. In D. Holtzhausen & A. Zerfass (Eds.), *The Routledge handbook of strategic communication* (pp. 303–311). Routledge.

Benoit, W. L. (2015). Image restoration theory. In W. Donsbach (Ed.), *The concise encyclopedia of communication* (p. 251). Wiley.

Bentham, J. (1961). *An introduction to the principles of morals and legislation*. Doubleday. (Original work published 1789).

Berger, J. (2012). *Contagious: Why things catch on*. Simon & Schuster.

Big data. (n.d.). *Gartner*. https://www.gartner.com/it-glossary/big-data

Blackburn, S. (2016a). Ethics. *The Oxford Dictionary of Philosophy*. Oxford, UK: Oxford University Press. http://www.oxfordreference.com/view/10.1093/acref/9780198735304.001.0001/acref-9780198735304-e-1149

Blackburn, S. (2016b). Morality. *The Oxford Dictionary of Philosophy*. Oxford, UK: Oxford University Press. http://www.oxfordreference.com/view/10.1093/acref/9780198735304.001.0001/acref-9780198735304-e-2075

Boren, M. (2018, April 16). Arrests at Starbucks in Philadelphia: Highlights from the fallout and protests Monday. *Philadelphia Inquirer/Daily News*. http://www.philly.com/philly/news/starbucks-arrests-philadelphia-black-men-racial-profiling-protests-live-updates-20180416.html

Borgatti, S., Everett, M., & Johnson, C. (2014). *Analyzing social networks*. SAGE.

Bortree, D., & Seltzer, T. (2009). Dialogic strategies and outcomes: Analysis of advocacy groups' Facebook profiles. *Public Relations Review*, 35(3), 317–319.

Boss, J. (2014, July 21). 4 ways to embrace adaptability. *Forbes*. https://www.forbes.com/sites/jeffboss/2014/07/21/5-ways-to-embrace-adaptability/#20aa3d765c49

Boss, J. (2015, September 3). 14 signs of an adaptable person. *Forbes.* https://www.forbes.com/sites/jeffboss/2015/09/03/14-signs-of-an-adaptable-person/#734fb6e116ea

Brinker, D. L., Gastil, J., & Richards, R. C. (2015). Inspiring and informing citizens online: A media richness analysis of varied civic education modalities. *Journal of Computer Mediated Communication, 20*(5). https://doi.org/10.1111/jcc4.12128

Brito, M. (2013). *Your brand: The next media company.* Que Publishing.

Bryant, J., & Monge, P. (2008). The evolution of the children's television community, 1953–2003. *International Journal of Communication, 2,* 160–192.

Bronn, P. S. (2008). Corporate reputation and the discipline of corporate communication. In C.E. Carroll (Ed.), *The handbook of communication and corporate reputation* (pp. 53-61). John Wiley & Sons, Inc.

Buber, M (1971). *I and thou.* Touchstone.

Burnes, B., (2004). Kurt Lewin and the planned approach to change: A re-appraisal. *Journal of Management Studies, 41*(6), 977–1002.

Burns, J. M. (1978). *Leadership.* Harper & Row.

Carlson, N. (2011, November 10). Design that inspired Steve Jobs. *Business Insider.* https://www.businessinsider.com/here-are-some-big-gorgeous-photos-of-industrial-designs-steve-jobs-truly-loved-2011-11

Carroll, A. B. (1979). A three-dimensional conceptual model of corporate performance. *The Academy of Management Review, 4*(4), 497. http://ezaccess.libraries.psu.edu/login?url=https://search-proquest-com.ezaccess.libraries.psu.edu/docview/210940874?accountid=13158

Carroll, A. B. (2008). A history of corporate social responsibility: Concepts and practices. In A. Crane, A. Mc Williams, D. Matten, J. Moon, & D. S. Siegel (Eds.), *The Oxford handbook of corporate social responsibility* (pp. 19–46). Oxford University Press.

Carroll, B., & Levy, L. (2010). Leadership development as identity construction. *Management Communication Quarterly, 24*(2), 211–231. https://doi.org/10.1177/0893318909358725

Castells, M. (2000). *The rise of the network society: The information age: Economy, society, and culture.* Wiley-Blackwell.

CBS/AP (2018, May 2). Two black men arrested in Philadelphia Starbucks reach settlement with coffee chain, city. *CBS Philly.* https://philadelphia.cbslocal.com/2018/05/02/starbucks-financial-settlement-rashon-nelson-donte-robinson/

Cheng, K. (June 19, 2013). Zappos: A case study in work environment design. *Deloitte Insights.* https://www2.deloitte.com/us/en/insights/topics/talent/zappos.html

Chesebro, J. (2014). *Professional communication at work: Interpersonal strategies for career success.* Routledge.

Chewning, L.V. (2015). Measuring the enactment of IRT via social media: What are organizations and stakeholders saying during crisis? In J.R. Blaney and L. Alwine (Eds.), *Putting image repair to the test: Quantiative applications of image restoration theory.* (pp.133–156). Lexington Books.

Chewning, L. V. (2016). Moving beyond corporate social responsibility to community and citizenry: Galvanizing social, reputational and sociotechnical capital for change. International Public Relations Research Conference. Miami, FL. https://a5522a3d-553d-4677-86c2-c4e5275200c1.filesusr.com/ugd/27a53c_f9e0941a0ccb4ad09d89254b8e56bb54.pdf

Chin, J. & Trimble, J. (2015). *Diversity and leadership.* SAGE. https://doi.org/10.4135/9781483368801

Choi, Y., & Lin, Y.S. (2009). Consumer responses to Mattel product recalls posted on online bulletin boards: Exploring two types of emotion. *Journal of Public Relations Research, 21*(2), 198–207.

Cialdini, R. B. (2009). *Influence: Science and practice* (5th ed.). Pearson.

City of Philadelphia (2018, April 19). Mayor's statement on the Starbucks incident. https://beta.phila.gov/2018-04-19-mayors-statement-on-the-starbucks-incident/

Claridge, T. (n.d.). What is linking social capital? *Social Capital Research and Training.* https://www.socialcapitalresearch.com/what-is-linking-social-capital/

Cleland, D. I., & Ireland, L, R. (2006). The evolution of project management. In D. Cleland & R. Gareis (Eds.), *The global project management handbook* (pp. 3-18). McGraw-Hill Professional.

Corkery, M. (2017). At Walmart Academy, training better managers. But with a better future? *The New York Times.* https://www.nytimes.com/2017/08/08/business/walmart-academy-employee-training.html?smid=tw-nytimes&smtyp=cur

Cornell, C. (2015). The 4 steps of a communication audit. International Association of Business Communicators. https://www.iabc.com/the-4-key-steps-of-a-communication-audit/

Coombs, W. T. (2006). Crisis management: A communicative approach. In C. H. Botan & V. Hazleton (Eds.), *Public relations theory II* (pp. 171–197). Lawrence Erlbaum.

Coombs, W. T. (2007). Protecting organization reputations during a crisis: The development and application of situational crisis communication theory. *Corporate Reputation Review, 10*(3), 163–176. http://dx.doi.org.ezaccess.libraries.psu.edu/10.1057/palgrave.crr.1550049

Coombs, W. T. (2012). *Ongoing crisis communication: Planning, managing, and responding* (3rd ed.). SAGE.

Coombs, W. T., & Holladay, S. J. (2010). *PR strategy and application: Managing influence.* Wiley-Blackwell.

Coombs, W. T., & Holladay, S. J. (2015). Strategic intent and crisis communication. In D. Holtzhausen & A. Zerfass (Eds.), *The Routledge handbook of strategic communication* (pp. 497–507). Routledge.

Cornelissen, J. (2014). *Corporate Communication: A guide to theory & practice.* SAGE.

Costco. (n.d.). About us. https://www.costco.com/about.html

Craig, R. T. (1999). Communication theory as a field. *Communication Theory, 9*(2), 119–161.

Creswell, J. (1998). *Qualitative inquiry and research design: Choosing among five traditions.* SAGE.

Cresswell, J., & Draper, K. (2018, May 9). Nike exodus of managers grows to 11 after inquiry. *The New York Times*, p. B1.

Cresswell, J., Draper, K., & Abrams, R. (2018, April 28). Women at Nike revolt, forcing change at last. *New York Times*, p. A1.

CSIMarket (n.d.). Costco wholesale sales per employee. https://csimarket.com/stocks/COST-Revenue-per-Employee.html

Cutlip, S. M., & Center, A. H. (1952). *Effective public relations.* Prentice Hall.

Czarnecki, S. (2017, June 6). Timeline of a crisis: United Airlines. *PRWeek.* https://www.prweek.com/article/1435619/timeline-crisis-united-airlines.

Daft, R. L. & Lengel, R. H. (1986). Organizational information requirements, media richness, and structural design. *Management Science, 32*(5), 554–571.

de Vries, R. E., Bakker-pieper, A., & Oostenveld, W. (2010). Leadership = communication? The relations of leaders' communication styles with leadership styles, knowledge sharing and leadership outcomes. *Journal of Business and Psychology, 25*(3), 367–380. http://dx.doi.org.ezaccess.libraries.psu.edu/10.1007/s10869-009-9140-2

Deardorff, D. K. (2006). Identification and assessment of intercultural competence as a student outcome of internationalization. *Journal of Studies in International Education, 10*, 241–266.

Deardorff, D. K. (2009). Synthesizing conceptualizations of intercultural competence: A summary of emerging themes. In D. K. Deardorff (Ed.), *The SAGE handbook of intercultural competence* (pp. 264–269). SAGE.

Deetz, S., Tracy, S., Simpson, & J. L. (2000). *Leading organizations through change.* SAGE.

Deigh, J. (2010). *An introduction to ethics.* Cambridge University Press.

Dell. (2017, May 31). Rakia and her Dell small business tech advisor [Video]. https://www.youtube.com/watch?v=Z16nZiVKd-c

Dewey, John (1938). *Experience & Education.* Kappa Delta Pi.

Dietrich, G. (2014). *Spin sucks*. Pearson.

Dimaggio, P. J., & Powell, W., (1983). The iron cage revisited: Institutional isomorphism and collective rationality in organizational fields. *American Sociological Review, 48*(2), 147–160.

Doerfel, M. L., Lai, C.-H., & Chewning, L. V. (2010). The evolutionary role of interorganizational communication: Modeling social capital in disaster contexts. *Human Communication Research, 36*, 125–162.

Draper, K., & Cresswell, J. (2018, May 6). Nike's chief vows changes after claims of workplace harassment and bias. *The New York Times*, p. A24.

Dunlop, W. L. (2017). The narrative identity structure model (NISM). *Imagination, Cognition and Personality, 37*(2), 153–177. https://doi.org/10.1177/0276236617733825

Dweck, C., (2006). *Mindset: The new psychology of success*. Random House.

Dweck, C. (2016, January 13). What having a growth mindset really means. *Harvard Business Review*. http://thebusinessleadership.academy/wp-content/uploads/2017/03/What-Having-a-Growth-Mindset-Means.pdf

Easter, M., & Dave, P. (2017, June 18). Remember when Amazon only sold books? *Los Angeles Times*. https://www.latimes.com/business/la-fi-amazon-history-20170618-htmlstory.html

Elving, W. J. (2012). Corporate communication positioned within communication studies. *Corporate Communications, An International Journal*: The journal and its history, scope and future developments. *The Review of Communication, 12*(1), 66–77.

Etherington, D. (2014, March 17). Apple's Jony Ive seeks product inspiration in unlikely places, heads a team of just 15. Tech Crunch. https://techcrunch.com/2014/03/17/apples-jony-ive-seeks-product-inspiration-in-unlikely-places-heads-a-team-of-just-15/

Fachin, F. F., & Davel, E. (2015). Reconciling contradictory paths: Identity play and work in a career transition. *Journal of Organizational Change Management, 28*(3), 369–392. https://doi.org/10.1108/JOCM-01-2014-0012

Farber, M., (2017, April 11). Video shows man being dragged off overbooked flight. *Fortune*. http://fortune.com/2017/04/10/united-airlines-overbooked-flight-video/

Fairhurst, G. T., & Connaughton, S. L. (2014). Leadership: A communicative perspective. *Leadership, 10*(1), 7–35. https://doi.org/10.1177/1742715013509396

Falkow, S. (2014, December 30). Why mobile content strategy is important to PR. BtoC. https://www.business2community.com/public-relations/mobile-content-strategy-important-pr-01107863

Fayol, H. (1917). *Administration industrielle et générale; Prévoyance, organization, commandement, coordination, controle*. H. Dunod et E. Pinat.

Fishbein, M, & Azjen, I. (1975). *Belief, attitude, intention, and behavior: An introduction to theory and research*. Addison-Wesley.

Fishbein, M., Triandis, H., Kanfer, F. H., Baum, A., Revenson, T. A., & Singer, J. E. (2001). Factors influencing behavior and behavior change. In (A. Baum, T. Revenson, and J. Singer, Eds.), *Handbook of health psychology* (pp. 3–18), Lawrence Erlbaum.

Fombrun, C., & Van Riel, C. B. M. (2004). *Fame and fortune: How successful companies build winning reputations*. FT Prentice Hall.

Fortin, J. (2018, May 2). 2 black men settle with Starbucks and Philadelphia over arrest. *The New York Times*. https://www.nytimes.com/2018/05/02/us/starbucks-arrest-philadelphia-settlement.html

Fortin, J. (2018, May 20). A new policy at Starbucks: People can sit without buying anything. *The New York Times*. https://www.nytimes.com/2018/05/20/business/starbucks-customers-policy-restrooms.html

Freberg, K. (2019). *Portfolio building exercises in social media: Exercises in strategic communication*. SAGE.

Freeman, R. E. (1984). *Strategic management: A stakeholder approach*. Harper Collins.

Freeman, R. E., Harrison, J. S., Wicks, A. C., Parmar, B. L., & De Colle, S. (2010). *Stakeholder theory: A state of the art*. Cambridge University Press.

Friedman, M. (1970, September 13). The social responsibility of business is to increase its profits. *The New York Times*, pp. SM12.

Gartner. (n.d.). Big data. https://www.gartner.com/en/information-technology/glossary/big-data.

Gergen, K, J. (1994). *Realities and relationships: Soundings in social constructionism.* Harvard University Press.

Gergen, K. J. (2015). *An invitation to social construction* (3rd ed.). SAGE.

Gersick, C. J. (1991). Revolutionary change theories: A multilevel exploration of the punctuated equilibrium paradigm. *The Academy of Management Review, 16*(1), 10–36.

Gert, B. (2015a). Applied ethics. In R. Audi (Ed.), *The Cambridge dictionary of philosophy* (3rd ed.). Cambridge University Press. http://ss360.libraries.psu.edu.ezaccess.libraries.psu.edu/cgi-bin/ssredirpg?D=7F9&U=http%3A%2F%2Falias.libraries.psu.edu%2Feresources%2Fproxy%2Flogin%3Furl%3Dhttps%3A%2F%2Fsearch.credoreference.com%2Fcontent%2Fentry%2Fcupdphil%2Fapplied_ethics%2F0%3FinstitutionId%3D725

Gert, B. (2015b). Morality. In R. Audi (Ed.), *The Cambridge dictionary of philosophy* (3rd ed.). Cambridge University Press. http://ss360.libraries.psu.edu.ezaccess.libraries.psu.edu/cgi-bin/ssredirpg?D=7F9&U=http%3A%2F%2Falias.libraries.psu.edu%2Feresources%2Fproxy%2Flogin%3Furl%3Dhttps%3A%2F%2Fsearch.credoreference.com%2Fcontent%2Fentry%2Fcupdphil%2Fmorality%2F0%3FinstitutionId%3D725

Giddens, A. (1986). *The constitution of society: Outline of the theory of structuration.* University of California Press.

Gilbert, S. (2012). *The story of Walmart.* Creative Education.

Gioia, D. A., Schultz, M., & Corley, K.G. (2000). Organizational Identity, Image, and Adaptive Instability. *The Academy of Management Review. 25*(63).

Gladwell, M. (2000). The tipping point: How little things can make a big difference. Little, Brown and Company.

Goei, R., & Boster, F. J. (2005). The roles of obligation and gratitude in explaining the effect of favors on compliance. *Communication Monographs, 72*(3), 284–300. https://doi-org.ezaccess.libraries.psu.edu/10.1080/03637750500206524

Goei, R., Massi Lindsey, L. L., Boster, F. J., Skalski, P. D., & Bowman, J. M. (2003). The mediating roles of liking and obligation on the relationship between favors and compliance. *Communication Research, 30*(2), 178–197. https://doi.org/10.1177/0093650202250877

Goffman, E. (1959). *The presentation of self in everyday life.* Doubleday.

Goffman, E. (1974). *Frame analysis: An essay on the organization of experience.* Harvard University Press.

Goluboff, R. L. (2018, April 20). Starbucks, LA Fitness and the long, racist history of America's loitering laws. *The Washington Post.* https://www.washingtonpost.com/news/post-nation/wp/2018/04/20/starbucks-la-fitness-and-the-racist-history-of-trespassing-laws/?utm_term=.46bab4cdc465

Govindarajan, V., & Srinivas, S. (2013). The innovation mindset in action: 3M Corporation. *Harvard Business Review.* https://hbr.org/2013/08/the-innovation-mindset-in-acti-3

Goodman, J. D. (2019, February 14). Amazon pulls out of planned New York City headquarters. *The New York Times.* https://www.nytimes.com/2019/02/14/nyregion/amazon-hq2-queens.html

Granovetter, M. (1995). *Getting a job: A study of contacts and careers.* Chicago, IL: University of Chicago Press.

Green, D. (2018). Walmart learned a valuable lesson a decade ago—and it's a warning for huge companies like Amazon. *Business Insider.* http://www.businessinsider.com/walmart-reputation-improvement-warning-for-amazon-2018-2

Greenwood, R., Suddaby, R., & Hinings, C. R. (2002). Theorizing change: The role of professional associations in the transformation of institutionalized fields. *Academy of Management Journal, 45*(1), 58–80.

Grossman, D. (2012). *You can't not communicate.* Little Brown Publishing.

Grunig, J. E., & Huang, Y-H. (2000). From organizational effectiveness to relationship indicators: Antecedents of relationships, public relations strategies, and relationship outcomes. In J. A. Ledingham and S. D. Bruning (Eds.), *Public relations as strategic management: A relational approach to the study and practice of public relations* (pp. 23–53). Lawrence Erlbaum.

Grunig, J. E., & Hunt, T. (1984). *Managing public relations.* CBS College Publishing.

Gulati, R., & Gargiulo, M. (1999). Where do interorganizational networks come from? *American Journal of Sociology, 104*(5), 1439–1493.

Hallahan, K. (2015). Chapter 16: Organizational goals and communication objectives in strategic communication. In D., Holtzhausen, & Zerfass (Eds.), *The Routledge handbook of strategic communication* (pp. 244–266). Routledge.

Hallahan, D., Holtzhausen, D., van Ruler, B., Vercic, D. & Sriramesh, K. (2007). Defining strategic communication. *International Journal of Strategic Communication, 1*(1), 3–35.

Harvard Business Review Staff. (2014, November). How companies can profit from a growth mindset. *Harvard Business Review.* https://hbr.org/2014/11/how-companies-can-profit-from-a-growth-mindset

Harvey, W. S., Morris, T., & Müller Santos, M. (2017). Reputation and identity conflict in management consulting. *Human Relations, 70*(1), 92–118. https://doi.org/10.1177/0018726716641747

Heath, D., & Heath, C. (2006). *Made to stick: Why some ideas survive and others die.* Random House.

Helms, M. M., & Nixon, J. (2010). Exploring SWOT analysis-where are we now? *Journal of Strategy and Management, 3*(3), 215–251. http://dx.doi.org.ezaccess.libraries.psu.edu/10.1108/17554251011064837

Higgins, M., & Kram, K. E. (2001). Reconceptualizing mentoring at work: A developmental network perspective. *Academy of Management Journal, 26*(2), 264–288.

Holtzhausen, D., & Zerfass, A. (2013). Strategic communication: Pillars and perspectives of an alternative paradigm. In K. Sriramesh, A. Zerfass, & J-N Kim (Eds.), *Public relations and communication management: Current trends and emerging topics.* Routledge.

Holtzhausen, D., & Zerfass, A. (2015). Strategic communication opportunities and challenges of the research area. In D. Holtzhausen, & A. Zerfass (Eds.), *The Routledge handbook of strategic communication* (pp. 3–17) Routledge.

Hon, L. C., & Grunig, J. E. (1999). *Guidelines for measuring relationships in public relations.* Institution for Public Relations.

Hootsuite. (2018, September 11). A long list of social media statistics that you need to know in 2018. Hootsuite Blog. https://blog.hootsuite.com/social-media-statistics-for-social-media-managers/

Hsieh, T. (2010). *Delivering happiness.* Business Plus.

Huitt, W., Hummel, J., & Kaeck, D. (2001). Assessment, measurement, evaluation, and research. *Educational Psychology Interactive.* http://www.edpsycinteractive.org/topics/intro/sciknow.html

Hursthouse, R., & Pettigrove, G. (2016). Virtue ethics. In E. N. Zalta (Ed.), *The Stanford encyclopedia of philosophy* (Winter 2016 ed.). https://plato.stanford.edu/archives/win2016/entries/ethics-virtue/.

IABC. (n.d.). IABC Foundation. https://www.iabc.com/about-us/iabc-foundation/

Ibarra, H., & Barbulescu, R. (2010). Identity as narrative: Prevalence, effectiveness, and consequences of narrative identity work in macro work role transitions. *The Academy of Management Review, 35*(1), 135–154. https://doi.org/10.5465/AMR.2010.45577925

Ibarra, H., & Lineback, K. (2005). What's your story? *Harvard Business Review, 83*(1), 64–71.

ICMR (n.d.). The benchmarking story. ICMR: IBS Center for Management Research. http://www.icmrindia.org/free%20resources/casestudies/xerox-benchmarking-2.htm

Influencer Marketing Hub. (n.d.). What is influencer marketing? A look at the next big thing. *Influencer Marketing Hub.* https://influencermarketinghub.com/what-is-influencer-marketing/

Irwin, N. (2016). How did Walmart get cleaner stores and higher sales? It paid its people more. *The New York Times.* https://www.nytimes.com/2016/10/16/upshot/how-did-walmart-get-cleaner-stores-and-higher-sales-it-paid-its-people-more.html?_r=0

Isaacson, W. (2011). *Steve Jobs.* Simon & Schuster.

Johnson & Johnson. (n.d.). Our credo. https://www.jnj.com/about-jnj/jnj-credo

Johansson, C., Miller, V. D., & Hamrin, S. (2014). Conceptualizing communicative leadership. *Corporate Communications, 19*(2), 147–165. http://dx.doi.org.ezaccess.libraries.psu.edu/10.1108/CCIJ-02-2013-0007

Johnson, K. (2018, April 14). Starbucks CEO: Reprehensible outcome in Philadelphia incident. https://news.starbucks.com/views/starbucks-ceo-reprehensible-outcome-in-philadelphia-incident

Johnson, K. (2018, April 15). A follow-up message from Starbucks CEO in Philadelphia. https://news.starbucks.com/views/a-follow-up-message-from-starbucks-ceo-in-philadelphia

Kant, I. (1964). *Groundwork of the metaphysic of morals* (H. J. Paton, Trans.). Harper and Row, (Original work published 1785).

Kant, I. (1965). *The metaphysical elements of justice: Part I of the metaphysics of morals* (J. Ladd, Trans.). Hackett Pub. Co. (Original work published 1780).

Kantor, J., & Streitfeld, D. (2015, August 15). Inside Amazon: Wrestling big ideas in a bruising workplace. *The New York Times.* https://www.nytimes.com/2015/08/16/technology/inside-amazon-wrestling-big-ideas-in-a-bruising-workplace.html

Katz, D. & Kahn, R. L. (1978). *The social psychology of organizations.* Wiley.

Kelnhofer, S. (2018, May 22). After drawing criticism, Starbucks clarifies new 'bathroom policy.' *The Western Journal.* https://www.westernjournal.com/after-drawing-criticism-starbucks-clarifies-new-bathroom-policy/

Kent, M., & Taylor, M. (1998). Building a dialogic relationship through the World Wide Web. *Public Relations Review, 24*(3), 321–334.

Kent, M., & Taylor, M. (2002). Toward a dialogic theory of public relations. *Public Relations Review, 28*(1), 21–37.

Kenyon Bulletin Archive. (2005). This is water. http://bulletin-archive.kenyon.edu/x4280.html

Ki, E. (2015). Chapter 21: Relationship cultivation strategies in strategic communication. In D. Holtzhausen and A. Zerfass (Eds.), *The Routledge handbook of strategic communication* (pp. 328–336). Routledge.

Kissel, P., & Büttgen, M. (2015). Using social media to communicate employer brand identity: The impact on corporate image and employer attractiveness. *Journal of Brand Management, 22*(9), 755–777. https://doi.org/10.1057/bm.2015.42

Knight, P. (2016). *Shoe dog.* Scribner.

Koerth-Baker, M. (2018, May 29). A half-day of diversity training won't change much for Starbucks. *FiveThirtyEight.* https://fivethirtyeight.com/features/a-half-day-of-diversity-training-wont-change-much-for-starbucks/

Kohlberg, L. (1973). The claim to moral adequacy of a highest stage of moral judgment. *Journal of Philosophy, 70*(18), 630–646. https://doi.org/10.2307/2025030. JSTOR 2025030.

Kolowich, L. (n.d.). What is a whitepaper? FAQs. HubSpot Blog. https://blog.hubspot.com/marketing/what-is-a-whitepaper-examples-for-business

Krajeski, J. (2008, September 19). This is Water. *The New Yorker.* https://www.newyorker.com/books/page-turner/this-is-water

Kram, K. E. (1985). *Mentoring at work: Developmental relationships in organizational life.* Scott Foresman.

La Monica, P. R. (2015, December 23). The best CEOs of the year are. *CNN Money.* https://money.cnn.com/gallery/investing/2015/12/23/best-ceos-2015/index.html

Lane, R. (2018, September 4). Bezos unbound: Exclusive interview with the Amazon founder on what he plans to conquer next. *Forbes.* https://www.forbes.com/sites/randalllane/2018/08/30/bezos-unbound-exclusive-interview-with-the-amazon-founder-on-what-he-plans-to-conquer-next/#11d202be647b

Levin, D. Z., Walter, J., & Murnighan, K. (2011). Dormant ties: The value of reconnecting. *Management and Organizations, 22*(4), 929–939.

Levinas, E. (1998). *Otherwise than being* (A. Lingis, Trans.). Duquesne University Press.

Lewin, K. (1947). Frontiers in group dynamics. *Human Relations, 1,* 5–41.

Lin, N. (2001). Building a network theory of social capital. In N. Lin, K. S. Cook, & R. S. Burt (Eds.), *Social capital: Theory and research* (pp. 3–24). Aldine De Gruyter.

Lipari, L. (2009). Ethics theories. In S. W. Littlejohn, & K. A. Foss (Eds.), *Encyclopedia of communication theory* (Vol. 1, pp. 352–355). SAGE. http://link.galegroup.com.ezaccess.libraries.psu.edu/apps/doc/CX3201900125/GVRL?u=psucic&sid=GVRL&xid=3ddd3d2e

Littlejohn, S. W., & Jabusch, D. M. (1982). Communication competence: Model and application. *Journal of Applied Communication Research, 10*(1), 29–37.

Lutz, A. (2014, September 30). Costco's simple strategy for outperforming Wal-Mart and Target. *Business Insider.* https://www.businessinsider.com/costcos-simple-strategy-2014-9

Manian, R., & Naidu, S. (2009). India: A cross-cultural overview of intercultural competence. In D. K. Deardorff (Ed.), *The SAGE handbook of intercultural competence* (pp. 233–248). SAGE.

Mark, J. (2010, July 14). Heraticlus of Ephesus. *Ancient History Encyclopedia.* https://www.ancient.eu/Heraclitus_of_Ephesos/

Martin, C. (n.d.). Informational interviewing. Monster.com. https://www.monster.com/career-advice/article/informational-interviewing

Marx, W. (2017, December 4). Artificial intelligence and PR: What you need to know. *BSB PR Sense Blog.* https://b2bprblog.marxcommunications.com/b2bpr/artificial-intelligence-and-pr

Marx, W. (2018, November 20). 12 powerful trends that will shape your strategy for 2019. *BSB PR Sense Blog.* https://b2bprblog.marxcommunications.com/b2bpr/pr-trends-pr-strategy

Matsakis, L. (2018, November 13). Amazon's HQ2 hunger games are over, and Jeff Bezos won. *Wired.* https://www.wired.com/story/amazon-hq2-over-jeff-bezos-won/

Mayfield, J., & Mayfield, M. (2016). Leadership communication: Reflecting, engaging, and innovating. *International Journal of Business Communication, 54*(1), 3–11.

McAdams, D. P. (1996). Personality, modernity, and the storied self: A contemporary framework for studying persons. *Psychological Inquiry, 7,* 295–321.

McAdams, D. P. (1999). Personal narratives and the life story. In L. Pervin and O. John (Eds.), *Handbook of personality: Theory and research* (2nd ed., pp. 478–500). Guilford Press.

McCann, E. (April 14, 2017). United's apology: A timeline. *The New York Times.* https://www.nytimes.com/2017/04/14/business/united-airlines-passenger-doctor.html.

McCarthy, J. (Feb. 7, 2018). Majority remains satisfied with acceptance of gays in U.S. Gallup. https://news.gallup.com/poll/226781/majority-remains-satisfied-acceptance-gays.aspx

McCroskey, J. C., & Young, T. J. (1981). Ethos and credibility: The construct and its measurement after three decades. *Central States Speech Journal, 32,* 24–34.

McGlade, C. (2017, October 25,). 3M—What's in a name? *Thomas.* https://www.thomasnet.com/articles/daily-bite/3m-what-s-in-a-name-/

McGregor, J. (2018, April 19). Anatomy of a PR response: How Starbucks is handling its Philadelphia crisis. *The Washington Post.* https://www.washingtonpost.com/news/on-leadership/

wp/2018/04/19/anatomy-of-a-pr-response-how-starbucks-is-handling-its-philadel-phia-crisis/?utm_term=.e2070578c68c

McGregor, J., & Seigel, R. (March 31, 2018). Starbucks's racial-bias training has another goal. *The Washington Post.* https://www.washingtonpost.com/news/on-leadership/wp/2018/05/31/starbucks-racial-bias-training-has-another-goal/

Meah, A. (n.d.) 33 inspiring Lao Tzu quotes. *Awaken the Greatness Within.* https://awakenthegreatnesswithin.com/33-inspiring-lao-tzu-quotes/

Mease, J. J. (2016). Embracing discursive paradox: Consultants navigating the constitutive tensions of diversity work. *Management Communication Quarterly, 30*(1), 59–83.

Medina-López-Portillo, A., & Sinnigen, J. H. (2009). Interculturality versus intercultural competence in Latin America. In D. K. Deardorff (Ed.), *The SAGE handbook of intercultural competence* (pp. 249–263). SAGE.

Men, L. R. (2014a). Strategic internal communication: transformational leadership, communication channels, and employee satisfaction. *Management Communication Quarterly, 28*(2), 264–284. https://doi.org/10.1177/0893318914524536

Men, L. R. (2014b). Why Leadership Matters to Internal Communication: Linking Transformational Leadership, Symmetrical Communication, and Employee Outcomes. *Journal of Public Relations Research, 26*(3), 256–279. https://doi-org.ezaccess.libraries.psu.edu/10.1080/1062726X.2014.908719

Meyrowitz, J. (1985). *No sense of place: The impact of electronic media on social behavior.* Oxford University Press.

Meyersohn, N. (2018, August 21). How Costco thrives in the Amazon era. *CNN.* https://www.cnn.com/2018/09/14/business/costco-warehouse-kirkland-signature-amazon-retail/index.html

Mill, J. S. (1861). *Utilitarianism* (edited with an introduction by R. Crisp). Oxford University Press, 1998.

Miller, K. (2015). *Organizational communication: Approaches and processes* (7th ed.). Cengage.

Mintzberg, H., Ahlstrand, B., & Lampel, J. (1998). *Strategy safari: A guided tour through the wilds of strategic management.* Free Press.

Mitchell, R. K., Agle, B. R., & Wood, D. J. (1997). Toward a theory of stakeholder identification and salience: Defining the principle of who and what really counts. *Academy of Management Review, 27*(4), 853–866).

Monge, P., & Contractor, N. (2003). *Theories of communication networks.* Oxford University Press.

Morrissey, J. (2018, June 17). Mobile apps are musts for most brands, as long as users like them. *The New York Times.* https://www.nytimes.com/2018/06/17/business/media/mobile-apps-advertising.html

Moosmüller, A., & Schönhuth, M. (2009). Intercultural competence in German discourse. In D. K. Deardorff (Ed.), *The SAGE handbook of intercultural competence* (pp. 209–232). SAGE.

Morial, M. H. (2018). Starbucks arrests show implicit bias is hiding in plain sight. *The Philadelphia Tribune.* http://www.phillytrib.com/commentary/starbucks-arrests-show-implicit-bias-is-hiding-in-plain-sight/article_07eeebb7-90a2-5cf0-afef-d3285d1c5a08.html

Morsing, M. (2017). CSR communication: What is it? Why is it important? In A. Rasche, M. Morsing, & J. Moon (Eds.), *Corporate social responsibility* (pp. 281–306). Cambridge University Press.

Murphy, M., & Dweck, C. (2016). Mindsets shape consumer behavior. *Journal of Consumer Psychology, 16*(1), 127–136.

National Investor Relations Institute. (2003). About NIRI. *NIRI.* https://www.niri.org/about-niri

Neff, J. (2011). Sleeping giant at Walmart wakes—Its vast workforce. *Ad Age.* http://adage.com/print/231210

NodeXL. (n.d.). Codeplex archive. *Codeplex.* https://archive.codeplex.com/?p=nodexl

Northouse, P.G. (1997). *Leadership: Theory and practice.* (7th ed.). SAGE.

O'Connell, J., & McCartney, R. (2018, November 13). It's official: Amazon splits prize between Crystal City and New York. *The Washington Post*. https://www.washingtonpost.com/local/amazon-hq2-decision-amazon-splits-prize-between-crystal-city-and-new-york/2018/11/13/d01ec4de-e76e-11e8-b8dc-66cca409c180_story.html?utm_term=.accb213549c9

Ovide, S. (2018, November 13). Amazon may have outsmarted itself with HQ2 tactics. *Bloomberg*. https://www.bloomberg.com/opinion/articles/2018-11-13/amazon-hq2-tech-giant-may-have-outsmarted-itself-with-tactics

Owen, M. (2018, November 20). Jony Ive discusses fragile ideas leading to design of iPhone, App Store. *Apple Insider*. https://appleinsider.com/articles/18/11/20/jony-ive-discusses-fragile-ideas-leading-to-design-of-iphone-app-store

Owens, E. (2018, May 12). At Starbucks, Yale and everywhere else, being black in America really is this hard. *CNN*. https://www.cnn.com/2018/05/10/opinions/while-black-at-yale-and-starbucks-owens-opinion/index.html

Patel, D. (2017). How micro-influencers are challenging outdated models of employee' social value. *Forbes*. https://www.forbes.com/sites/deeppatel/2017/08/10/how-micro-influencers-are-challenging-outdated-models-of-employees-social-value/#1c32a9004276.

Pearce, W. B. (1994). *Interpersonal communication: Making social worlds*. Harper Collins.

Pearce, W. B. & Cronen, V. E. (1980). *Communication, action and meaning: The creation of social realities*. Praeger.

Pearce, W. B. & Pearce, K. (1998). Transcendent storytelling: Abilities for systemic practitioners and their clients. *Human Systems, 9*, 167–185.

Peterson, A., (2018, September 26). The big deal about big data and PR. *Prime Research*. http://prime-research.com/en/2018/09/big-deal-big-data-pr/

Peterson, H. (2016). Walmart is copying one of Costco's winning strategies—and it's working. *Business Insider*. http://www.businessinsider.com/walmart-is-investing-more-in-employees-2016-10

Petty, R. E., & Cacioppo, J. T. (1986). *Communication and persuasion: Central and peripheral routes to attitude change*. Springer-Verlag.

Pollitt, C. (2014). An inside view of Walmart's digital communications strategy. *Social Media Today*. https://www.socialmediatoday.com/content/inside-view-walmarts-digital-communications-strategy

Powell, W. W. (1990). Neither market nor hierarchy: Network forms of organization. *Research in Organizational Behavior, 12*, 295–336.

Prochaska J. O., & DiClemente C. C. (1983). Stages and processes of self-change in smoking: Towards an integrative model of change. *Journal of Clinical Psychology, 51*, 390–395.

Project Management Institute. (2017). *PMBOK guide: A guide to the project management body of knowledge* (6th ed.). PMI.

Project Management Institute. (n.d.). www.pmi.org

PRSA. (n.d.). About PRSA. https://www.prsa.org/about/about-prsa/

Putnam, R. D. (2000). *Bowling alone: The collapse and revival of American community*. Simon & Schuster.

Ramo, J. C. (1999, December 27). *Jeffrey Preston Bezos: 1999 person of the year. Time*. http://www.time.com:80/time/poy/bezos.html

Richmond, V. P., & McCroskey, J. C. (2009). *Organizational communication for survival: Making work, work* (4th ed.). Pearson.

Ringen, J. (2018, April 17). Nike has a new digital playbook and it starts with sneakerheads. *Fast Company*. https://www.fastcompany.com/40547805/nike-has-a-new-digital-playbook-and-it-starts-with-sneakerheads

Roberts, M. (2018, May 23). Starbucks' new bathroom policy is a callback to its founding credo. *The Washington Post*. https://www.washingtonpost.com/blogs/post-partisan/wp/2018/05/23/starbucks-imagines-a-utopia/?utm_term=.c78b854fcebe

Rost, J. C. (1991). *Leadership for the twenty first century*. Praeger Publishers.

Rowley, T. J. (1997). Moving beyond dyadic ties: A network theory of stakeholder influences. *The Academy of Management Review, 22*(4), 887–910.

Rumelt, R. P. (2011). *Good strategy bad strategy: The difference and why it matters*. Crown Business.

Saks, M. (2016). A review of theories of professions, organizations and society: The case for neo-Weberianism, neo-institutionalism and eclecticism. *Journal of Professions and Organizations, 3*, 170–187.

Salovey, P., & Mayer, J. D. (1990). Emotional intelligence. *Imagination, Cognition and Personality, 9*, 185–211.

SAS (n.d.). SAS Sentiment Analysis. https://www.sas.com/en_us/software/sentiment-analysis.html

Schmidt, S. (2017, October 16). #MeToo: Harvey Weinstein case moves thousands to tell their own stories of abuse, break silence. *The Washington Post*. https://www.washingtonpost.com/news/morning-mix/wp/2017/10/16/me-too-alyssa-milano-urged-assault-victims-to-tweet-in-solidarity-the-response-was-massive/?noredirect=on&utm_term=.2050870d684c

Scholz, M. (2017, July 7). The three-step process that's kept 3M innovative for decades. *Fast Company*. https://www.fastcompany.com/40437745/the-three-step-process-thats-kept-3m-innovative-for-decades

Schramm, W. (1954). How communication works. In W. Schramm (Ed.), *The process and effects of mass communication*. University of Illinois Press.

Schwab, S. (2011). Finding your brand voice. *Social Media Explorer*. http://socialmediaexplorer.com/content-sections/tools-and-tips/finding-your-brand-voice/

Scott, D. M. (2013). *The new rules of marketing & PR* (4th ed). John Wiley & Sons, Inc.

Sederevicuite, K., & Valentini, C. (2011). Towards a more holistic stakeholder analysis approach. Mapping known and undiscovered stakeholders from social media. *International Journal of Strategic Communication, (5)*, 221–239.

Seeger, M., & Ulmer, R. (2002). A post-crisis discourse of renewal: The cases of Malden Mills and Cole Hardwoods. *Journal of Applied Communication Research, 30*, 126–142.

Segran, E. (2018, May 2). Why Americans still love Nike even after its workplace scandals. *Fast Company*. https://www.fastcompany.com/40566617/why-americans-still-love-nike-even-after-its-workplace-scandals

Sehl, K. (2019, April 22). Social share of voice: what it means and how to get more of it. *Hootsuite Blog*. https://blog.hootsuite.com/how-to-increase-share-of-voice/

Shaughnessy, B. A., Treadway, D. C., Breland, J. W., & Perrewé, P. L. (2017). Informal leadership status and individual performance: The roles of political skill and political will. *Journal of Leadership & Organizational Studies, 24*(1), 83–94. https://doi.org/10.1177/1548051816657983

Shleyner, E. (2018, June 18). 19 social media metrics and how to track them. *Hootsuite Blog*. https://blog.hootsuite.com/social-media-metrics/

Short, K. (2013, November 19). 11 reasons to love Costco that have nothing to do with shopping. *Huffington Post*. https://www.huffingtonpost.com/2013/11/19/reasons-love-costco_n_4275774.html

Shumate, M., Fulk, J., & Monge, P. (2005). Predictors of the international HIV-AIDS INGO network over time. *Human Communication Research, 31*(4), 482–510. https://doi.org/10.1093/hcr/31.4.482

Shumate, M., & O'Connor, A. (2010). The symbiotic sustainability model: Conceptualizing NGO-corporate alliance communication. *Journal of Communication, (60)*, 577–609.

Siegel, R. (2018, April 19). 'They can't be here for us': Black men arrested at Starbucks tell their story for the first time. *The Washington Post*. https://www.washingtonpost.com/news/business/wp/2018/04/19/they-cant-be-here-for-us-black-men-arrested-at-starbucks-tell-their-story-for-the-first-time/?utm_term=.05e16a53537f

Siegel, R., & Horton, A. (2018, April 17). Starbucks to close 8,000 stores for racial-bias education on May 29 after arrest of two black men. *The Washington Post*. https://www.washingtonpost.com/news/business/wp/2018/04/17/starbucks-to-close-8000-stores-for-racial-bias-education-on-may-29-after-arrest-of-two-black-men/?utm_term=a02d7b69e58d

Silva, D., Chuck, E., & Radford, M. (2018, April 17). Starbucks CEO meets with two black men arrested in Philadelphia store. *NBC News*. https://www.nbcnews.com/news/us-news/two-black-men-arrested-philadelphia-starbucks-meet-ceo-n866291

Strauss, A., & Corbin, J. (1998). *Basics of qualitative research: Techniques and procedures for developing grounded theory*. SAGE.

Sinnott-Armstrong, W. (2015). Consequentialism. In E. N. Zalta (Ed.), *The Stanford encyclopedia of philosophy* (Winter 2015 ed.). https://plato.stanford.edu/archives/win2015/entries/consequentialism/

Soderquist, D. (2005). *The Walmart way*. Nelson Business.

Solis, B. (2010). The social media style guide: 8 steps to creating a brand persona. *Engage*. http://www.briansolis.com/2010/06/the-social-media-style-guide-8-steps-to-creating-a-brand-persona-2/

Solomon, M. (2018, September 15). How Zappos delivers WOW customer service on each and every call. *Forbes*. https://www.forbes.com/sites/micahsolomon/2018/09/15/the-secret-of-wow-customer-service-is-breathing-space-just-ask-zappos/#603256ae1b2c

Starbucks (n.d.). Our mission, our values. https://www.starbucks.com/about-us/company-information/mission-statement

Starbucks (2018, April 14). Starbucks response to incident in our Philadelphia store. https://news.starbucks.com/views/starbucks-response-incident-in-philadelphia-store

Starbucks (2018, April 17). Starbucks to close all stores nationwide for racial-bias education on May 29. https://news.starbucks.com/press-releases/starbucks-to-close-stores-nationwide-for-racial-bias-education-may-29

Statistic Brain Research Institute. (n.d.) Walmart company statistics. https://www.statisticbrain.com/wal-mart-company-statistics/

Stephens, K. K. (2007). The successive use of information and communication technologies at work. *Communication Theory*, *17*(4), 486–507.

Stephens, K. K., Sornes, J. O., Rice, R.E., Browning, L. D., & Saetre, A. S. (2008). Discrete, sequential, and follow-up use of information and communication technology by experienced ICT users. *Management Communication Quarterly*, *22*, 197–231.

Stone, B. (2013, June 7). Costco CEO Craig Jelinek leads the cheapest, happiest company in the world. *Bloomberg*. https://www.bloomberg.com/news/articles/2013-06-06/costco-ceo-craig-jelinek-leads-the-cheapest-happiest-company-in-the-world

Stone, Z. (2013, June 14). Is Costco secretly a social enterprise? *Fast Company*. https://www.fastcompany.com/2682280/is-costco-secretly-a-social-enterprise

Sullivan, M. (2016, August 15). What I learned working with Jony Ive's team on the Apple watch. *Fast Company*. https://www.fastcompany.com/3062576/what-i-learned-working-with-jony-ives-team-on-the-apple-watch

Szreter, S., & Woolcock, M. (2004). Health by association? Social capital, social theory, and the political economy of public health. *International Journal of Epidemiology*, *33*, 650–667.

Tang, L., Gallagher, C. C., & Bie, B. (2015). Corporate social responsibility communication through corporate websites: A comparison of leading corporations in the United States and China. *International Journal of Business Communication*, *52*(2), 205–227. https://doi.org/10.1177/2329488414525443

Taylor, K. (2017). Walmart has spent more than $18 million on tear-jerking ads to fix its infamous reputation. *Business Insider*. http://www.businessinsider.com/walmart-spent-18-million-on-reputation-repair-ads-2017-8

Telegraph (2011, October 6). Steve Jobs: Timelines. https://www.telegraph.co.uk/technology/steve-jobs/8810045/Steve-Jobs-timeline.html

Temin, D., (2017, April 11). How United became the world's most hated airline in one day. *Forbes.* https://www.forbes.com/sites/daviatemin/2017/04/11/how-united-became-the-worlds-most-hated-airline-in-one-day/#7f20747f61f2

Tetzeli, R. (2017, December). Why Jony Ive is Apple's design genius. *Smithsonian Magazine.* https://www.smithsonianmag.com/innovation/jony-ive-apple-design-genius-180967232/

The state of mobile search–statistics and trends. (2019, January 7). *GoGulf.* https://www.go-gulf.com/blog/mobile-search/

Thomas, L. (2018). Amazon grabbed 4 percent of all US retail sales in 2017, new study says. *CNBC.* https://www.cnbc.com/2018/01/03/amazon-grabbed-4-percent-of-all-us-retail-sales-in-2017-new-study.html

Tjan, A.K. (July 14, 2010). Four lessons on culture and customer service from Zappos CEO, Tony Hsieh. *Harvard Business Review.* https://hbr.org/2010/07/four-lessons-on-culture-and-cu.

Tolbert, P. S., & Zucker, L. G. (1996). The institutionalization of institutional theory [Electronic version]. In S. Clegg, C. Hardy, & W. Nord (Eds.), *Handbook of organization studies* (pp. 175–190). SAGE.

Tornoe, R. (2018, April 16) What happened at Starbucks in Philadelphia? *Philly.com.* http://www.philly.com/philly/news/starbucks-philadelphia-arrests-black-men-video-viral-protests-background-20180416.html

Tushman, M. L., & Romanelli, E. (1985). Organizational evolution: A metamorphosis model of convergence and reorientation. *Research in Organizational Behavior, 7,* 171–222.

van Dijk, T. A. (1980). *Macrostructures: An interdisciplinary study of global structures in discourse, interaction, and cognition.* Lawrence Erlbaum.

van Maanen, J. (1998). *Qualitative studies of organizations.* SAGE.

van Riel, C.B.M. (1997). Research in corporate communication: An overview of an emerging field. *Management Communication Quarterly, 11*(2), 288–309.

van Riel, C.B.M, & Fombrun, C. J. (2007). *Essentials of corporate communication.* Routledge.

Veil, S. R. Reno, J., Freihaut, R., & Oldham, J. (2015). Online activists vs. Kraft Foods: A case of social media hijacking. *Public Relations Review, 41,* 103–108.

Verill, A. (2017, April 24). A Zappos lesson in customer service metrics. *Software Advice.com.* https://www.softwareadvice.com/resources/zappos-lesson-customer-service-metrics/

Vickery, A. J. (2018). Listening enables me to connect with others: Exploring college students' (mediated) listening metaphors. *International Journal of Listening, 32*(2), 69–84.

Vocoli. (2015, October 1). Thinking outside the big box: How Costco wins with happy employees and investors. https://www.vocoli.com/blog/october-2015/thinking-outside-the-big-box-how-costco-wins-with-happy-employees-and-investors/

von Bertalanffy (1968). *General system theory: Foundations, development, applications.* George Braziller.

Wahba, P. (2017, January 6). Sam's Club CEO out amid tough Costco battle. *Fortune.* http://fortune.com/2017/01/06/sams-club-ceo-costco/

Waters, R. D., Burnett, E., Lamm, A., & Lucas, J. (2009). Engaging stakeholders through social networking: How nonprofit organizations are using Facebook. *Public Relations Review, 35*(2), 102–106.

Weick, K. E. (1995). *Sensemaking in organizations.* SAGE.

Weiner, B. (2006). *Social motivation, justice, and the moral emotions: An attributional approach.* Lawrence Erlbaum.

Weiner, M., & Kochhar, S. (2016a). *Irreversible: The public relations big data revolution. IPR: Institute for Public Relations*. https://instituteforpr.org/irreversible-public-relations-big-data-revolution/

Weiner, M., & Kochhar, S., (2016b, October 16). Unleashing the power of big data in public relations. *My PRSA Publications*. http://apps.prsa.org/Intelligence/TheStrategist/Articles/view/11678/1152/On_the_Horizon_Unleashing_the_Power_of_Big_Data_in#.XGxXWOhKjIV

Winsor, M., & McCarthy, K. (April 19, 2018). Men arrested at Starbucks were there for business meeting hoping to change 'our lives.' *Abcnews.com*. https://abcnews.go.com/GMA/News/men-arrested-starbucks-business-meeting-hoping-change-lives/story?id=54578217

Young Entrepreneur Council. (2015, April 6). 12 ways to shift your mindset and embrace change. *Inc*. https://www.inc.com/young-entrepreneur-council/12-ways-to-shift-your-mindset-and-embrace-change.html

Yukl, G. A. (2006). *Leadership in organizations* (2nd ed.). Prentice-Hall.

Zakhem, A. J., Palmer, D. E., & Stoll, M. L. (2008). Introduction. In A. J. Zakhem, D. E. Palmer, & M. L Stoll (Eds.), *Stakeholder theory* (pp. 15–22). Prometheus.

Zavattaro, S. M. (2013). Expanding Goffman's theater metaphor to an identity-based view of place branding. *Administrative Theory & Praxis, 35*(4), 510–528. https://doi.org/10.2753/ATP1084-1806350403

INDEX